The New York Times

HOLIDAY CHEER CROSSWORD PUZZLES
Festive, Fun and Easy Puzzles

Edited by Will Shortz

ST. MARTIN'S GRIFFIN ☙ NEW YORK

www.stmartins.com

Puzzles 1–195 in this work were originally published in *The New York Times*
from January 1, 1997, to July 18, 2005. Copyright © 1997, 2004, 2005 by
The New York Times Company. All rights reserved. Reprinted by permission.
Puzzle 196, "Season's Greetings," copyright © 2006 by Randy Ross. Puzzle 197,
"Sing We Noel," copyright © 2006 by Nancy Salomon. Puzzle 198, "Christmas
Cover-up," copyright © 2006 by Patrick Merrell. Puzzle 199, "Dear Santa . . . ,"
copyright © 2006 by Nancy Nicholson Joline. Puzzle 200, "Little Holiday Helpers,"
copyright © 2006 by David J. Kahn.

ISBN-13: 978-0-312-36126-6
ISBN-10: 0-312-36126-2

First Edition: October 2006

10 9 8 7 6 5 4 3 2 1

Introduction

By tradition, every year around Christmas, *The New York Times* publishes at least one crossword related to the holiday. It may involve Christmasy puns, jokes, a holiday verse . . . you never know what. One year, on the day *after* Christmas, the *Times* had a crossword about returning Christmas gifts.

For this book we collected some lighthearted puzzles from the *Times*'s archives, which we think you'll enjoy around this time of year. Then we commissioned five brand-new Christmas-related crosswords specifically for this volume from some of the country's top puzzlemakers.

Randolph Ross, who created "Season's Greetings" (Puzzle #196), is a high school principal on Long Island. He has had almost a hundred crosswords published in the *Times* since May 21, 1991, when his first Sunday puzzle appeared in the paper. Once, when he was interviewed for a job as principal by a school board, the board was so intrigued by his crossword hobby that they spent more time asking him about that than they did his education credentials!

Nancy Salomon ("Sing We Noel," #197) is one of the most prolific *New York Times* crossword contributors. Her puzzles are noted for their fresh, lively vocabulary. She has mentored many beginning puzzlemakers by e-mail, working with them until they're able to be successful on their own. In addition to her solo efforts, Nancy has shared bylines with far more collaborators (many but not all of them novices) than anyone else in *Times* history—twenty-four and counting.

Patrick Merrell ("Christmas Cover-up," #198) is a professional cartoonist, humorist, author, and puzzlemaker—sometimes all at once. His hilarious 2005 book *Punchline Puzzles* contains fifty original crosswords, each of which includes the punchline to an accompanying cartoon. Patrick's puzzles are known for elegance, originality, and playful stretching of the crossword "rules."

Nancy Nicholson Joline ("Dear Santa . . . ," #199) is one of the longest-running *Times* crossword contributors. Her first puzzle appeared in the paper on March 27, 1986; her first Sunday in 1988. She's known for gentle humor and wide-open constructions. For years Nancy held the record for the lowest number of words (fifty-six) in a weekday *Times* puzzle. This record has since been superseded—but then at the time Nancy set this record, nobody used computer assistance.

David Kahn ("Little Holiday Helpers," #200) is a consulting actuary in New York City. His first *Times* crossword appeared on March 15, 1994, just after I started at the paper. David specializes in amazing, smack-your-forehead themes and constructions—"how did he do that?!" sort of things. The puzzle he created for this book has a handsome twist I think you'll enjoy.

Happy solving (and holidays) to you!

—Will Shortz

This volume includes five special Christmas-themed puzzles created by five of America's top crossword constructors!

Some of *The New York Times*'s best crossword constructors have come together to bring you five all-new, holiday-themed puzzles that are sure to brighten the season:

- Puzzle 196: "Season's Greetings" by Randy Ross
- Puzzle 197: "We Sing Noel" by Nancy Salomon
- Puzzle 198: "Christmas Cover-up" by Patrick Merrell
- Puzzle 199: "Dear Santa . . ." by Nancy Nicholson Joline
- Puzzle 200: "Little Holiday Helpers" by David J. Kahn

So sit back and solve the season away!

ACROSS

1 Genie's offering
5 Rascal
10 Final Four letters
14 Tops
15 Video companion
16 Cry of surprise
17 Fast-moving construction machine?
19 Film editor's technique
20 Sideshow spiel
21 Set of moral principles
23 Sniggled
26 Out of kilter
29 Watergate, e.g.
32 John of "Fawlty Towers"
33 Insolent
34 Hard-to-move painting
36 Hush-hush org.
37 Agreeable
38 Hemmed in
39 Open a bit
40 Family
41 Homer hero of '61
42 Isn't just a benchwarmer
43 Ending with web and sure
45 Returns from Venus, say
47 Displeased look
48 TV, radio, magazines, etc.
49 Comedian Anderson
51 Isn't fully upright
56 Mouthful of tobacco
58 Eat pizza?
61 Dance in a circle
62 Home of the brave
63 Historic ship
64 Jet black
65 "Awake and Sing!" playwright
66 Show on the face of it

DOWN

1 Yellow jacket
2 Davenport site
3 Fit of pique
4 Weight
5 Like some cows
6 Mongrel
7 Nabokov novel
8 Sought salt
9 Lay man?
10 Not at all
11 Cowardly Leno?
12 Roadie's tote
13 "Certainly, captain!"
18 Minuscule
22 Campus building
24 Worse, as excuses go
25 Hard to grasp
27 Joseph Addison output
28 Becomes frayed
29 13-Down speaker
30 Crazy antic?
31 Trick taker, often
32 One eyeing a canary, maybe
33 Express disdain
35 Do some landscaping
38 Rotten
39 Barley product
41 PC listing
42 Aristotle's teacher
44 Like most streets
46 Cotton threads
48 Sounded kittenish
50 Ratio phrase
52 Has complete domination over
53 Ron Howard role
54 Tar source
55 Coal site
56 Phi follower
57 Sweets
59 Make like
60 Rent out

by Richard Silvestri

2

ACROSS

1. The "A" in I.R.A.: Abbr.
5. Chili con ___
10. Do newspaper work
14. End of a fishing line
15. Sewing machine inventor Howe
16. Financial page inits.
17. Charles Lindbergh's feat across the Atlantic
19. Nameless, for short
20. Prehistoric
21. Marked down
22. "Friends, ___, countrymen"
24. Antlered deer
25. The City of Witches
26. Thin, as oatmeal
29. Game show player
32. See eye to eye
33. "It takes two" to do this
34. When repeated, a ballroom dance
35. Explore the seven seas
36. Emphatic ending with yes
37. Tennis score after deuce
38. Uncle: Sp.
39. External
40. Three sheets to the wind
41. Oratorio performers
43. Fake ducks
44. Martini garnish
45. Golf shirt
46. Present to Goodwill, e.g.
48. Is no more, informally
49. "That's it!"
52. At the drop of ___
53. Paul Scott tetralogy, with "The"
56. Formal ceremony
57. Rainbow ___
58. Dory or ferry
59. Cousin of a frog
60. Eye sores
61. Memorial Day weekend event, briefly

DOWN

1. Mock words of understanding
2. In the 40's, say
3. In the 20's, say
4. Certain boxing win, for short
5. Stalk vegetable
6. Desirable party group
7. Fixes illegally
8. "I'd rather not"
9. Alienate
10. Tooth cover
11. Batman and Robin
12. The Rolling Stones' "Time ___ My Side"
13. Hamilton bills
18. Marooned person's signal
23. Skillet lubricant
24. Rear of a sole
25. Less loony
26. "___ not, want not"
27. Once more
28. One of six Bach compositions
29. "Gay" city
30. Polished, as shoes
31. "Patton" vehicles
33. Sir or madam
36. Undermines
37. Sacramento's ___ Arena
39. Leave out
40. Atlanta-based airline
42. Pleased as punch
43. Krispy Kreme products
45. Excite, as curiosity
46. Bull's-eye hitter
47. The Buckeye State
48. "A thing of beauty is ___ forever"
49. Oodles
50. Noggin
51. Trial fig.
54. The "A" in MoMA
55. Baseball stat

by Gregory Paul

ACROSS

1 Thin-waisted flier
5 Lad's partner
9 Game player's cry
14 Teen People cover subject
15 Ashe Stadium org.
16 Congested, say
17 "___ Lisa"
18 Genesis brother
19 Bobby of the Black Panthers
20 Posters of a pop music icon?
23 Pie chart piece
24 Eastern "way"
25 Supermodel Carol
28 Weekend ice cream treat?
32 Shooter ammo
35 Ring
36 Relaxed
37 Baby in wool?
39 Pug or boxer
41 Ready for business
42 View
45 Tide type
48 Give it a shot
49 Vintner?
52 England's Isle of ___
53 J.F.K. Library architect
54 Greets the dawn
58 What makes a bivalve move?
61 Of the Vatican
64 Small combo
65 Moolah
66 Staring intently
67 "Zounds!"
68 Actor Estrada
69 Apartment sign
70 Trevi Fountain locale
71 Crummy grades

DOWN

1 Wusses
2 Be nuts about
3 ___ boom
4 Botanists' concerns
5 Swiss tourist destination
6 "Rush!"
7 To-do
8 Sensibleness
9 Stage a prison break
10 Ticks off
11 Hoops grp.
12 "My ___ Sal"
13 Word on a dollar
21 Quite a feat
22 Inits. on Mars
25 Trim to fit, perhaps
26 Light-show light
27 Itsy-bitsy
29 The old man
30 Dateless, say
31 Prefix with classical
32 Take second
33 Flow chart site
34 Sufficiently
38 ___ Paese cheese
40 Hair goo
43 Montague rival
44 Uno + dos
46 Apple pie order?
47 Llama land
50 Sob ___
51 Put on the line
55 Close shave
56 "Dallas" matriarch
57 Goes after
58 Rat's challenge
59 By logic, then . . .
60 Neeson of "Kinsey"
61 Soft touch
62 Going back in time
63 Buddy

by Kurt Mengel

4

ACROSS

1 Homes for hombres
6 Spongy cake
11 Radiator sound
14 Listing
15 Unified
16 "Blah, blah, blah . . ."
17 "My Big Fat Greek Wedding" star
19 Experience a brain cramp
20 "Our Lady" of the Roman Cath. Church
21 Pick up
22 Think tank nugget
23 Robe fabric
25 Definitely not Mr. Right
26 McGregor of film
30 2004 Olympics swimming star
32 Mormon doctrine since 1890
35 Do a 5K, say
36 Performing in the theater
37 Retire
41 Suffix with front
42 Give rise to
43 "Ninotchka" actress, 1939
47 Airline with a kosher menu
48 Places for pews
49 Congested-sounding
52 Just slightly
53 Depot: Abbr.
54 Chinese dish
59 Barbecue site
60 "Not a Pretty Girl" singer, 1995
62 "Die Meistersinger" heroine
63 Common childhood illness, once
64 Tears down
65 Three times, in an Rx
66 Construction girder
67 Atlanta university

DOWN

1 Pink-slips
2 Go ___ (tussle)
3 Locale for Anna
4 Part of T.A.E.
5 Get cracking
6 No longer edible
7 Noted 19th-century botanist
8 Anne ___ (Henry VIII's second)
9 Granny ___ .
10 50's monogram
11 Furrow filler
12 "Sophie's Choice" Oscar winner
13 Tough spot
18 Deli loaf
22 Siderite, for one
24 Winter coat
25 Place to throw garbage
26 Modern rock genre
27 Took the cake
28 Ques. follower
29 Saw
31 Sci-fi film of 1982
33 Highlanders, e.g.
34 Indian tourist stop
37 Turns right
38 ___ Harbour, Fla.
39 LAX posting, for short
40 First State: Abbr.
42 Old-timer
43 Lathered up
44 American Indian
45 Hindu incarnation
46 Down the road
50 Wisecracking TV alien
51 Ugarte's player in "Casablanca"
53 Brush off
55 Palindromic title
56 Automaker Ferrari
57 Pastry chef, at times
58 Like a yenta
60 "Who ___ to say?"
61 An end to sex?

by Adam Cohen

ACROSS

1 Spats
6 Poker variety
10 Theda —— of the silents
14 18-and-over
15 Sit for a shot
16 Catchall abbr.
17 Auto racer Andretti
18 Humorist Bombeck
19 K-12, in education
20 "If looks could kill" look
23 Dog sled driver
26 Former telecommunications giant: Abbr.
27 —— Luis Obispo
28 Bickering
29 Racetrack fence
32 Courtroom pledge
34 Coarse file
35 Helping hand
36 Big inits. in trucks
37 Welcome that's not so welcoming
43 Vienna's land: Abbr.
44 Fitting
45 Meditation method
46 Hoodwinks
48 Close angrily
49 The "O" in S.R.O.
50 George W., to George
51 Shirt or sweater
53 Tickles one's fancy
55 Snub
59 Merle Haggard's "—— from Muskogee"
60 Ponder
61 Not live
65 Just dandy
66 Away from land
67 Light on one's feet
68 Serve supper to
69 Geeky sort
70 Open the door to

DOWN

1 Tartan cap
2 Boise's state: Abbr.
3 Mink, for one
4 Pilot's pre-takeoff filing
5 Mink, for one
6 On —— (without a contract)
7 Pop singer Amos
8 Label on a street-corner box
9 Handed out cards
10 Symbol of redness
11 "Finally!"
12 Gung-ho
13 Non-earthling
21 Lines up
22 Jazz dance
23 Artist Chagall
24 Great Salt Lake state
25 Mexican's assent
30 Ventilate
31 Standard of perfection
33 "Stop behaving like a child!"
36 Start to fume
38 Hungers (for)
39 Number cruncher, for short
40 Charged particles
41 Gawk at, as on the beach
42 Thumbs-down votes
46 Gingersnap, e.g.
47 Connected to the Internet
48 Marital partner
50 Speak derisively
52 "What now?!"
54 Rock music genre
56 Monopoly card
57 Exploitative type
58 Show the way
62 Peach center
63 Samuel's mentor
64 Comfy room

by Kendall Twigg and Nancy Salomon

ACROSS

1 Protrudes
5 Stay to the finish
9 Harness racer
14 Straddling
15 Whale of a movie?
16 Be wild about
17 Hourly pay
18 Try to persuade
19 "The Thinker" sculptor
20 Title of a certain astronomy lecture
23 —— de France
24 Auction unit
25 Fraternal group
29 Custard dessert
31 Part-goat god
34 Funny Sherman
35 Call it a day
36 Fill beyond full
37 With 48-Across, practical advice for attending the lecture
40 Tolkien tree creatures
41 Bagpiper's wear
42 Augusta's home
43 Bandleader Brown
44 Gullible sorts
45 Astaire or Rogers
46 Roadie's load
47 In great shape
48 See 37-Across
56 Yule tune
57 Orange component
58 On the road
60 For all to see
61 Leap for Lipinski
62 Veg out
63 Withdraws gradually
64 Apportion, with "out"
65 Had down cold

DOWN

1 Paleontologist's discovery
2 Delta Center N.B.A. team
3 Like some pizza orders
4 Gush forth
5 Townies
6 Lost a lap?
7 "Vamoose!"
8 Hailer's cry
9 Person of the cloth
10 Vote to accept
11 Musical finale
12 —— the Red
13 Director Clair
21 1992 Joe Pesci title role
22 Party offering
25 Silents star Normand
26 Unescorted
27 Vegas coin-ops
28 Producers of 46-Downs
29 Rolls up, as a flag
30 Shopper's aid
31 Lose one's cool
32 Make amends
33 Fresher
35 Groucho remark
36 Mikita of hockey
38 Cousin of a giraffe
39 Valuable violin
44 Refines, as ore
45 Endearing facial feature
46 Squirrel's stash
47 Boneless cut
48 Flat-bottomed boat
49 Do roadwork
50 Neck of the woods
51 Many cyber-ads
52 Richness
53 Spill the beans
54 Actor McGregor
55 Stun
59 Bow wood

by Joan Yanofsky

ACROSS

1 À la mode
5 Street machine
10 Old late-night host
14 Subject for a censor
15 In play
16 Not playing
17 Comic Rudner
18 Mathematician Kurt
19 Make invalid
20 The length of a meter is based precisely on the amount of light emitted from this
23 Mother ___
24 Envelope abbr.
25 Breakfast bowlful
28 The second Mrs. Trump
31 Coeur d'___, Idaho
32 "The eternal teenager"
36 Maui memento
37 H. H. ___ (Saki's real name)
38 "Norma ___"
39 The Golden Flashes, in college sports
42 Ben's partner
44 MapQuest info
45 Stylists' solutions
46 Floored it
48 Card balance
49 1903 Shaw play
56 Supercaffeinated cola
57 Stand out
58 First name in 52-Down
59 Dairy aisle purchase
60 Calf catcher
61 Some Ivy Leaguers
62 Prince's school
63 Airheaded
64 Adam's third

DOWN

1 Stop
2 Rogaine user's desire
3 ___-bitty
4 Dictator player of 1940
5 Multiroofed structure
6 Stag
7 Middle of Caesar's boast
8 Times to party
9 Move, in Realtor-speak
10 Of vital importance
11 Take as one's own
12 Unfamiliar
13 Some election map shading
21 Audiophile's concern
22 Baby powder mineral
25 Columbo portrayer
26 Away from the wind
27 Jockey's strap
28 Diner freebies
29 Farm unit
30 "Citizen Kane" studio
32 Group of two
33 Airport postings: Abbr.
34 Coin classification
35 A and E, but not I, O or U
37 N.Y.C. subway overseer
40 Capital on the Delaware
41 Drink with a straw
42 Be in accord
43 Menu picks
45 Sportscast feature
46 Young salmon
47 Early: Prefix
48 Soprano-bass combos, maybe
50 Hardly Mr. Cool
51 Early sixth-century date
52 Some jazz singing
53 Fr. title
54 Landed
55 Car until 1957
56 "Mud"

by Roy Leban

8

ACROSS

1 Beginner
5 Ceiling support
9 Brass instruments
14 Crowd noise
15 The Bruins of the Pac Ten
16 Take by force
17 Just twiddling one's thumbs
18 Diagram
19 Juliet's beloved
20 Navel
23 Louisville Slugger
24 French president's residence
25 Critical
27 "Oh my goodness!"
30 Hippie happening
33 One of the Bushes
36 Not completely dissolved, as a drink mix
38 Online auction house
39 Collect
41 "Dear" letter recipient
42 Guitar bars
43 Pickle flavoring
44 Copier of a manuscript
46 Wide shoe specification
47 Mama Cass ___
49 Dirties
51 TV host Winfrey
53 Shines
57 F.B.I. employee: Abbr.
59 The Midwest, agriculturally speaking
62 Bar mitzvah officiator
64 Fitzgerald of scat
65 It ebbs and flows
66 Approximately
67 "Whatcha ___?"
68 Dublin's land, in poetry
69 School readings
70 Gulp from a bottle
71 Mexican sandwich

DOWN

1 Arapaho or Apache
2 Alpine song
3 Come from behind
4 Ultimatum words
5 Hobgoblin
6 Off-white
7 Landed (on)
8 Fox comedy series
9 Seek help from
10 Bob Hope tour grp.
11 Big stinger
12 ___ code (long-distance need)
13 Parking place
21 Safecrackers
22 Slick
26 Profess
28 Frisbee, e.g.
29 Mixes
31 "Must've been something ___"
32 Nasdaq rival
33 Green gem
34 Silents star Jannings
35 Vote depository
37 Threesome
40 Lingerie item
42 Guy
44 Christmas tree topper
45 Cosmic explosion
48 Satellite paths
50 Last six lines of a sonnet
52 Obeys
54 Director Kurosawa
55 Doc
56 Meeting transcriber
57 Smell ___ (be leery)
58 Kotter of "Welcome Back, Kotter"
60 Strike ___ blow
61 552, in old Rome
63 Except

by Barry C. Silk

ACROSS

1 Moulin Rouge dance
7 "That's hardly proper"
13 Shoulder adornment
15 Riviera resort
16 Fellow traveler
17 One of a Yule trio
18 Tees off
19 Inscribed stones
21 Onetime Ford model
22 Be more patient than
24 Consumer protection org.
27 "Mornings at Seven" playwright Paul
28 Brooklyn or the Bronx, informally
29 Dissenting votes
32 Ham or hamburger
33 Baby talk
35 Bar, at the bar
37 Matchsticks game
39 Strike caller
40 Overly stylish
42 Boot camp fare
44 Just manage, with "out"
45 Superman sans cape
46 Further amend
48 Droop
49 Leaf bisectors
50 Tony winner Caldwell
53 One of the Gorgons
54 Come down hard
55 From east of Europe
58 CN Tower city
61 Faint
62 Visitors to a justice of the peace
63 Part of a drum kit
64 Political pundit Myers

DOWN

1 Beany's cartoon pal
2 To the left, at sea
3 Appointed
4 Junkyard dogs
5 C.S.A. state
6 Composer Rorem
7 On the heels of
8 Not hard yet
9 "___ bien!"
10 President pro ___
11 Actress Thurman
12 Whole bunch
14 Antinuclear agreement
15 Use cusswords
20 Title of this puzzle
22 Pizazz
23 Play for a sap
24 "The Maltese Falcon" actor, informally
25 Babbling water
26 Trailblazer Daniel
28 ___ vivant
29 Makes out
30 Milo of "Barbarella"
31 Hurt bad
34 Kicks out
36 World Series mo.
38 Help settle
41 Metal in surgical tools
43 Sis or bro
47 Something drawn out
49 Copycat's words
50 Spaced (out)
51 More than eccentric
52 Irregularly notched
53 Crow's-nest spot
54 Bishop of Rome
55 Fitting
56 ___ Paulo
57 Doctrine
59 Moth-eaten
60 Shad delicacy

by David Diefendorf

ACROSS

1 Touches up
6 Sound of relief
10 High-five, e.g.
14 Place to lounge
15 Plot part
16 Hotel feature
17 "That's all ___!"
18 Four Freedoms subject
19 Spot
20 Rehearsed for a concert?
23 "What ___ now?"
24 Hard to comprehend
25 Org.
28 Poe's Arthur Gordon ___
30 The scarlet letter, e.g.
34 Shooting marble
35 Like most urban land
37 Canadian physician Sir William ___
38 Performed in a concert?
41 Follow ___ (sleuth)
42 "Soap" family
43 Uris hero
44 Arcade game
46 F.I.C.A. funds it
47 Eye problem
48 Commercial name suffix
50 Jazz group, often
52 Listened to a concert?
57 Bell curve figure
59 Pre-euro money
60 Therapeutic treatment, maybe
61 Jump over
62 Sainted fifth-century pope
63 Very cold
64 Put under?
65 Brewski
66 Elysian spots

DOWN

1 Bigger than big
2 Linda of soaps
3 Doohickey
4 Men's accessory
5 Drink mixes
6 Medicaid, for one
7 Clinched
8 K
9 Medal winners
10 Like some grins
11 Maiden
12 Saint Moritz sight
13 Work at
21 Wisconsin college
22 Rockies range
25 Taking one's cuts
26 French explorer La ___
27 Like dessert wines
29 Flat spots
31 Be a bad winner
32 ___-andrew (buffoon)
33 Golfer with an army
35 Signs in the sky
36 Tends to details, figuratively
39 It may be extended
40 "Here ___" (arrival words)
45 Seems suspicious
47 Went bad
49 Parting word
51 Public relations concern
52 "Eh"
53 Walked on
54 Exclusive
55 Poker player's declaration
56 Scoundrels
57 F.B.I. target, with "the"
58 Grounded Aussie

by Norm Guggenbiller

ACROSS

1 Drug buster, for short
5 Apartments
10 Arizona city
14 Mishmash
15 Scoundrel
16 Kuwaiti leader
17 Group voting the same way
18 Car from Japan
19 It may be carried with a guitar
20 Unexpectedly
23 Dismal, in poetry
24 Not just anger
28 "___ out!" (ump's call)
29 Mine finds
33 Grassy Argentine plains
34 Gap and Toys 'R' Us, e.g.
36 Verb not in the king's English
37 Unexpectedly
41 Pro ___ (proportionally)
42 Followed smoothly
43 Natural to a creature
46 Rocker David Lee ___
47 Sup
50 "Saturday Night Fever" group, with "the"
52 "Where the deer and the antelope play"
54 Unexpectedly
58 Shoot (by)
61 Decree
62 Family rooms
63 Detest
64 Delay leaving
65 Stow cargo
66 Reason to put a clothespin on your nose
67 Earl of ___, favorite of Queen Elizabeth I
68 Pitching stats, for short

DOWN

1 Opposite of everyone
2 That certain something
3 Violent troublemaker
4 Beverage with a marshmallow
5 Pledges' group, for short
6 ___ Ness monster
7 Flulike symptoms
8 Supercharged engine
9 Close tightly
10 Parking ticket issuer
11 Flightless Australian bird
12 Break a Commandment
13 "___ you there?"
21 Foam
22 Actress Hagen
25 Neat as ___
26 Jets or Sharks, in "West Side Story"
27 Not an exact fig.
30 Howard of "Happy Days"
31 Archer of myth
32 Waste conduit
34 Telescope user
35 Palm starch
37 Decrease gradually
38 "Can ___ true?"
39 Same old same old
40 Kind of jacket
41 "Spare" item at a barbecue
44 Snakelike fish
45 Erase
47 Make lovable
48 Slate
49 Present and future
51 Ice cream concoctions
53 Confuse
55 Some evergreens
56 Land unit
57 River to the underworld
58 Group with the rock opera "Tommy," with "the"
59 Owned
60 Judge Lance of the O. J. Simpson case

by Sarah Keller

12

ACROSS

1 The "one" in a one-two
4 White Rabbit's words
10 Médoc or muscatel
14 ___ Lingus
15 From Genève, par exemple
16 Emcee Trebek
17 Actress Peeples
18 A A
20 Columnist Maureen
22 They follow Aprils
23 The Joads, e.g., in "The Grapes of Wrath"
24 State capital since 1959
26 ___-a-brac
27 B B
33 Nasal partitions
36 Punxsutawney groundhog
37 Old Roman road
38 Sharer's word
39 Uses again, as Tupperware
42 Fairway position
43 "Mila 18" author
45 58-Down digs
46 With cunning
48 E E
51 Ste. Jeanne ___
52 And others
56 Accused's response
58 Defunct gridders' org.
61 Race of about 6.2 mi.
62 L L
65 Massachusetts' Cape ___
66 Aweather's opposite
67 Alchemist's potion
68 Carnival city
69 Duck's place
70 "Duck Soup" performers
71 Just hired

DOWN

1 Band-Aid co.
2 Kindergarten quintet
3 Muscleman's quality
4 Words before and after "rose"
5 10-Down dress
6 ___ fire (started burning something)
7 Pale as a ghost
8 General ___ chicken
9 Auction conclusion?
10 Hawaiian surfing mecca
11 In an unlawful way
12 Hawaii's state bird
13 Alimony senders, maybe
19 Eve's opposite
21 It may be something of great interest
25 Winged
26 Masquerader's event
28 ___ salts
29 Col. Potter of "M*A*S*H," to pals
30 Home of the N.B.A.'s Heat
31 Buzz's moonmate
32 ___ Poupon mustard
33 "Du jour" item
34 International money
35 Used a crowbar on
40 Cabinet dept. since 1979
41 Army N.C.O.
44 Ready for the post office
47 Hurdle for an aspiring J.D.
49 Canadian tribe
50 World traveler Bly
53 Pick up
54 Many a navel
55 "That's not news!"
56 End of filming
57 Angelic topper
58 The Bruins' sch.
59 Evening, in Paris
60 Comic Redd
63 Dream state, for short
64 High school yearbook sect.

by Martin Schneider

ACROSS

1 To the rear
4 Cold war winner
8 Raft wood
13 For
14 "You ___ kiddin'!"
15 Attach, in a way
16 With 38-Across, a punny riddle
19 Points in a lofty speech
20 Long tale
21 Simpson exclamation
22 Dummy
23 Short-sheeting and others
25 Slightly open
28 SeaWorld attraction
32 Things that are burned nowadays
35 Cousin of a bassoon
37 Moon of Mars
38 See 16-Across
41 Partner of above
42 Set straight
43 Dummy
44 Tobacconist's offering
45 "Baseball Tonight" channel
47 Fake
51 Like ripe cheeses
55 Each
58 Bush's alma mater
59 Designer Pucci
61 Answer to the riddle
64 Cajoles
65 PBS matters
66 Word with rolling or bowling
67 City whose daily newspaper is the Beacon Journal
68 Come together
69 Today, in Tijuana

DOWN

1 Ladybug's prey
2 Tolkien ring bearer
3 Sauna attire
4 Get exactly right
5 Pitches in
6 Explosive stuff
7 None of the above
8 Family pariah
9 Diving bird
10 Extraction from galena ore
11 Hardly thrilling
12 Pharaoh's symbol
15 Enter
17 Numbers to crunch
18 Ecol. watchdog
23 Where a queen may be crowned
24 Title chance
26 Restoration poet
27 In the sack
29 Start of an incantation
30 Tavern in "The Simpsons"
31 Plays for a fool
32 Baseball's "Georgia Peach"
33 Pacers' contest?
34 Eye problem
36 "Dig in!"
37 And
39 Muscle ___
40 White House resident, informally
46 Depilatory brand
48 Con artists' prey
49 Will Smith title role
50 Coffee break time, maybe
52 Informational symbol
53 Children's song refrain
54 Soft, like cotton
55 Typewriter type
56 "Star Wars" critter
57 Not just chuckle
59 Young newts
60 Fail to make
62 Useless tic-tac-toe row
63 Big time

by Zach Jesse

14

ACROSS

1 God of love
5 Diehard
9 Give the heave-ho
14 Audition goal
15 Pet on "The Flintstones"
16 Bravery
17 Start of a Yogi Berra quote
19 Online periodical, briefly
20 "This is only ___"
21 Ear part
23 Off the wall
24 Susan who wrote "Illness as Metaphor"
26 Peruvian beast
28 End of 17-Across
33 Russian leader of old
36 Knock the socks off of
37 African fly
38 ___ Lilly & Co.
39 Alternative to dial-up Internet: Abbr.
40 "Quiet!"
41 Cheerios ingredient
42 The "r" of "pi r squared"
44 When a plane is due to take off: Abbr.
45 B & B's
46 Start of a Yogi Berra quote
49 Mild cigar
50 New Haven collegians
54 Prefix with bytes or bucks
57 Out of control
59 Spice of life
60 Spend, as energy
62 End of 46-Across
64 Ditch digger's tool
65 Plant's start
66 Slightly
67 Play (around)
68 Bookie's quote
69 Telescope part

DOWN

1 Diva performances
2 "Live Free or Die," for New Hampshire
3 Mary-Kate and Ashley ___ (celebrity twins)
4 Antares, e.g.
5 Modifying word: Abbr.
6 Small container for liquids
7 Entail
8 Two-base hit
9 Christmas ___
10 The 1920's
11 Pen name for Charles Lamb
12 It's south of Mass.
13 Deuce topper
18 And others: Abbr.
22 Environmentalists' celebration
25 Boxer's weak spot
27 Beat to a pulp
29 Harry Potter's messenger bird Hedwig, e.g.
30 Lots and lots
31 "No man ___ island . . ."
32 New Jersey hoopsters
33 Actress Garr
34 Venetian blind part
35 Gives a hand
39 Old-fashioned showdown
40 TV classic "The ___ Erwin Show"
43 What bouncers check
44 Went from apes to humans
45 Prohibited
47 Melodious
48 Volcano flow
51 Seeing red
52 Big name in bottled water
53 Mails
54 Net material
55 Giant fair
56 Cyclist's choice
58 Monopoly card
61 Golf peg
63 Hwys.

by Kyle Mahowald

15

ACROSS

1 Headquartered
6 "Zounds!"
10 Links numbers
14 "Goodnight" girl of song
15 Six Flags attraction
16 Pull a sulky, perhaps
17 She appeared in "Thelma & Louise" with 24-Across
19 Top of the heap
20 Say "cheese," say
21 Cut and paste
23 Bard's "always"
24 She appeared in "The Witches of Eastwick" with 53-Across
27 Wide of the plate
29 Hospital fluids
30 G.I.'s mail drop
31 Opposite of sud
33 Aggressive, personalitywise
37 Sticks up
39 An absence of musical skill
42 Layered do
43 Quarterback's ploy
45 Writer Harte
47 Iron or gold source
48 Bonny one
51 Unrestricted, as mutual funds
53 He appeared in "A Few Good Men" with 63-Across
57 Big bird
58 Bounce back
59 Storage spot
61 Ankara native
63 Actor famously connected to many other actors
66 Canadian gas brand
67 Sign from above
68 Not straight
69 Marsh plant
70 Woods plant
71 Not o'er

DOWN

1 Megaproportioned
2 Mars, to the Greeks
3 Appears
4 "Annales" poet Quintus ___
5 Buys and sells
6 Mound stat
7 "What ___?!"
8 Nike rival
9 Hanker for
10 School org.
11 Rainbow-shaped
12 Star-crossed lover of fiction
13 Violinist Isaac
18 Exactly right
22 Lip-puckering
25 "Quo Vadis?" emperor
26 Second half of a vote
27 Propels a shell
28 Well-versed in
32 Society girl
34 Tyre's ancient land
35 Be worthy of
36 Got mellower
38 Polio vaccine developer
40 Suffix with buck
41 Map out again
44 Classic Welles role
46 Antinuclear treaty
49 Fed up with
50 Hatch a plot
52 Represent with symbols
53 Shortstop Derek
54 Elicit a chuckle from
55 Say "@#$%!"
56 Hang like a hummingbird
60 Stallion-to-be
62 Down for the count
64 Overnight spot
65 Ultimate degree

by Kurt Mengel

ACROSS

1 Dark cloud
5 Twelve Oaks neighbor
9 1994 Nobel Peace Prize sharer
14 Pope from 440 to 461
15 Drew on
16 Get past
17 Composer Khachaturian
18 Not opt.
19 It'll keep you up
20 Mali dancewear?
23 Pal of Roo
24 Itty bit
25 Boss's Day mo.
28 East ___, Conn.
30 Represent
32 Biblical verb
36 Response to a Nebraskan's gag?
38 On the horizon, maybe
41 Really steamed
42 Japanese plaything?
44 Hawaii's state bird
45 What 10's represent
46 Loaf parts
49 Rock's Nugent
50 One-third of a hat trick
52 Key with four sharps
57 Hawaiian doozy?
59 Raise the roof
62 Novelist Jaffe
63 Seed coat
64 Third of nine
65 Jenna or Barbara Bush
66 Relocate
67 Mandela's native tongue
68 "Now, about . . ."
69 Tram loads

DOWN

1 Home ___
2 Eagle's home
3 Like some good soil
4 Dance at a bar?
5 Holiday roast
6 Playing ___ (court activity)
7 Mass for the dead
8 Beef up
9 Airport convenience
10 Baseball family name
11 Popular brew, for short
12 Swearing-in words
13 ___ Percé
21 www address
22 Orem native
25 Grown-up
26 Comic Myron
27 Disgruntled player's demand
29 Mr. of mysteries
31 Comparison word
32 Jazz cat's command
33 "+" pole
34 Reprimanded gently
35 "Hey there!"
37 Boundless time
39 Hill where Jesus was crucified
40 Green tea type
43 Shows age, in a way
47 Presidential middle name
48 Mustangs' sch.
51 Trunk artery
53 9-Down company
54 "12 Angry Men" role
55 Antipasto morsel
56 Hoyle's listings
57 Primitive homes
58 Condo, e.g.
59 V-chip target
60 "Oh, sure!"
61 Conquistador's prize

by John Underwood

ACROSS

1 Hatch plots
7 Busy activity
11 Little devil
14 Broadway musical based on Dickens
15 In the thick of
16 Lao-tzu principle
17 Gets noticed, as an actor?
19 Mustache site
20 Paradises
21 —— Kong, China
22 Hawkeye player on "M*A*S*H"
23 "The Nutcracker" attire
25 Resentful
27 Cable film channel
30 Gets noticed, as an acrobat?
33 Newspaperman William Randolph ——
35 Book before Job
36 "It was —— mistake!"
37 Tiny hill builder
38 Tizzy
41 Noisy insect
44 Harmonize
46 Gets noticed, as a chef?
49 "Harper Valley ——"
50 Napping
51 Count ——, villain in Lemony Snicket books
53 Neighbor of Niger
54 Get —— a good thing
57 Telegraph pioneer
61 Do-it-yourselfer's purchase
62 Gets noticed, as an artist?
64 Sign after Cancer
65 Period after dark, in ads
66 Shabby
67 Go wrong
68 Ever and ——
69 Causing goosebumps

DOWN

1 Not all
2 Dressed
3 Nature walk
4 Super Bowl or the Oscars, e.g.
5 Boo-boos
6 Mesozoic, for one
7 Mexican serving
8 Mysterious sign
9 Nutcake
10 Poetic tribute
11 "We'll find it"
12 Whom a dragon threatens in a fairy tale
13 Certain 1960's paintings
18 Synagogue
22 Swear (to)
24 When repeated, "For shame!"
26 Suffix with devil
27 "Now I see!"
28 Gibson who directed "The Passion of the Christ"
29 Texas Instruments product
31 Horne and Olin
32 Grounded jet, for short
34 Reared
37 Org. for tooth doctors
39 Bankbook abbr.
40 Drink with one lump or two
42 Middle grade
43 Headache queller
44 Have headaches, say
45 Trolley
46 Witch's laugh
47 More grayish
48 Truck scale units
52 Blacksmith's workplace
55 Defense grp. since 1949
56 Actor Wilson of "Shanghai Noon"
58 Monotonous learning
59 Give this for that
60 Nervously irritable
62 Paternity identifier
63 Bowlike line

by Levi Denham

18

ACROSS

1 Banned orchard spray
5 Obey
9 Problem with eyeliner
14 "Smooth Operator" singer
15 With the bow, in music
16 Small songbirds
17 Welcome forecast for Santa
18 Undecided
19 Chopin's Mazurka in ___
20 Double-H of magic
23 "Old MacDonald" refrain
24 Not precise
28 Rwandan people
32 Kind of counter
33 Double-H of film
37 ___ list
38 Author Umberto
39 Nocturnal lizards
42 Sparks's home: Abbr.
43 Birth place
45 Double-H of politics
47 "Seinfeld" role
50 Sawyer of morning TV
51 Secret pros
53 Game where you might hear "7 come 11"
57 Double-H of literature
61 Holy war
64 Prefix with distant
65 Emphatic type: Abbr.
66 To no ___ (unsuccessfully)
67 Imperfect gravy feature
68 Works of Michelangelo
69 Cinéma vérité, e.g.
70 Test areas
71 Forest growth

DOWN

1 "Steady ___ goes"
2 Molokai porch
3 Like a lot
4 Put another way
5 Biblical verb
6 Suffix with smack
7 Neutral shade
8 Title boy of old comics
9 Al Jolson standard
10 Handyman
11 Migratory fish
12 Santa ___
13 Letter run
21 Babies
22 Gerund suffix
25 A long, amateurish piano recital, maybe
26 Gave up
27 Cache
29 It's definite
30 Quite
31 Signed
33 Lumberjack
34 Cause of an intestinal problem
35 Willy of "Death of a Salesman"
36 "Beloved" writer Morrison
40 Popular laundry detergent
41 Matched, after "in"
44 Outcome of merciless teasing?
46 "Yoo-hoo!"
48 Christmas tree dropping
49 Miscalculate
52 Bloodhound's sense
54 Jetsons' dog
55 High school exams, for short
56 Two-time U.S. Open tennis champ
58 Water color
59 Without feeling
60 Cheese ___
61 English sports car, informally
62 "___ Got the World on a String"
63 Solo in space

by Elizabeth C. Gorski

ACROSS

1 Nerd
6 Colorless
10 Sign of poor schoolwork
14 Philly footballer
15 ___ of Sandwich
16 Plains cylinder
17 Strasbourg school
18 Nay sayer
19 Bell sound
20 Places for American Beauties
23 Slalom
24 "Country Grammar" rapper
25 Cleaned up
27 Dolt
30 Tarzan portrayer Ron
31 Proof part, sometimes
32 Pals
34 Military strength in the sky
37 Cloak for Claudius
38 What the starts of 20- and 53-Across and 11- and 29-Down are
40 Intoxicating Polynesian drink
41 Painting with crashing waves, maybe
43 Rosie of "White Men Can't Jump"
44 Mode of hobo transportation
45 Conflict
47 Buffalo-to-Rochester dir.
48 Modern phone feature
50 Enjoy greatly
52 Little ___, who sang "The Loco-Motion"
53 Breakfast staple
58 Bunks
60 Food product that melts
61 Died down
62 Computer correction command

63 An eclipse, some think
64 Static ___
65 Charon's river
66 Snickers alternative
67 Hardly easygoing

DOWN

1 Bucks and does
2 Baylor's home
3 They may be involved in shouting matches
4 Popular 1990's sitcom
5 "Saturday Night Fever" trio
6 So very much
7 Lustful
8 "Vissi d'___," "Tosca" song
9 Horse focusers
10 Mind-reading skill, for short
11 Colorful dishes
12 Goofball
13 Like a rock
21 Everyone
22 Cesspool
26 Sign of an engine problem
27 Follower of John
28 Pump
29 Wealthy boyfriend, perhaps
31 Dogpatch diminutive
33 Kenyan tribe
34 Wonderment
35 On a par
36 Tear down

38 Dance venue
39 Photo ___
42 "Ta-ta!"
43 Speak so the back row can hear
45 Conestogas
46 Michigan, e.g., in Chicago: Abbr.
48 Picture puzzle
49 Shot put or 100-meter dash
50 Curl one's lip
51 Moscow money
54 ___ mater
55 Wading bird
56 1/100 of a euro
57 Like some modern filmmaking
59 White or Red follower

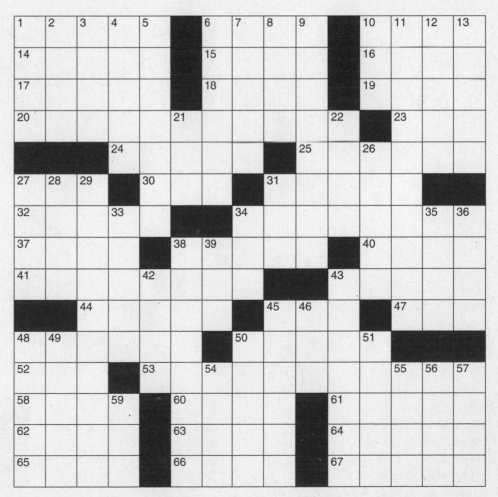

by Jay Giess

20

ACROSS

1 Swear to
5 "What's the ___ that can happen?"
10 Nose (out)
14 Ending with hard or soft
15 Baker who sang "Sweet Love," 1986
16 Shed one's skin
17 Many a homecoming attendee
18 Work over, as a ship
19 Fat of the lamb
20 "Draw one," in diner slang
23 Wildebeest
24 English dog
25 Straight from the garden
27 Rewrites
30 Broken arms may go in them
33 Foul callers
36 Irrelevant, as a point
38 Jump for joy
39 A barber has to work around it
40 Faculty member
42 Burn ___ crisp
43 First-class
45 Radio tuner
46 Glimpse
47 Gym shoes, for short
49 "Golden Boy" playwright Clifford
51 Clothesline alternative
53 Wrestler
57 Companion for Tarzan
59 "Sun kiss," in diner slang
62 Holds close
64 Oak-to-be
65 Gaming table fee
66 Hence
67 ___ four (teacake)
68 Marsh plant
69 Clutter
70 Perfect places
71 Luke Skywalker's mentor

DOWN

1 ___ plane (military craft)
2 Comparison shopper's quest
3 Blow one's top
4 Channel surfers' gadgets
5 Violation of the Geneva Convention
6 "___'Clock Jump" (1930's hit)
7 Jazz phrase
8 Not flexible
9 Idaho produce, informally
10 Ambulance inits.
11 "Life preservers," in diner slang
12 Secluded valley
13 "___, Brute?"
21 Gave dinner
22 Moray catcher
26 Half a dozen
28 Land hopper
29 Prefix with logical
31 Ladleful of unappetizing food
32 Command to Fido
33 Foes of Dems.
34 Make, as money
35 "Flop two," in diner slang
37 Sen. Cochran of Mississippi
40 Capital where the yen is capital
41 Periodic table listings
44 Deface
46 Ocean inlet
48 South-of-the-border shawl
50 ___ Mahal
52 Went like the wind
54 Sal of "Rebel Without a Cause"
55 Played on stage
56 "I ___ vacation!"
57 Throat-clearing sound
58 Unadulterated
60 Written reminder
61 Smile
63 "Send help!"

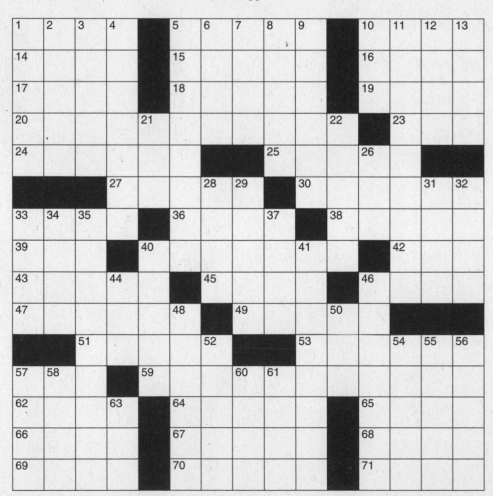

by Gregory E. Paul

ACROSS
1 Philosopher William of —
6 Kid around with
10 Helgenberger of "CSI"
14 "Naughty you!"
15 Wheel shaft
16 Radio "good buddy"
17 All smiles
18 Quilters' parties
19 "Elephant Boy" boy
20 Crops up
22 Hatchling's home
24 Actor Herbert of "Pink Panther" films
25 One way to stand
26 Purge
28 Dense fog
30 Cheese in a ball
32 Lee's uniform color
34 Shrewd
35 Kosher —
36 Amount left after expenses
37 Feted with sherry, say
38 Woman associated with seven other answers in this puzzle
41 Loathe
43 "You've got mail" co.
44 Houlihan portrayer
48 Way up or down
49 B'way hit signs
50 Mambo king Puente
51 Kodak inventor
53 "What's up, —?"
55 Bro. or sis.
56 Utmost
57 Chop —
59 Observant ones
61 Clump of hair
63 Good buy
65 — home (out)
66 In alignment
67 Poet Pound
68 Poetry Muse
69 Joad family's home state: Abbr.
70 Part of a Fifth Ave. address
71 A bit stupid

DOWN
1 Circular in form
2 Acting out of a phrase
3 London or Lisbon
4 Sound boosters
5 Mob figure Lansky
6 Sharp left or right
7 Yoked team
8 Ready to turn in
9 "Steppenwolf" author
10 TV hosts, briefly
11 Mother-of-pearl source
12 Hoopster's grab
13 In a cranky mood
21 Milano Mr.
23 Not spoken
27 Prepared to shoot in a shootout
29 Least crazy
31 Bad, as a tennis shot
33 Doing battle
37 W.W. I president
39 Benchmarks
40 Where the boyz are
41 Founder of modern Turkey
42 Given to blushing
45 Bug
46 Say over
47 "War and Peace" author
48 Directed at
49 Tormented by pollen, say
52 Poet W. H. —
54 Funnel-shaped
58 Ball material
60 Corrida charger
62 Tetley product
64 Nonprofessional

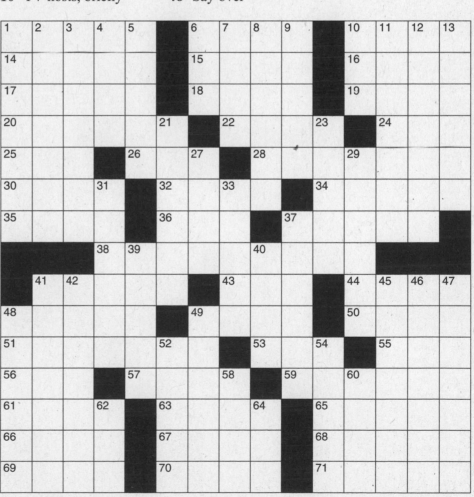

by John Underwood

22

ACROSS

1 Blast from the past?
6 Artsy Manhattan area
10 Pest control brand
14 ——-off coupon
15 Pizazz
16 It's west of the Isle of Man
17 Ad come-on #1
20 Suffix with buck
21 The Virgin Is., e.g.
22 Lace into
25 Washington's —— Stadium
27 Moon of Mars
31 See 23-Down
34 Left Bank locale
35 Fine arbitrarily
36 Fair-hiring abbr.
38 Show off one's biceps
39 Fallen Russian orbiter
40 Men's accessories
43 Young newt
44 "How sweet ——!"
46 Cable Superstation
47 Arrow poison
49 Israeli desert region
51 With 29-Down, ad come-on #3
53 Lover of Aphrodite
55 Mouse's place
56 2.0 grades
57 Knotted, scorewise
59 Grow tiresome
61 Ad come-on #4
68 "Hold it ——!"
69 Shade provider
70 Nary a soul
71 Carol time
72 Short hours of operation?
73 Ohm's symbol

DOWN

1 Coolers, for short
2 Sri Lanka export
3 Ltr. container
4 Clambake clam
5 Mikhail Romanov, e.g.
6 Detonate
7 "That —— Devil Called Love"
8 Doe's mate
9 Right turn ——
10 Get intelligence from
11 Intelligence grp.
12 Table scrap
13 Born in France
18 Surrender
19 "—— Tu" (1974 hit)
22 Endurance
23 With 31-Across, ad come-on #2
24 Explorer Vespucci
26 Stays current
28 Car rental info
29 See 51-Across
30 Hockey teams, e.g.
32 School mo.
33 Louis XIV, e.g.
37 Makes unreadable, in a way
41 Fall back
42 Catch some rays
45 Get older
48 Ping-Pong locale
50 In —— (occurring naturally)
52 Opened wide
54 Navratilova rival
58 Fargo's state: Abbr.
60 "—— extra cost!"
61 Roll-call call
62 Buckeyes' sch.
63 Rolodex no.
64 "—— got an idea"
65 Underwater eggs
66 It's east of the Isle of Man: Abbr.
67 Bounding main

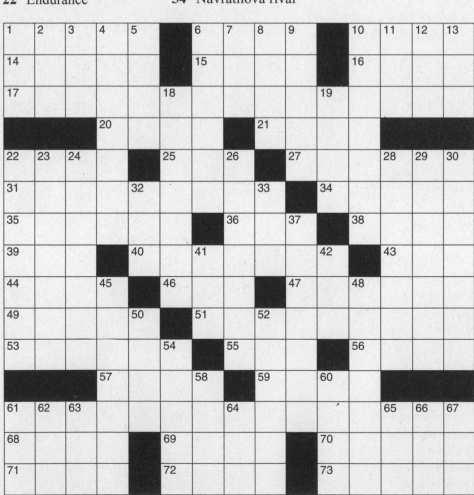

by Michael Shteyman

ACROSS

1 Trophies and such
7 Give at no charge, as a hotel room
11 Hypodermic units, for short
14 Magical drink
15 Cousin of a bassoon
16 "Roses —— red . . ."
17 1981 Mel Gibson film, with "The"
19 Fellows
20 Go in
21 Basic beliefs
23 Gorbachev was its last leader: Abbr.
26 404 in old Rome
28 Niagara source
29 —— de mer
30 The Ocean State
33 —— donna
35 They split when they're smashed
36 Motorcycle attachment
39 English pool game
43 Sign up for more issues
45 Scoundrel
46 Arrived like Michael in an old song?
51 Decimal base
52 Spoken
53 Singer Turner
54 Penny
55 Actress Roberts and others
58 Electrical pioneer
60 Explosive initials
61 Had the passenger seat
66 Winning 1-Across can make this grow
67 Blue-green
68 Fancy home
69 Room with an easy chair
70 Master thespians they're not
71 Like a professional haircut

DOWN

1 Mo. before May
2 Court
3 —— disadvantage (handicapped)
4 Equestrian
5 Sad
6 Grab
7 Bullfight
8 Kimono sash
9 Not worth debating
10 French father
11 Kodak, e.g.
12 Lowlife
13 Felt
18 Make a change in the decor
22 "Full" or "half" wrestling hold
23 Diamond V.I.P.'s
24 Delhi dress
25 Moved on ice
27 Dog docs
30 Zoomed
31 Charged particle
32 Cig
34 Just
37 Commercial suffix with Tropic
38 Remainder
40 Smith who sang "God Bless America"
41 Not odd
42 Landlord's due
44 Bleaches
46 Went bad
47 Juice source
48 Malicious
49 Change for a five
50 Epidermal eruptions
54 Feline
56 Part of McDonald's logo
57 Bean type
59 Disoriented
62 Hoover ——
63 Lass
64 Western tribe
65 Actor Beatty

by David Pringle

24

ACROSS
1 Nasty habits
6 Homes for hermanos y hermanas
11 "Dracula" creature
14 Blaze of glory
15 African wader
16 Emissions watchdog: Abbr.
17 See 29-Across
19 Dollop
20 Redder, as a tomato
21 Empire State Building style
23 Butcher's cut
25 Bigheads
27 Repeat performance?
28 Semicircle
29 Beginning of a daffy-nition of 17-Across
32 Winter warmer
34 Discover
35 Paid respect to
38 A cheap way to fly
42 Kisses in Castile
44 W.W. II conference site
45 Daffy-nition, part 2
50 For example
51 No in Nuremberg
52 Cambodian currency
53 Eight: Prefix
54 Ballroom dance
57 Chutzpah
59 U.S./Eur. divider
60 End of the daffy-nition
64 Runner Sebastian
65 Old sporty Toyota
66 Pertaining to an arm bone
67 You can get a bang out of it
68 Data processing command
69 — coil (electrical device)

DOWN
1 American Legion member
2 Rocks at the bar
3 Like much office work
4 Option at a fast-food restaurant
5 "That's enough!"
6 Pay with plastic
7 Feel bad
8 Results of dives
9 Mimic
10 Separate into whites and darks, e.g.
11 Beautify
12 Military helicopter
13 No-nos
18 High-schooler
22 Durbin of Hollywood
23 Young woman
24 Killer whale
26 Barn bird
29 Many a time
30 Cereal grain
31 Area of land
33 Classical Flemish painter
36 Inexact fig.
37 Lintel support
39 Perceives
40 Troublemaker
41 Something to swing on a string
43 — Lanka
45 Not broken up
46 Formulator of the law of universal gravitation
47 Shrinking —
48 Desire strongly
49 A Baldwin brother
53 Little egg
55 Copy, as a film
56 New York City archbishop
58 Drubbing
61 Golf's — Elder
62 Mule of song
63 Large time piece?

by Sarah Keller

ACROSS

1 "The Sopranos" network
4 Big dos
9 Varnish ingredient
14 It's measured in minutes
15 Multiple choice options, perhaps
16 Come up
17 Oscar Wilde, notably
18 College basketball coach who was the subject of "A Season on the Brink"
20 Alpine event
22 Have an impact on
23 "Fooled Around and Fell in Love" singer, 1976
26 Piggy
29 "The Witches" director Nicolas
30 —— Jeanne d'Arc
31 Some N.C.O.'s
32 Celerity
35 Gym wear
37 "Different Seasons" author
39 Inferior, slangily
41 Directly show where
42 Tusked beast
43 Mideast grp.
44 Black-and-white predator
48 Arrange
49 Pseudonym in detective fiction
53 Spade player, familiarly
55 It begins with an equinox
56 Half a famous dance team
60 44-Across's milieu
61 Slippers of sorts
62 Attire for Mr. Peanut
63 Like 31-Across
64 —— four

65 One of the black keys on a piano
66 Skid row affliction

DOWN

1 Mooring rope
2 S.O.S alternative
3 Staff interval
4 Libreville's land
5 "Little Boy" in 8/6/45 news
6 Shot having a 14-Across
7 Wall St. worker
8 Reaper's tool
9 Incurred, as charges
10 Journalist Sevareid
11 Red Skelton specialty
12 Sort of: Suffix
13 Take home
19 Hootchy-——
21 Match alternative
24 Panama, e.g.: Abbr.
25 Ring site?
27 The Little Giant
28 20-Across path
31 Dispatched
33 1950's political inits.
34 Wire wearer
35 Do a 20-Across
36 Sports datum
37 It'll keep you in your place
38 Queen who wrote "Leap of Faith"
39 The so-called Tiffany Network
40 Weeder's need
43 "The magic word"
45 Got more life from
46 Dental compound
47 They're history
49 Discharge, in a way
50 Form of ID: Abbr.
51 W.W. II conference site
52 Jason's journey, e.g.
54 "The —— Love" (R.E.M. hit)
56 Devilkin
57 Wish undone
58 Coppertone rating: Abbr.
59 1960's chess champ

by Alan Arbesfeld

26

ACROSS

1 Jazz style
6 Reclusive actress Greta
11 Sandwich initials
14 Tehran native
15 Perfect
16 Karel Čapek play
17 Rooming house offering
19 Whiz
20 Tints
21 Tasteless
23 Large monkeys
27 Happy-face symbols
29 Peter of "Lawrence of Arabia"
30 Cuban dance music: Var.
31 Make up (for)
32 Rent
33 ___ King Cole
36 "___ Lama Ding Dong" (1961 nonsense hit)
37 Nullifies
38 Author Ferber
39 Mrs., in Madrid
40 Like the weather around lighthouses, often
41 Open, as a package
42 Ed of "The Honeymooners"
44 Carve
45 Golf attendants
47 Prayer book
48 Country bumpkins
49 Et ___ (and others)
50 Part of a college e-mail address
51 Like a native
58 Bro's sibling
59 Tape deck button
60 Ham it up
61 Asian holiday
62 Cosmetician Lauder
63 Dork

DOWN

1 Baby's mealtime garment
2 Afore
3 Naughty
4 ___ case-by-case basis
5 Tiny puncture
6 Scoffs
7 Fusses
8 Stephen of "The Crying Game"
9 Drinker's place
10 Antiquated
11 Drilling tool
12 Like a rabbit's foot, supposedly
13 Deuce toppers
18 Sand hill
22 Priest's robe
23 Wild swine
24 ___ of roses
25 Economic cycle
26 Mrs. Chaplin
27 Disreputable
28 Rumple
30 King's time on the throne
32 Apple's apple and Chevron's chevron
34 Win by ___
35 Levy imposer
37 Cast a ballot
38 Letter accompanier: Abbr.
40 Toy loved by dogs
41 Without assistance
43 Wordsworth creation
44 "The proof ___ the pudding"
45 Toothpaste brand
46 War hero Murphy
47 Dish
49 Suffix with accept
52 Breakfast drinks, briefly
53 No longer working: Abbr.
54 Mercedes competitor
55 Fish eggs
56 Summer on the Seine
57 Belle of a ball

by Alison Donald

ACROSS

1 "Qué ___?"
5 1970's White House name
11 Revolutionary Guevara
14 Often
15 There are eight in a cup
16 ___ Luthor, of "Superman"
17 Evangelist and friend of presidents
19 ___ pro nobis
20 1956 Elvis hit that went to #2
21 Sun. talk
22 Mil. weapon that can cross an ocean
23 Some short plays
25 Nosh
27 French composer Erik
29 Turned sharply
32 Diplomat's asset
35 "Tickle me" guy
37 Parenthetical comment
38 Part of H.R.H.
39 Word that can follow the ends of 17- and 62-Across and 11- and 34-Down
41 Break a commandment
42 On ___ (winning)
44 Vaccines
45 Understands
46 "Forget about it!"
48 Art supporter
50 Words of agreement
52 German thoroughfare
56 Huck Finn's transport
58 Digital readout, for short
60 Walk nonchalantly
61 ___ Baba
62 Takes no chances

64 Word with pool or port
65 Go back to a favorite book
66 Pitcher
67 Language suffix
68 Antsy
69 Some cameras, for short

DOWN

1 Picasso or Casals
2 "March comes in like ___ . . ."
3 Figure out
4 As a minimum
5 Energetic one
6 Part of E.U.: Abbr.
7 Genetic molecules
8 Flu symptoms
9 Becomes aware of
10 Mil. award
11 How bidding proceeds in bridge
12 Basil or oregano
13 Midterm, e.g.
18 Gym site, for short
22 Prepares, as Champagne
24 ___ Marner
26 Banned apple spray
28 Show host
30 Get to work on Time
31 TV rooms
32 Holier ___ thou
33 Prefix with space
34 Dangerous thing to be caught in
36 Gumbo vegetables
39 Dressed
40 First and Second Avenues area, in Manhattan
43 Ransack
45 Spectacles
47 Common allergen
49 Part of Q.E.D.
51 Words of compassion
53 Wrap
54 Morley of "60 Minutes"
55 Observers
56 Preakness, for one
57 "Woe is me!"
59 Not natural
62 In favor of
63 Droop

by Richard Chisholm

ACROSS

1 Guy Fawkes Day mo.
4 Flora and fauna
9 In a lather?
14 Big time
15 Translator's obstacle
16 "Alfie" actress, 2004
17 Path to enlightenment
18 Place to take off in lighter-than-air craft?
20 Mid seventh-century year
22 Caught, in a way
23 50's monogram
24 Like some wonders
27 Like W. C. Fields's nose
30 Community news source in Belgium?
33 July 1944 battle site
34 "Agnus ___"
35 Name in plastic
38 Animator?
42 Early Chinese dynasty
43 Ode title starter
44 "Must've been something ___"
46 Row of cavalry barracks?
50 Street cleaner
53 Pick up
54 Omega symbolizes it
55 "A.S.A.P.!"
58 Just out
59 Satirical blog item?
63 Stanford-Binet figs.
66 Cornhusker city
67 Xbox user
68 Whole bunch
69 Formal turndown
70 "Them"
71 Med. insurance group

DOWN

1 ___ Percé Indians
2 It's extracted
3 Martha's 1960's backup group
4 Book lover's prefix
5 Gilbert & Sullivan princess
6 Some museum hangings
7 Painted metalware
8 Organism with pseudopods
9 Railroad stop: Abbr.
10 "Alley ___!"
11 Brazilian novelist Jorge
12 Concealed
13 "Holy cats!"
19 "Movin' ___" ("The Jeffersons" theme)
21 Salt, for one
24 Cries of pain
25 "Certainly"
26 List heading
28 Strauss of denim
29 Nielsen of "Rocky IV"
31 "The Matrix" role
32 Old Ford
36 Give some to
37 Web site?
39 Ballpark rollout
40 Syllable from Curly
41 Cape Town coin
45 Capable, slangily
47 Prefix with drome
48 1990's rock genre
49 Halter?
50 Wise old head
51 Frisbee maker
52 Lazarus and Goldman
56 Ending with time or life
57 ___ office
60 Key letter
61 Toil in a trireme
62 Half of a yr.
64 Iranian city
65 ___-cone

by Leonard Williams

ACROSS

1 Ones filling out 1040's, for short
5 Dangers
10 Fed. workplace watchdog
14 Nimble
15 Irish-born actor Milo
16 San —— Obispo, Calif.
17 —— avis
18 Téa of "Hollywood Ending"
19 Greek war god
20 Longtime ABC daytime drama
23 Thought things over
24 "C'est si ——"
25 Little white lie
28 Classic children's nursery song
33 BB's and bullets
34 Rowed
35 Lays down the lawn
39 Made a statement on a stack of Bibles?
42 "—— of the D'Urbervilles"
43 Hatred
45 Best buds
47 1970 Jack Nicholson film
53 Folk singer DiFranco
54 Genetic info
55 "It's —— nothing"
57 1952 George Axelrod Broadway farce, with "The"
62 Gangster's blade
64 Butchers' offerings
65 Slowish
66 Finish a drive?
67 Capri and Wight
68 City near Provo
69 "You said it, brother!"
70 "This is —— ..." (radio announcement)
71 Memo

DOWN

1 PC storage accessory
2 Treat for an elephant
3 Once more
4 More hackneyed
5 Massage intensely
6 "Yes, it's clear now"
7 Attempt to score
8 Obi-Wan —— of "Star Wars"
9 Poetic command before "O Ship of State!"
10 Former king of Norway
11 Guaranteed to succeed
12 Hurry
13 Nitwit
21 Bright thought
22 Prefix with European
26 Summer coolers
27 Mattress holders
29 Letters on an ambulance
30 Audi rival
31 Nutso
32 Welcome ——
35 Davenport
36 Father of Thor
37 Creating dissension
38 Seek damages
40 Hip-hop
41 Nickname for a 59-Down student
44 —— Griffin, 1960's–80's talk show host
46 Scorch
48 Deficiency of red blood cells
49 Most reasonable
50 Attachable, as sunglasses
51 Matador charger
52 Bulb holder
56 Moon to June
58 Smooth
59 College where an athlete might wear a "Y"
60 Summers on the Riviera
61 Helper: Abbr.
62 Health resort
63 —— and cheese

by Sarah Keller

30

ACROSS

1 Document burial place
5 Marilyn Monroe mark
9 Full range
14 Like ideal cactus climate
15 E-garbage
16 Degrade
17 Something to play in Kinshasa?
19 Increased, as the score
20 "Come in!"
21 Baby bug
23 Moo goo —— pan
24 Fresh talk
26 From time immemorial
28 Eye part
31 Regained consciousness
33 Like "fuzz" for "police"
34 Rock band equipment
35 High do
38 Beaujolais, e.g.
39 Letters that make you feel important?
42 Unbridged area
43 Cribbage markers
45 Alternative to gin or vodka
46 TV viewer's aid
48 Away, but not completely off-duty
50 Sidestepped
51 French-born satirist Hilaire
53 Author Dinesen
54 Meyers of "Kate & Allie"
55 Live's partner
58 "Phooey!"
62 —— de Mayo
64 Intermediary (or a title for this puzzle)
66 Rivers' destination
67 Cry from the pews
68 Start of a magician's cry
69 Foul
70 Cincinnati team
71 Freeway exit

DOWN

1 Place for a smile
2 Wrinkle remover
3 Buildup on a suit jacket
4 Sidles through a doorway
5 Chow mein additive
6 October birthstones
7 Tibetan priest
8 Reason to call 911: Abbr.
9 Bodywork place
10 Lawyers' org.
11 The Lord's tropical fruit?
12 Run-of-the-mill
13 Not very hot
18 Grove fruit
22 Some Anne Rice characters
25 Bless the food
27 J.F.K. posting, for short
28 Request of an invitee, briefly
29 Nobelist Wiesel
30 Romantic ballroom queues?
31 Bedouin's mount
32 Doctors' org.
36 Hourly charge
37 Guest column
40 Olive ——
41 Acerbic pianist Oscar
44 John Belushi was originally on it: Abbr.
47 Start a battle
49 Any of the original 13
51 Breakfast strip
52 Author Jong
53 Laid up
56 Thickening agent
57 Vatican's home
59 —— Hart, sitcom title character
60 Presidential time
61 Go bananas
63 Friskies eater
65 Nav. rank

by Lee Glickstein and Nancy Salomon

ACROSS

1 Evergreen trees
5 Hammer part
9 Fit for a king
14 Massage target
15 Inauguration highlight
16 Dress type
17 . . . Boo or yoo follower
19 Jazz singer Carmen
20 "I should say ___!"
21 Actress Gaynor
22 Leaves high and dry
23 Certain OPEC minister
25 Gravity-powered vehicle
27 Lorraine's neighbor
29 Online activity
30 Functioned as
33 Unwitting tools
34 Snowy locale in a Frost poem
35 Currently "in"
36 Hightailed it
37 Manifests
38 Kind of package
39 B & B
40 Up
41 "I ___ Right to Sing the Blues"
42 Wolf's home
43 After the whistle
44 Green eggs and ham profferer, in Dr. Seuss
45 Rigatoni relative
46 Puzzles solved with a pencil
47 Circular dinner order
50 Actor's minimum
52 Atomic
55 Lies against
56 . . . Reagan's first interior secretary
58 Camp craft
59 Tall story
60 Elvis's middle name
61 Steps lightly
62 New York county
63 Lucy Lawless role

DOWN

1 Open wide
2 Cavern feature
3 . . . Oldtime radio station in a 1990's AMC series
4 Prepared
5 Trig function
6 "Chicago Hope" actress
7 Completely
8 . . . Inventor of the sewing machine
9 Certain plane engines
10 Charlton Heston title role
11 Lass
12 Art sch. class
13 Venerable Virginia family
18 Some Apples
24 Sperry's partner
26 Little shavers
27 Sap sucker
28 "Mule Train" singer, 1949
29 Onetime "Masterpiece Theatre" host
30 . . . Massachusetts birthplace of the 19th-century feminist Elizabeth Packard
31 Cardiology concern
32 Robert Fulton power source
34 . . . English river, site of the ruins of Tintern Abbey
37 Big blow
38 Rain or shine preceder
40 Pen names
41 Stares
44 Like some solutions
45 Alphabetically last top 40 rock artist
46 Polynesian language
47 Warsaw ___
48 Construction beam
49 New Mexico Indian
51 Scorch
53 George Orwell's alma mater
54 Sicilian peak
57 Candle dripping

by Stanley Newman

ACROSS

1 "Show Boat" author Ferber
5 Sheep cries
9 Sense much used in a bakery
14 Stick-to-itiveness
15 Pac 10 member
16 Shire of "Rocky"
17 Strong wind
18 Metric weight
19 Back street
20 Forecast maker
23 Leader known for his "little red book"
24 Quantity: Abbr.
25 Lucy of "Charlie's Angels," 2000
28 Slugger called the Sultan of Swat
31 Commendation
36 Gaelic tongue
38 Crystal ball user
40 Sea duck
41 "Melrose Place" actress
44 Loos who wrote "Gentlemen Prefer Blondes"
45 Wire screen
46 Fill up
47 Episodes of "Friends" and "Seinfeld," now
49 Within a stone's throw
51 Acid, in the 60's
52 700, on monuments
54 Actor Stephen
56 Motorcyclist's wear, often
63 Final authority
64 Extol
65 Former Baathist state
67 "You're ___ talk!"
68 "Do you come here often?," e.g.
69 Scrabble piece
70 Accelerator or brake
71 Pindar writings
72 Scored 100 on

DOWN

1 Fabergé collectible
2 Shout at a shootout
3 River with Blue and White tributaries
4 Special forces unit
5 Crazy, slangily
6 Farm division
7 Having wings
8 Brazilian dance
9 TV series with Klingons and Romulans
10 Having XY chromosomes
11 Scat queen Fitzgerald
12 Place
13 Place
21 Road topper
22 "Steee-rike!" caller
25 Franz who composed "The Merry Widow"
26 In an old song, the "I'll see you in my dreams" girl
27 Carrier that acquired Piedmont
29 Period in office
30 Beauty of Troy
32 Is sick
33 Perfect
34 Theater reservations
35 Missed the mark
37 "___, Brute?"
39 Switch-hitter known as Charlie Hustle
42 Screwdriver or wrench
43 Pantomime game
48 Educ. site
50 ___ room
53 Yo-Yo Ma's instrument
55 Japanese dog
56 Swim meet division
57 Gazed at
58 "The Thin Man" dog
59 Police action
60 Father's Day month
61 Guitarist Clapton
62 Story
63 Soak (up)
66 Mathematical proof letters

by Randall J. Hartman

ACROSS

1 Morocco's capital
6 "Oh, my stars!"
10 Recipe amt.
14 They're not PC
15 Inner: Prefix
16 Pro ___ (one way to divide things)
17 African language family
18 Close
19 They can be refined
20 Ford explorer?
23 Jock: Abbr.
26 Sailor's affirmative
27 Mississippi city where Elvis was born
28 Hospital's ___ center
30 Positioned
32 Far Eastern bread
33 "The Hours" role for which Nicole Kidman won an Oscar
36 Genre for Aretha Franklin
37 Dashboard inits.
38 Pupil's locale
41 Billiards great
46 Org. with a complex code
48 ". . . ___ the whole thing!"
49 Rejoinder to "Am, too!"
50 With grace
52 Computer monitor: Abbr.
53 Bout enders, for short
54 Ambassadors and such, or an appropriate title for this puzzle
58 Ambience
59 Det. Tiger or N.Y. Yankee
60 Blow one's lid
64 Kind of mile: Abbr.
65 Cry out
66 Where the Decalogue was received
67 Shade trees
68 Talk back to
69 Ability

DOWN

1 Josh
2 Physician's org.
3 Roll-on brand
4 When Hamlet sees the ghost
5 Literally, "harbor wave"
6 One often seen in a turban
7 Fit for drafting
8 Ollie's partner
9 Friend of Hamlet
10 Jamboree group
11 Longtime Massachusetts congressman
12 Writer Shelby
13 Give, as a gene
21 Actress Cannon
22 Sport in which Israel won its first Olympic medal
23 Off-roaders, for short
24 ZZ Top, musically
25 Reckless
29 Trademarked fruit name
30 Discontinuance
31 Seuss's "Horton Hears ___"
34 "___ a man with seven wives"
35 Popular cereal or magazine
39 Langston Hughes poem
40 Discontinued fliers, quickly
42 River past Luxor
43 Rejects
44 Protective covering
45 Unaffected
46 Demented
47 Initiation, for one
51 French political divisions
52 Marine ___
55 Nolo contendere, e.g.
56 Unagi, in a sushi bar
57 Best-selling author Larson
61 Prefix with cycle
62 Chum
63 Up to, informally

by Kevan Choset

ACROSS

1 Exemplar of grace
5 Bidder's site
9 Fancy duds
14 Stay near the shore, say
15 1963 film "___ la Douce"
16 Eyeball benders
17 Pierce portrayer on TV
18 C
19 Raggedy Ann and friends
20 What a scary Doris Day did on the film set?
23 Cried a river
24 Congressional committee subject
27 Slippery sort
28 Nursery noise
30 Lather
31 More miffed
34 Talking birds
36 60's muscle car
37 What the lexicographer/dairy expert did?
40 Ring master?
41 Family nickname
42 Adam of "The O.C."
43 Air ball, e.g.
45 Math ordinal
46 RR depot
47 Sounded like a chick
49 Oracle site
52 What the paranoid C.I.A. publicist did?
56 Diet guru Jenny
58 Temple University team, with "the"
59 Snack with a lickable center
60 In reserve
61 River Kwai locale, formerly
62 Gem for some Libras
63 More together
64 Hill inhabitants
65 Auditioner's goal

DOWN

1 Give and take
2 Dylan Thomas's home
3 Build on
4 Weak brew
5 Tower designer
6 Hair twist
7 Gallic girlfriend
8 Prison exercise area
9 Beckett's no-show
10 Historical periods
11 Stern lecture
12 www bookmark
13 N.B.A. stats: Abbr.
21 Land south and west of the Pyrenees
22 Post-op program
25 Referred to
26 Bedtime request
28 See 29-Down
29 With 28-Down, noted 20th-century American artist, informally
31 Little rascal
32 Kukla's puppet pal
33 Scream and holler
34 Breath freshener
35 Understated
38 Bankrolls
39 Magician's secret exit
44 Repair, as film
46 Quakes
48 Fired up
49 C sharp equivalent
50 Comedic horn honker
51 Ultimate goal
53 Sluggin' Sammy
54 Victor's cry
55 Fish dish
56 Comedian Bill, for short
57 Some strands in a cell

by Richard Leva and Nancy Salomon

ACROSS

1 Jane Austen novel
5 Chopper blade
10 Friend
13 Meat cuts behind the ribs
15 Give the slip
16 Pharmaceutical giant —— Lilly
17 Poker instruction
19 —— v. Wade (1973 Supreme Court decision)
20 Elapsed time
21 Slowly merged (into)
23 Filling maker: Abbr.
24 Saudi export
25 "The final frontier"
27 Slots instruction
31 Burn with hot liquid
34 His and ——
35 Cousin of an ostrich
36 "Piece of cake!"
37 Diamond weight
39 Mojave-like
40 Mornings, for short
41 Boot bottom
42 Devoutness
43 Roulette instruction
47 Paris divider
48 Versatile truck, informally
49 —— King Cole
52 Carafe size
54 Step-up
56 Critic —— Louise Huxtable
57 Craps instruction
60 Chess pieces
61 Clear the blackboard
62 Breed of red cattle
63 Mammal that sleeps upside-down
64 Shut out
65 New Jersey five

DOWN

1 Castilian hero
2 Pitcher's place
3 Pitchers' gloves
4 Prelude to a deal
5 Carmaker's woe
6 Racetrack
7 Road goo
8 Strange
9 Closes again, as an envelope
10 Keep working hard
11 —— vera
12 Told a whopper
14 Hide from view
18 Like Darth Vader
22 11-pointer in blackjack
25 Queens ballpark
26 Sassy
27 Work at, as a trade
28 Pitched
29 Send forth
30 New York's Giuliani
31 The world has seven of them
32 Where soldiers stay overnight
33 Helper
37 Harry ——, Columbia Pictures co-founder
38 Sheltered, nautically
39 Be under the weather
41 How 007 does not like martinis
42 Squinted
44 Formerly known as
45 Orion, with "the"
46 Leave one's mark on
49 Unsophisticated
50 High-class tie
51 Parenting challenges
52 Ewe's baby
53 "I had no ——!"
54 Rick's love in "Casablanca"
55 Paradise lost
58 It's north of Calif.
59 Research room

by Gordon Seaberg

36

ACROSS

1 The Beatles or the Stones
5 Penny
9 When repeated, a city in Washington
14 Inter ___
15 Penny, maybe, in poker
16 With 3-Down, French-born diarist
17 57-Across song about a request in a gene lab?
20 Not pro
21 Senescence
22 Prefix with dermal
25 Rocky hill
26 Prepare for printing
27 Prefix with gliding
29 Change over at a factory
31 Pulitzer or Tony, as for 57-Across
33 Star of Scorpio
37 57-Across song about a request in the maritime supply store?
40 Varnish ingredient
41 Dye chemical
43 Pouilly-___ (white wine)
46 Individual
47 Board game from India
51 Shade tree
53 Dover's state: Abbr.
54 Slothful
55 Word said twice before "Don't tell me!"
57 Noted Broadway composer
63 With 68-Across, what Fred MacMurray had in a 1960's sitcom
64 007

65 Famed lab assistant
66 Old catalog maker
67 Swear
68 See 63-Across

DOWN

1 ___-relief
2 Pint at a pub
3 See 16-Across
4 20th-century art movement
5 Synagogue singer
6 Whole
7 A degree
8 Golf bag item
9 Light switch surrounder
10 Battery end
11 Actress Turner and others
12 Lord or vassal
13 It's a plus in accounting
18 C.D. earnings: Abbr.
19 Howler
22 Mileage rating grp.
23 Manhandle
24 Pitcher Hideki ___
26 Honky-___
28 Give ___ for one's money
30 Heads' opposite
32 Small sharks
34 Followers of pis
35 Alleviated
36 Fence crossing
38 "Get it?"

39 53, in old Rome
42 Patriots' org.
44 Some patches
45 African antelopes
47 Fence features
48 ___ drop of a hat
49 Old Oldsmobile
50 Wishful one
52 Central
56 The one here
58 Brian Williams's employer
59 Old French coin
60 Bigheadedness
61 Charged particle
62 ___ Butterworth's

by Stephen Budiansky

ACROSS

1 Actress Thompson
5 Dye-yielding plant
9 Humble in position
14 Baseball great —— Speaker
15 Paradoxical Greek
16 Far from 9-Across
17 Actors Holm and McKellen
18 Annual Broadway event
20 Travolta musical
22 Woolly, e.g.
23 Met debutante of 1956
26 Talking computer of film
29 Bikini, for one
30 War stat.
31 Coin rating
32 Aware of
34 Baffin Islander
36 Theme of this puzzle
40 Dunk, e.g.
41 Sp. miss
42 "The Time Machine" people
43 Mattress problem
44 "Vive ——!"
49 Pick up
50 Football's Gang Green
53 Play too broadly
55 Online newsgroup system
56 Predatory players
60 Follower of H.S.
61 Crop up
62 Trusses
63 Shuttle protector
64 Like Waldorf salad apples
65 Goofball
66 Cheap digs: Abbr.

DOWN

1 Scarlet letter, e.g.
2 Genesis landfall
3 Moolah
4 Tear into
5 Cortez's victim
6 Start of some movement names
7 "Vacancy" shower
8 New Orleans campus
9 Defeater of Holyfield, 1999, for the world heavyweight title
10 Pearl Buck heroine
11 Terrier type
12 India inc.?
13 "Indeed"
19 Moira's player in "On the Beach"
21 Respectful greeting
24 Mine, in Marseille
25 Tennis's Davenport
27 —— brat
28 Bossy but generous type, supposedly
31 "Suspicion" studio
33 Wash. setting
34 Erhard movement
35 Menaces, in a way
36 Corduroy rib
37 Understood by few
38 Hit the trails
39 So
40 Pray
43 Having had a good workout
45 Spits out
46 Painter of bathers
47 Verdi opus
48 Yucca fibers
50 Beat (out)
51 Ordinal ending
52 ——-Finnish War
54 Gds.
56 Dirty dog
57 "Exodus" hero
58 "Road" film destination
59 G, e.g., but not H

by Alan Arbesfeld

ACROSS

1 Lavish entertainment
5 At a distance
9 Russian country house
14 Realtor's unit
15 Exploration org.
16 Actor Hawke
17 Title for Jesus
20 Chi-town team
21 Slimmer's regimen
22 Contents of Bartlett's
23 Peddle
24 Mows
25 Lightest-colored
28 Pre-dye hair shade, often
29 Revolutionary Guevara
32 Champion tennis servers
33 Russia's ___ Mountains
34 "Slow down!"
35 1976 Walter Matthau/Tatum O'Neal movie
38 Private investigators, for short
39 Iranian money
40 Africa's Sierra ___
41 Suffix with book or freak
42 Baseball glove
43 Expired
44 Smooth, as a drive
45 One of the three H's in a summer weather forecast
46 Gas rating number
49 Coarse fiber
50 "Ugh!"
53 1958 best seller by William J. Lederer and Eugene Burdick
56 Concise
57 Shakespeare's stream
58 Major-___ (bigwig)
59 Name on a deed
60 Store
61 One more time

DOWN

1 Chief parts of adipose tissue
2 Sound in a long hallway
3 Big-mouthed carnivorous dinosaur, for short
4 Hosp. brain readout
5 Make sacred
6 No longer bright
7 Aide: Abbr.
8 The old college cheer
9 Second-in-command
10 One of the Three Musketeers
11 Atkins of country music
12 Big-eared hopper
13 "No ifs, ___ or buts"
18 Texas oil city
19 Is, in math
23 Predicate parts
24 Words moving along the bottom of a TV screen
25 Singer Page
26 Suffers after overexercise
27 Bloodsucker
28 Terrific
29 Total confusion
30 Singer Lena or Marilyn
31 Relaxed
33 Come together
34 Tearful
36 Twaddle
37 Sports jacket
42 Christmas display sight
43 Underlying
44 Temporary halt
45 Comedy
46 Director Preminger
47 Prepare to swallow
48 Beach bird
49 Coffee, slangily
50 Universally known figure
51 Arrived
52 "Well, what do you ___?!"
54 Thanksgiving side dish
55 Boise's home: Abbr.

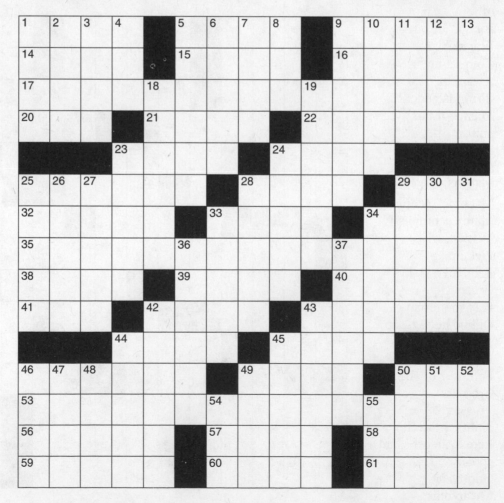

by Janet R. Bender

ACROSS
1 Sign at an A.T.M.
5 Smooth
11 Afternoon social
14 Slender instrument
15 Without delay
16 Columnist Buchwald
17 Actress Moore
18 Ringers
20 Freshwater fish with silvery scales
22 For each
23 Cone producer
25 Punch hard
28 Tiny bit
29 Ringers
33 Actress Hatcher
34 Vessel of 1492
35 Ringers
42 Calais concept
43 Ones with war stories
45 Ringers
51 Tater
52 Butcher's, baker's or candlestick maker's
53 Western tribe member
54 Equips with metal plating
57 Indispensable
59 Ringers
62 Hit the spot
65 Air hero
66 In abundance
67 Some investments, for short
68 Noted Turner
69 Aft ends
70 Certain cobras

DOWN
1 Cape —
2 Justice Fortas
3 Shade maker for a siesta
4 —— to the throne
5 Deli meat
6 Kind of clock or number
7 Additionally
8 Voter's finger stainer
9 Scholastic sports grp.
10 Cry of pain
11 Assume responsibility for
12 Raises
13 Confused
19 Late afternoon on a sundial
21 Educated guess: Abbr.
23 Hale
24 Checked a license, informally
26 Trigonometric function
27 Director Kazan
30 Quick drink
31 Old cable TV inits.
32 Jokester
36 Indy 500 locale
37 Summer N.Y. hrs.
38 Hula hoops?
39 A Gabor
40 Habitués
41 Manuscript annotation
44 Copenhagen-to-Prague dir.
45 Evergreen
46 All excited
47 Favorite
48 Rule
49 Showy blooms
50 Encountered
51 Nasser's successor
55 Semis
56 Ella Fitzgerald specialty
58 Largest of seven
60 Barley brew
61 Craggy prominence
63 Utilize
64 Double-180 maneuver

by Gene Newman

ACROSS

1 Fraternity letter
4 Battery contents
8 Oldtime actress Todd
14 Personal
15 Goof off
16 Attack
17 Stop on it
18 No neatnik
19 Anxiety
20 Cartier's Christmas creation?
23 In any way
24 Stat for Sammy Sosa
25 Thimblerig thing
27 Meal
30 Ones soon to leave the ivied halls: Abbr.
31 Subcompact
32 American Revolutionary portraitist
34 Illegal act, in slang
35 Capote's least favorite road sign?
39 Olympus competitor
40 "I'm in!"
41 Just
42 "Noble" element
43 Woven fabrics
48 Narc's employer: Abbr.
49 Fall from grace
50 12 chimes
51 Songbird's lament?
57 Sounded like a Persian
58 Point to the right
59 Driver's org.
60 Shed
61 Shade of green
62 Comic strip cry
63 Didn't go straight
64 Scored the same
65 Like few counties nowadays

DOWN

1 Drink at the Duke's Head
2 Deviate
3 Completely committed
4 Likewise
5 Massage target for a runner
6 Popular shirt maker
7 Actress Mazar
8 All ___
9 City on the Hong River
10 Tied
11 Absolute
12 "Le Cid" composer
13 Got the fare down
21 Chapter of history
22 Collar
26 Run on TV
28 Hand measure
29 Hué New Year
30 Swings around
31 Wild West
33 Big name in fashion
34 Montana Indian
35 Johnny Unitas wore it
36 Norman's home
37 Diminutive, as a dog
38 Rug rat
39 Silent agreement
42 Prepared for action
44 Gerund maker
45 Lit
46 More protracted
47 Sly
49 Computer honcho Wozniak
52 Jedi ally
53 Play Shylock
54 Hideaway
55 Man, but not woman
56 Be hot and bothered
57 Miss after marriage

by Richard Silvestri

ACROSS

1 French cleric
5 Enthusiasm
9 Slightly open
13 "Time ___,"1990's sci-fi TV series
14 1950's candidate Stevenson
16 Art ___
17 56-Across figure
19 Bushy do
20 Birds' homes
21 Stabbed
23 Job application attachments
24 "Bird on ___," 1990 Mel Gibson movie
25 Carrier to Sweden
26 Before: Abbr.
27 Necessary: Abbr.
30 ___ Parks, former "Miss America" host
33 Two under par
34 Man's nickname that's an alphabetic run
35 W.C., in England
36 56-Across figure
38 Metal in rocks
39 Popular card game
40 When some TV news comes on
41 Change for a five
42 Superman's symbol
43 Brings into play
44 Singer Sumac
46 Faux pas
48 Fierce one
52 Vance of "I Love Lucy"
54 Place to buy a yacht
55 Mimicked
56 S. Dakota monument
58 ___ of Man
59 Happening
60 Johnson who said "Ver-r-r-y interesting!"

61 Loads
62 Puts in extra
63 Spick-and-span

DOWN

1 Battling
2 Indian who may be 1-Down
3 Foundation
4 Tire out
5 Cutups
6 A sphere lacks them
7 Computer keys: Abbr.
8 Neighbor of a Vietnamese
9 Firefighter Red
10 56-Across figure
11 Farm unit
12 Crucifix
15 Place to dip an old pen
18 "___ la Douce," 1963 film
22 Actor David of "Separate Tables"
24 Laser gas
26 Walks outside the delivery room?
28 To be, in France
29 Opposite of an ans.
30 Ocean-colored
31 Millions of years
32 56-Across figure
33 Set foot in
36 Mrs. Bush
37 "My treat!"

41 One who rows, rows, rows the boat
44 Breadmakers' needs
45 Algebra or trig
47 Disneyland attractions
48 Headed (for)
49 Taking out the trash, for one
50 Heart line
51 Chirp
52 Colorado resort
53 ___ facto
54 Partner of born
57 Dam project: Abbr.

by Sherry O. Blackard

ACROSS

1 Retreats
7 Dry, as wine
10 It leaves marks on asphalt
14 Triumphant cry
15 Word often said twice before "again"
16 Numbers game
17 She wed George Washington
20 Niagara Falls' prov.
21 Karel Čapek play
22 Church nooks
23 Where Washington relaxed
28 Wrath
29 Pi preceder
34 Friend in the Southwest
37 Forsaken
39 Ready for picking
40 State defense organization headed by Washington
43 Its flight attendants' greeting is "Shalom"
44 Magician's start
45 Word prefixed with poly-
46 Edison's New Jersey lab locale
48 "Welcome" site
49 Where Washington's forces wintered
55 Defense aid
59 Writer Fleming
60 Time Warner merger partner
61 Colonial force headed by Washington
66 —— Stanley Gardner
67 Belfry flier
68 —— corpus
69 Faculty head
70 Not just tear up
71 "Tristram Shandy" author

DOWN

1 Televised sign in football stands
2 Hersey's bell town
3 Love of artistic objects
4 D.C. summer clock setting
5 Fed. biomedical research agcy.
6 Deprive of food
7 Fab Four drummer
8 Directional suffix
9 Dancer Charisse
10 Old record problem
11 Popular sneakers
12 "Picnic" playwright
13 Female deer
18 —— date
19 Rajah's wife
24 Carp
25 "Star Trek: T.N.G." counselor
26 Bellini opera
27 Prefix with potent
30 "The Count of Monte ——"
31 Film director Martin
32 Mayberry boy
33 Close
34 Swear to
35 Actor O'Shea
36 Investments usually held for yrs. and yrs.
37 Kind of suit found in a courtroom
38 Sculling need
41 Queen in "The Lion King"
42 Page (through)
47 Chapter 57
48 Avian talkers
50 Needing a good brushing, say
51 Ingest
52 Scarcer
53 Beatnik's encouragement
54 "Family Ties" mom
55 Served past
56 Oral tradition
57 "To Live and Die ——"
58 Bingo call
62 Peacock network
63 Musical talent
64 Long.'s opposite
65 Face on a fiver

by Ed Early

ACROSS
1 Chest adornment
6 Candidate for rehab
10 Somewhat, in music
14 Really go for
15 Boffo review
16 Apricot-shaped
17 Valentine's Day pastries?
19 Make rhapsodic
20 Top of a suit?
21 Mrs. Chaplin
22 Hardly suited for Mensa
23 Director Craven
24 Rainy months?
27 Sword handles
29 Pickled delicacies
30 A lot of binary code
32 Asian nurse
33 — mater (brain covering)
36 Subtly added mistakes? . . . or a title for this puzzle
41 Part of marbling
42 Wild revelry
43 Rainfall measure
44 Suffix with buck
45 Areas usually decorated with stained glass
48 Attempt to score in hockey?
52 New Deal inits.
55 Viking attire
56 Teen spots?
57 Sibling, e.g.: Abbr.
58 "Yikes!"
59 Fork in a mountain pass?
62 Zola heroine
63 ". . . — sum"
64 Try to bite
65 They lack refinement
66 It's held at eateries
67 "Later, dude!"

DOWN
1 Colorful parrot
2 Draw forth
3 Horse player's buy
4 "Exodus" hero
5 Went first
6 Father of the Titans
7 Port south of Osaka
8 Time to revel, perhaps
9 Hi-— graphics
10 Pretend to be
11 Pizza places
12 Playground retort
13 Bygone
18 Stallion, once
22 Indian metropolis
25 2004 Boston conventioneers, informally
26 One of a Navy elite
28 Sun Devils' sch.
30 Clocked out
31 Anti-Brady Bill org.
32 In the least
33 Line of suits?
34 "Monsters, —" (2001 animated film)
35 Bone china component
37 Column style
38 Will or fist preceder
39 Really eager
40 Pizza
44 Nike rival
45 Blessing evoker
46 Swimming site
47 Suds holders
48 Minutes taker, maybe
49 Indiana senator Richard
50 Really dumb
51 Needing a lift
53 5/8/45
54 Prince Valiant's lady
59 Hesitation sound
60 Public radio host Glass
61 Compete

by Lee Glickstein

44

ACROSS
1 Livens (up)
5 Snapshot
10 Bedazzles
14 Away from the wind
15 Home run king Hank
16 Retail store
17 Glib responses
19 On the ocean
20 Baffled
21 Canines or bicuspids
23 New Haven collegians
24 Personal bugbear
27 Observer
30 Quattros, e.g.
31 Some sports cars
34 Take into custody
37 Supreme Diana
38 Go bad
39 Indy service break
41 Sport ___ (all-purpose vehicle)
42 Med. school subj.
44 Caviar source
45 Price add-on
46 Subway handhold
48 Make into law
50 Kind of stove
53 Smooch
56 Major company in metallic products
57 Drink often served with a lemon twist
60 Skin woe
62 Portfolio hedges
64 Eliot or Frost
65 One of the nine Muses
66 "Lohengrin" soprano
67 Drags
68 Heroic tales
69 Not shallow

DOWN
1 Mama's partner
2 Fill with joy
3 Flower feature
4 Protect, as freshness
5 Free ticket
6 Hems' partners
7 Source of iron or lead
8 Rich pastry
9 Beginning
10 Not an expert
11 Exhausted
12 Before, in verse
13 Depot: Abbr.
18 "Forget it!"
22 Clean air org.
24 "Blue Hawaii" star
25 Far-reaching view
26 "The Private Lives of Elizabeth and ___" (1939 film)
28 Common newspaper nickname
29 Art Deco designer
31 Understand
32 Jay Silverheels role
33 Go back to square one
35 Surprise greatly
36 Roman robe
40 Bundle
43 Things held by Moses
47 Chest muscle, for short
49 Neatened
51 Easy strides
52 Designer Ashley
54 Item worn around the shoulders
55 Pick up on
57 Teensy bit
58 Navy noncoms, for short
59 "Rush!" order
60 It may be a walk-up: Abbr.
61 Dove's sound
63 Children's game

by Marjorie Berg

ACROSS

1 Film mogul Louis B. (whose company mascot was 26-Across)
6 "Funny!"
10 Hard to fluster
14 Mrs. David O. Selznick, daughter of 1-Across
15 Assist in wrongdoing
16 Hodgepodge
17 One lacking courage
19 On the briny
20 ___ Tuesday
21 Take the first step
23 Poland's Walesa
25 Tam sporter
26 Roarer in film intros
29 Sty fare
31 Eucalyptus-loving "bears"
35 Drive-thru dispenser, maybe
36 Gazetteer statistic
38 Sporty Mazda
39 Courage seeker in a 1939 film
43 Top man in the choir?
44 ___ proprietor
45 SSW's opposite
46 Fake
48 Crowe's "A Beautiful Mind" role
50 Suffix with chariot
51 Pack and send
53 Reply to "That so?"
55 Deuterium and tritium, to hydrogen
59 Make unreadable, for security
63 Island near Java
64 One feigning courage
66 Tied in score
67 "___ homo"
68 Put ___ in one's ear
69 An earth sci.
70 Not fake
71 Cake sections

DOWN

1 Fail to catch
2 Keystone's place
3 Reunion number
4 Sign up
5 Superman player George
6 Barn loft contents
7 Basics
8 Puts on the burner
9 Tear into
10 Formal jacket feature
11 What's more
12 In ___ of
13 A drawbridge may span one
18 Render harmless, perhaps, to 26-Across's kin
22 Hardly cramped
24 Round dances
26 Starbucks order
27 Old anesthetic
28 Prophetic signs
30 Argentina's Juan
32 Frankie or Cleo
33 Do penance
34 Less dotty
37 Ike's two-time opponent
40 Exerting little effort
41 Straight: Prefix
42 Former Georgia governor Maddox
47 Sleeping bag closer
49 Suggest subtly
52 Treaty result
54 "Star Wars" genre
55 "___ to differ"
56 Except for
57 Promise product
58 Shelter org.
60 Gape at
61 Whitetail, e.g.
62 Notable times
65 Slithery swimmer

by Gilbert H. Ludwig

ACROSS

1 Strip —
5 Favored by God
10 Wielding a peeler, maybe
14 Locket shape
15 Instant message sender, perhaps
16 Disney lioness
17 Purse item
18 Popular group dance
20 Like dessert wines
22 Top-2% group
23 "Ich bin — Berliner"
24 Travelers' org.
26 Plod along
28 Toasters do it
34 River islet
35 Farmer's letters?
36 Salinger title girl
40 Desk set item
44 Van —, Calif.
45 Enter again
46 Neighbor of Braz.
47 Four-runner?
51 Break into parts, as a monopoly
54 Hoo-ha
55 Notebook maker
56 Unwelcome forecast
60 Potter's potions professor
64 One with a half-interest
67 Laundry item
68 Earthen pot
69 Commercial prefix with liner
70 Grant for a film?
71 Lone Star State sch.
72 Rodeo critter
73 Girl or boy lead-in

DOWN

1 Comfy footwear
2 Swear to
3 — duck
4 Lands' End competitor
5 Dickensian epithet
6 Warp-and-weft machine
7 Actress Sommer
8 Glimpsed
9 Soap opera meetings
10 A Beatle bride
11 In one's natural state
12 Movie set light: Var.
13 John of "Miracle on 34th Street"
19 Peel
21 1970's Japanese P.M. — Fukuda
25 Not "fer"
27 Worked with
28 — Crunch
29 Place
30 Humble response to praise
31 Pick up
32 Felt under the weather
33 Taints
37 Most of it nowadays is filtered
38 — mortals
39 Many an M.I.T. grad: Abbr.
41 U.S.A.F. rank
42 "Nana" author
43 Old oath
48 Sign of disuse
49 Self-assurance
50 Friend on "Friends"
51 Exquisite trinket
52 Letter-shaped fastener
53 Prepare to get shot?
57 Water holder
58 Course on insects, for short
59 Fork-tailed flier
61 "I smell —"
62 Left side
63 "Only Time" singer
65 Quick rest
66 Bird in the "Arabian Nights"

by James M. Jenista and Dana McLemore

ACROSS

1 Look (at), as stars
5 Artist's suffix with land or sea
10 Tortoiselike
14 "___ Around" (#1 Beach Boys hit)
15 Breaking a bad one is good
16 El ___, Tex.
17 ___-a-brac
18 Big kitchen appliance maker
19 Eight, in Spain
20 Wife of King David
22 Prepare to pop the question
23 Nova Scotia clock setting: Abbr.
24 June 14
26 Hamburger meat
30 Peter who was a seven-time Oscar nominee
32 Last full month of summer
34 Departure's opposite: Abbr.
35 Penny
39 Cheater's aid
40 Yellowish shade
42 Asian nurse
43 President before Wilson
44 Australian hopper, for short
45 Igloo dweller
47 "To be or not to be" soliloquist
50 Woman of "Troy"
51 One taking flight
54 That, in Tijuana
56 Scent
57 "Days of Our Lives," for one
63 "The World According to ___"
64 Ne plus ___
65 Slightly

66 Feminine suffix
67 Full . . . and happy about it
68 Mideast's ___ Strip
69 Active one
70 Cursed
71 School before middle school: Abbr.

DOWN

1 Any of the Bee Gees
2 Taj Mahal site
3 Time, in Mannheim
4 Work on glass, say
5 Former Iranian leaders
6 Awoke
7 Basic rhyme scheme
8 "H.M.S. ___"
9 Third letter after delta
10 Light dessert
11 Donned skates, e.g., with "up"
12 Actor Milo
13 Sheeplike
21 Declares
22 ___ Kan (pet food)
25 Peter who played Mr. Moto
26 Agreement
27 Atmosphere
28 End-of-week cry
29 Noisy public speaker
31 California/Nevada lake
33 Singer nicknamed the Velvet Fog
36 Oscar winner Jannings
37 Partner of rank and serial number
38 Ending with tele-
41 Side dish at KFC
46 "Scram!"
48 Old Turkish title
49 Ripper
51 Ran amok
52 Poetry Muse
53 Talent
55 Ditchdigger's tool
58 Director Preminger
59 Newspaper unit
60 And others, in footnotes
61 Completely demolish
62 One who raised Cain
64 Inits. in Navy ship names

by Christina Houlihan Kelly

48

ACROSS
1 Actor Damon
5 Great buy, slangily
10 Go yachting
14 Met solo
15 Inventor Nikola
16 Ides of March utterance
17 Timid creature
18 Big name in chips
19 "Hud" Oscar winner
20 Actor Ben with the gang?
23 ——-mo
25 Cornhusker State: Abbr.
26 Like good soil
27 Chops to bits
29 Best Actress winner for "Million Dollar Baby"
31 Really enjoyed
32 Democratic honcho Howard
33 Roadside sign
36 Marathoner Frank with candy?
40 Layer?
41 Richly adorn
42 Easy mark
43 Nutty as a fruitcake
45 Motor City hoopster
46 Mel Ott, notably
48 Several eras
49 Unlock, poetically
50 Novelist Evan with a small smooch?
54 Man Friday, e.g.
55 Publicist's concern
56 Workbook segment
59 Puts into play
60 "Our Gang" dog
61 Mower maker
62 Document content
63 Dorm annoyance
64 Cashless deal

DOWN
1 "Spy vs. Spy" magazine
2 "You —— here"
3 Gets soused
4 Pucker-producing
5 Metro entrances
6 Potato sack wt., maybe
7 Renaissance family name
8 K.C. Royal, e.g.
9 Space cadet's place
10 Author/illustrator Maurice
11 First-stringers
12 Europe's "boot"
13 Quiet time
21 Like a stumblebum
22 —— compos mentis
23 Not just a success
24 Like a ballerina
28 Despicable sort
29 Serta competitor
30 Harry Potter accessory
32 Icicle former
33 Become familiar with
34 Fabulous author
35 "Funny Girl" composer Jule
37 Voyages in vain?
38 Place for a title
39 Used to be
43 Up-to-the-minute
44 White Monopoly bill
45 "I yam what I yam" speaker
46 False front
47 Encyclopedia volume
48 Landscaper's tool
50 —— monde
51 "You said it!"
52 Defense grp.
53 Roster removals
57 Lyrical Gershwin
58 Blouse, e.g.

by Deb Amlen

49

ACROSS

1 Light ——
6 Defender of some unpopular causes, in brief
10 "Jabberwocky" starter
14 Father —— Sarducci of "S.N.L."
15 Game delayer
16 "I can't —— thing!"
17 Comedy troupe since the 60's
20 Org. with bomb-sniffing dogs
21 Gull-like predator
22 Enter cautiously
23 The Joads, e.g.
25 Features of some cell phones
26 Breakfast bowlful
28 "Really?!"
29 Milk: Prefix
30 Gives a rap
31 Hogwarts letter carrier
34 Bellicose god
35 Propelled a shell
36 Peau de —— (soft cloth)
37 Part of w.p.m.
38 Orbital point
39 —— nova
40 Slips on a slip
42 Housekeeper, at times
43 Lights into
45 Margaret Mead study site
46 From there
47 Geeky sort
48 Nashville sch.
51 Momentous
54 Double contraction
55 Egyptian Christian
56 Bubbling over
57 Poetic adverb
58 Gas brand in Canada
59 Like unwashed rugs

DOWN

1 Fuji competitor
2 Exec
3 Military part-timers
4 Chemical suffix
5 "William Tell" composer
6 Giant slain by Hermes
7 Water-to-wine site
8 Beyond tipsy
9 Cold
10 Prickly plant
11 London rail hub
12 Places in the heart
13 Composer Camille Saint-——
18 Swedish chain
19 Chair designer Charles
24 Hobby shop stock
25 Nuclei
26 Brouhaha
27 Bern's river
28 MTV teen toon
30 Broadway rosters
32 Cheeky
33 Shakespearean king
35 Shimmer
36 Passable
38 "If I Were —— Man"
39 Short end of the stick
41 Blusterer
42 1960's–70's Dodge
43 Had home cooking
44 Parasol's offering
45 Brief tussle
47 Drops off
49 Piqued state
50 Beyond homely
52 Sounds from Santa
53 Baseball card stat.

by Rob Richardson

50

ACROSS

1 Baldwin of the silver screen
5 Recur, as arthritis
10 Father of Seth
14 Actress Hatcher
15 Computer item with a tracking ball
16 Aura being picked up
17 Possibly prompting a reply like 25-, 47- or 62-Across
20 Supersede
21 Immature insects
22 Rink surface
23 Rep.'s opponent
24 Singer Sumac
25 "What?!"
31 Companion of Tarzan
32 It's good only for its waste value
33 T-bone or porterhouse
37 Not so much
39 Noted Tombstone family, once
41 Ancient Roman censor
42 Like beer at a bar
44 River's mouth
46 Sign outside a hit show
47 "What?!"
50 Railroad stop: Abbr.
53 End of a proof
54 Chem. thread
55 Meat-packing pioneer
57 Chosen one
62 "What?!"
64 Slugger Sammy
65 Sailor's "Halt!"
66 "The Thin Man" wife
67 European car
68 Nigeria's largest city
69 Son of Seth

DOWN

1 "___ additional cost!"
2 Pope after Benedict IV
3 Folies Bergère designer
4 Kind of acid
5 Atmosphere, as in a restaurant
6 For both sexes
7 Toothpaste holder
8 "It's no ___!"
9 Shotgun shot
10 State unequivocally
11 Split (up)
12 At right angles to a ship
13 Jason's ally and lover, in myth
18 Killer whales
19 Poetic feet
23 Horse with a spotted coat
25 Sign of a saint
26 Unlock
27 Toward sunset
28 Swapped
29 Sheik's bevy
30 And others: Abbr.
34 Facility
35 Gillette brand
36 Wacko
38 Problem with an old sofa
40 Hollywood hopefuls
43 Resentment
45 "Li'l ___" (Al Capp strip)
48 Springlike
49 "Phèdre" playwright
50 Final approval
51 Custer cluster
52 Entertain
56 Kind of history
57 For men only
58 Studebaker's fill-up, maybe
59 Daffy Duck or Porky Pig
60 Continental currency
61 Those: Sp.
63 Eggs

by Robert Malinow

51

ACROSS

1 Frisks, with "down"
5 Muhammad's birthplace
10 Elisabeth of "Leaving Las Vegas"
14 Ranch unit
15 Pong maker
16 Hoopster Malone
17 "All I Wanna Do" singer, 1994
19 Toledo's lake
20 Pekoe server
21 Luggage attachment
23 Threw in
24 French article
26 Like woolen underwear?
27 Salsa scooper-uppers
29 Sun. delivery
30 Yeats or Keats
33 Boys' or girls' room, in London
34 Attack by plane
37 Cleansed (of)
38 First U.S. chief justice
40 Hide-hair link
41 No longer in style
43 Press for payment
44 Palm reader, e.g.
45 Hither's partner
46 Rigid bracelet
48 Bill of fare
50 Needle hole
51 Gut course
55 All riled up
57 Rich's partner
58 Say "Uncle!"
59 "Network" star
62 On the ocean
63 No longer in style
64 Add kick to
65 Flat rate?
66 Late actor Davis
67 Chapters of history

DOWN

1 Orzo, e.g.
2 Had a yen
3 Radial pattern
4 Eve's tempter
5 Fountain offering
6 Catchall abbr.
7 Cougar or Lynx
8 Hags
9 Sony competitor
10 Summer pest, informally
11 "The Bridge" poet
12 Dickens's —— Heep
13 Mournful poem
18 Luke Skywalker's mentor
22 Like the air around Niagara Falls
24 "Looks like trouble!"
25 Lunchtime, for many
28 Congealment
30 Country club figure
31 Mideast export
32 Singer with the 1988 #1 country hit "I'm Gonna Get You"
34 Acted the fink
35 Antagonist
36 Flub
38 Leigh of "Psycho"
39 Month for many Geminis
42 Difficult spot
44 Mariner's measure
46 Guardian Angels toppers
47 Table extension
48 New dad's handout
49 Biscotti flavoring
52 Salvage ship's equipment
53 New Mexico's state flower
54 Cookout leftovers?
56 —— facto
57 For the asking
60 Profs' helpers
61 Yalie

by Gail Grabowski

52

ACROSS
1 Service unit
7 Itinerary abbr.
10 Blunders
14 Garner of jazz
15 "Get it?"
16 Nair competitor
17 Watergate judge John
18 Biblical jawbone source
19 Way off
20 "No kidding!?"
23 Give, as odds
25 Untrustworthy sort
26 Up ___ (trapped)
27 Really attractive
32 Tolkien creature
33 Stop by
34 Hugs, in a letter
35 Drugs, briefly
36 Trip to the Bahamas, e.g.
40 "Doonesbury" character based on Hunter S. Thompson
43 Rock's Bon Jovi
44 Pushed hard
48 Genetic material
49 "The Mothers-in-Law" co-star
52 Bone: Prefix
54 Bend shape
55 European carrier
56 Jimmy Carter autobiography
61 Zilch
62 Narrow inlet
63 Habituates
66 Blue-pencil
67 Creature with a tiny waist
68 Bar request
69 "___ Dinah" (Frankie Avalon's first hit)
70 Range units: Abbr.
71 Word spelled phonetically by the starts of 1-, 20-, 27-, 36-, 49- and 56-Across

DOWN
1 French possessive
2 "___ tu" (Verdi aria)
3 In formation
4 Rope fiber
5 Develop sores
6 Dabble in
7 Biblical twin
8 Hardy heroine
9 Ricky player in '50s TV
10 Put on the books
11 Grid coin tosser
12 Collide with, in a way
13 D and C, in D.C.
21 Like Nasdaq trades
22 Xanthippe, e.g.
23 Peggy with the 1958 hit "Fever"
24 Novelist Rand
28 Job for Perry Mason
29 Chanteuse Lena
30 Marker
31 "There's ___ in 'team'"
35 Old World blackbird
37 1977 double-platinum Steely Dan album
38 Playing hard to get
39 More morose
40 Blotted (out)
41 Expose to the sun
42 Grasshopper's cousin
45 Stomach-related
46 Stat. for Pedro Martinez
47 Letters on a shingle
49 "Kitchy-___!"
50 Waggle dance performer
51 Victoria's prince
53 Related maternally
57 Vehicle on rails
58 Glasses option
59 Boaters and bowlers
60 Muslim mystic
64 Yellowstone herd member
65 Like some grins

by Holden Baker

ACROSS

1 Brown shade used in old photos
6 Having protected feet
10 Postal delivery
14 Deal maker
15 2:00 or 3:00
16 Skin breakout
17 Head/legs separator
18 Cathedral area
19 Box office take
20 Short-lived success
23 Affirm
26 Congo, formerly
27 Lunch or dinner
28 Hand: Sp.
31 Furthermore
32 Vintage designation
33 Oscar winner for "Scent of a Woman"
35 Short-lived success
40 Octagons, hexagons, etc.
41 The "E" of Q.E.D.
43 Greek cross
46 "___ a man with seven wives"
47 Counterpart of midterms
49 Mary of old films
51 Close of a swimming race
52 Short-lived success
56 10th-grader, for short
57 Skater Lipinski
58 Ballet rail
62 Cleveland's lake
63 Give off
64 Elicit
65 What a detective follows
66 Kind of room
67 Paper size larger than "letter"

DOWN

1 Used a pew
2 Swelled head
3 The "p" of r.p.m.
4 To the degree that
5 Makes amends
6 Former Iranian rulers
7 Mesa dweller
8 Evict
9 Picked from the stack of cards
10 ___ cum laude
11 Maine's ___ National Park
12 Summer office worker
13 Looked lecherously
21 Founded: Abbr.
22 Atmosphere layer
23 Be inquisitive
24 Atoll protector
25 Iridescent gem
28 "Olympia" painter
29 Deeds
30 Disease research org.
33 Prop for Santa
34 NAFTA concept
36 Collar site
37 Lunch meat
38 Asia's shrinking ___ Sea
39 "The Lion King" lion
42 Cooking meas.
43 It's on the fringe
44 Toward land
45 Perfect world
47 Blubber
48 Sanford of "The Jeffersons"
50 Marveled aloud
51 Atty.-to-be exams
53 News bit
54 Tattle on
55 Small beam
59 Alternative to a bare floor
60 "His Master's Voice" sloganeer
61 Sushi fish

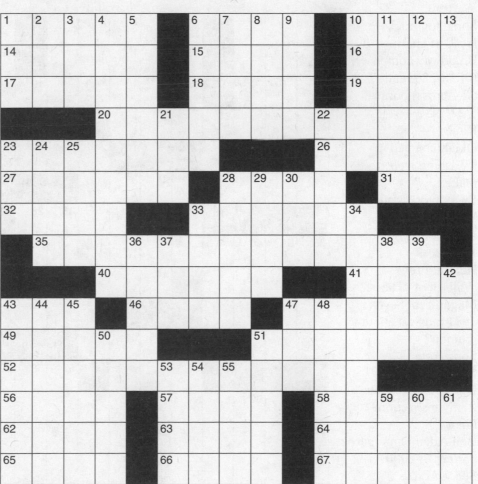

by Mike Torch

ACROSS

1 Hardwood tree
4 Nosed (out)
9 With 69-Across, song from 20-Across
14 Give the umpire grief
15 Mr. Moto player
16 Kid's retort
17 Big inits. in TV comedy
18 1979 musical about a half-mad barber
20 1970 musical about marriage
22 Fury
23 U.S.: Abbr.
24 See 51-Across
29 Container with a screw-top
33 ___ vera
34 Some toy trucks
37 Head of Haiti
38 Broadway composer (of 18-, 20- and 57-Across) born 3/22/1930
43 Rime
44 Oklahoma native
45 "Wishing won't make ___"
46 Encounter, as success
51 With 24-Across, song from 18-Across
55 Height: Prefix
56 Wallach of "The Magnificent Seven"
57 1971 musical about a reunion
60 Song from 57-Across
65 Unforgettable Cole
66 Army inspection?
67 Giant
68 Bell Atlantic merger partner of 2000
69 See 9-Across
70 Refine, as metal
71 One of the Chaplins

DOWN

1 Early 80's political scandal
2 California winemaking county
3 Noted resident of Baker Street
4 "Born Free" lioness
5 Like the answer to this clue
6 Lady Jane ___
7 Before, in verse
8 Jeans material
9 Aspirin maker
10 CPR giver, for short
11 Skater Midori
12 Give the go-ahead
13 The Almighty
19 Noteworthy time
21 Specialist
24 Annoying
25 It's sworn at a swearing-in
26 Peter Fonda title role
27 Reply to the Little Red Hen
28 Consider
30 Utmost
31 Average guys
32 ___ Domini
35 First-rate
36 Old dagger
38 Climb, as a pole
39 Canine from Kansas
40 Bridge hand
41 Ship's front
42 Richard Gere title role
47 ___-Mart
48 Cake toppers
49 Pact
50 Entertained
52 "Die Lorelei" poet
53 Under the weather
54 Light rhythms
57 Party
58 Kind of exam
59 Advanced
60 C.D. holder, maybe
61 Alice's sitcom boss
62 H.S. course
63 "Mazel ___!"
64 Not her

by David J. Kahn

NOTE: As a demonstration of speed puzzle construction at the 28th Annual American Crossword Puzzle Tournament, on March 11, 2005, in Stamford, Connecticut, Mike Shenk took a theme proposed by the audience and created this puzzle, start to finish, without computer-assisted fill, in 60 minutes. Later, in a race to solve it, Trip Payne of Boca Raton, Florida, finished first, in three minutes. About two-thirds of the audience completed the puzzle correctly within the 15-minute time limit.

ACROSS

1 Desert flora
6 Coated candy
11 Interstice
14 Wolf pack member
15 Without company
16 Outback runner
17 Vegetarian tennis star?
19 Surfing site
20 They're underfoot
21 All in
23 Greet the opposing team
26 Vanna's partner
27 Gets along
29 Tibias' ends
31 Culminating point
32 Femme fatale
33 Choral work
34 Doc bloc, for short
37 Volunteer's words
38 Bone connector
39 Thick cut
40 Kareem, once
41 Misanthrope
42 Roberts of "Mystic Pizza"
43 Camera card contents
45 Mass parts
46 Sunday paper section
48 Memorial Day setting
49 Course start
50 Bound to experience
51 Goes belly-up
53 Rockies tree
54 Vegetarian film critic?
60 Popular season on the Riviera
61 Drove to distraction
62 Austin Powers's father
63 Curious George creator H. A. ___
64 Demands
65 Sharpshooting Shaq

DOWN

1 New reporter
2 Penny portrait
3 Runner Sebastian
4 Does a doily
5 Answer to a knock
6 "American Buffalo" playwright
7 Yodelers' milieu
8 Hide-hair link
9 Modern evidence
10 Camper's gear
11 Vegetarian film critic?
12 Change the Constitution
13 Tie up a boat
18 Sighed cry
22 Sulky state
23 Pesto base
24 In reserve
25 Vegetarian talk show star?
27 Poet's concern
28 Fresh
30 Cariou of "Sweeney Todd"
31 Shipping areas
33 Itty-bitty bugs
35 L. L. Bean's home
36 Lower
38 Wise fellow
39 Catch some rays
41 Kind of turn
42 "Leading With My Chin" author
44 6 on a phone
45 First born?
46 Drummer's partner
47 Bring together
48 Hotel staffers
51 Hightailed it
52 It's got you covered
55 Beatitudes verb
56 Island strings
57 Epoch
58 Salonga of "Miss Saigon"
59 Wing

by Mike Shenk

ACROSS

1 Is in a play
5 Layers
11 Tool with teeth
14 Jacket
15 Rang, as bells
16 Swiss canton
17 Famous large deep-blue rock
19 Brooch
20 An hour before midnight
21 Illegally seized
23 Filled with joy
26 Game played on 64 squares
27 Say more
30 Sly maneuver
31 Prophet
32 Make void
34 Money in Mexico
36 Strikebreaker
39 Shows for the first time
41 Yield to desire
43 Similar (to)
44 Cry in court
46 Ordinary
47 Pub projectile
49 Prosperity
51 Maidenform product
52 Hindu social division
54 Admit to wrongdoing
56 Calm down
58 Injuries near beehives
62 Savings for old age, for short
63 Military decoration
66 Get ___ of (toss out)
67 Rubs out
68 "Bye"
69 Cheer for a matador
70 Puts trust in, with "on"
71 Site of Napoleon's exile

DOWN

1 Dull hurt
2 Refrigerate
3 Put on reel-to-reel
4 Jobs in the computer field
5 Kind of column
6 Alternative to coffee
7 Male sheep
8 For all to hear
9 Sawbucks
10 Bring forth as evidence
11 Site for eating and entertainment
12 7-Down, astrologically
13 Orchestra section
18 Greek oracle site
22 Kind of monkey
24 ___-turvy
25 Hurricane's center
27 Shade of blue
28 Drop, as a doughnut in milk
29 "Just Shoot Me" co-star
31 Daughter's opposite
33 Half of Congress
35 Medium, large and extra-large
37 Ice cream thickening agent
38 Lugosi who played Dracula
40 Hollywood filming locale
42 Minnesota port
45 7-Down's mate
48 Autumn farm worker
50 Estimate the value of
52 Egypt's capital
53 Shower bringer
54 Wild
55 Jigsaw puzzle element
57 Without a doubt
59 Hammer's target
60 Take hold of
61 Portico in Greek architecture
64 Letter before omega
65 ___ jeans

by Elizabeth Babikan

ACROSS
1 Stared stupidly
6 Light bulb units
11 Sweetums
14 Simple counters
15 Potato growers' home
16 Big galoot
17 Convince a G.I.?
19 Cause to fret
20 Peruvian range
21 Not naked
23 Was dependent
26 Bunt result, maybe
27 Like the Wolfman
28 It goes under a top
30 "The Republic" philosopher
31 Work units
32 Secure position
34 Baseball bat wood
35 Random attack
36 Evidence in a paternity suit
39 No pieces of cake
41 Masterstroke
42 Water balloon sound
44 Wind up or down
45 Tropical lizard
46 "As Good As It Gets" film studio
48 Hit on the noggin
49 Gymnast Mary Lou
50 Go-between
52 Frequently, in verse
53 Refuse to work on the weekend?
58 Actor Billy —— Williams
59 Gives off
60 Hosiery shade
61 Blunder
62 "Belling the Cat" author
63 Casino array

DOWN
1 Burner fuel
2 Justice Fortas
3 Chum
4 Elongated pastries
5 Mickey Mouse operation?
6 Sly trick
7 Tacks on
8 Mai ——
9 Bara of old films
10 Touchy subject
11 Dine on some fish?
12 Gift-giver's urging
13 Abutting
18 Uneven?
22 Unit in a terrorist organization
23 Perlman of "Cheers"
24 Corn units
25 Burn trash?
26 Washed
28 Irritate
29 Violinist's application
32 London forecast
33 Sounds from Santa
35 Set sail
37 Microwave, slangily
38 Like two peas in ——
40 Hops-drying oven
41 Like some air-conditioning
42 Walked briskly
43 Like better
45 Rant and rave
47 Japanese cartoon art
48 Track action
50 Concerning
51 [You don't mean . . . !]
54 Rejoinder to " 'tain't!"
55 Dynamic ——
56 Quick to learn
57 Thumbs-up response

by Victor Fleming and Nelson Hardy

58

ACROSS

1 Cousin of a cockatoo
6 Read on the run
10 Lip
14 Sultanate citizen
15 Shower square
16 Fall preceder
17 Informal head cover
18 Housing ___
19 First name in architecture
20 One who gets a piece of the pie?
23 Kind of sauce
27 Religious commemoration
28 Fearful
30 Baltimore partner
32 Ticked off
33 Allude
35 Copy
38 Borderline logic?
42 Ring site
43 Cockamamie
44 Roll
45 Sing the praises of
46 Kind of ring
49 Bee-related
52 Ally in movies
53 "Stay away from the swamp grass"?
58 Poe product
59 Bridge
60 It may be well-taken
65 Pastry chef's aide
66 2003 A.L. M.V.P., familiarly
67 Displaced person
68 Some M&M's
69 Bank (on)
70 Durable fabric

DOWN

1 In style
2 Start of a Latin conjugation
3 Elevator part
4 Baptist leader?
5 Passamaquoddy home
6 Formal accessory
7 Double checker
8 Rival of Björn
9 Parcel
10 Sound setup
11 Final Four site
12 Horse fathers
13 Wear
21 Poetic conjunction
22 Combusted
23 Try a tidbit
24 Luau greeting
25 Not so common
26 Palm, e.g.
29 Huge worry
30 Did in
31 Part of H.M.S.
34 Many millennia
35 To the left or right
36 Put forward
37 Diary note
39 "Cheers" role
40 Savanna sight
41 Tissue additive
45 Some brews
47 Key abbr.
48 Masticated
49 Moving
50 Sign of the 1960's
51 Sat around
54 Open a bit
55 Scale start
56 Old fiddle
57 Dr. Jones, to friends
61 Fire truck accessory
62 Canterbury can
63 Elm City collegian
64 "Stand" band, 1989

by Richard Silvestri

ACROSS

1 Boss
6 Pepsi, for one
10 Not check or charge
14 Event with bucking broncos
15 Banned orchard spray
16 Prefix with suction
17 Woody of "Manhattan"
18 Take a breather
19 Norway's capital
20 "See you later"
21 Check mate?
24 Beyond doubt
25 Some linens
26 Balance beam?
31 "Yow!"
32 Cry heard on a fairway
33 Catch, as a perp
36 Before-test work, informally
37 Simple song
39 Super-duper
40 Brit. word reference
41 Ferris wheel or bumper cars
42 Join
43 Firm offer?
46 Illinois city symbolizing middle America
49 Refusals
50 Vegas spread?
53 Person in a zebra-striped shirt, informally
56 Opposite of gave
57 Whom the cheerleaders cheer
58 Hit musical set in Argentina
60 ___ fixe (obsession)
61 Suffix with major
62 Katey of "Married . . . With Children"
63 Loch ___ monster
64 Film unit
65 Stable enclosure

DOWN

1 One who complains, complains, complains
2 "___ smokes!"
3 Doing nothing
4 Wide shoe designation
5 Cheese dishes
6 Aladdin's transportation
7 Butter substitute
8 Glasgow gal
9 Beautiful skill
10 Deal finalizer
11 Grocery pathway
12 Leave, slangily
13 B-ball
22 Mess up
23 "How do I love ___?"
24 Tread
26 Mispelled, for misspelled, e.g.
27 Irish republic
28 Barely made, with "out"
29 Frequently
30 Kiddie
33 Pinot ___ (wine)
34 Voting no
35 When repeated, Road Runner's sound
37 Fiasco
38 Dictator Amin
39 Relatives of termites
41 Completely botch
42 Futile
43 Car stoppers
44 Tooth layer
45 Boar's mate
46 Yeltsin's successor as leader of Russia
47 Eat away at
48 Woodwinds
51 Red Rose
52 $5.15/hour, e.g.
53 Latvia's capital
54 Footnote abbr.
55 Autumn
59 Dyemaker's container

by Christina Houlihan Kelly

60

ACROSS

1 Throat problem
5 Amorphous movie monster
9 "Quo ___?"
14 Prom night wheels
15 Capital of Italia
16 "No way!"
17 Dermal flare-up
18 Black-bordered news item
19 More up-to-date
20 "Right now!"
23 Gun rights grp.
24 Mandela's org.
25 Rte. recommenders
26 Porker's place
27 Death, to Dylan Thomas
33 Fam. member
34 Morales of "N.Y.P.D. Blue"
35 Newsman Jim
38 Steams up
40 Where a train pulls in: Abbr.
42 Lamarr of film
43 Hobo's ride, perhaps
46 Ad award
49 Book collector's suffix
50 Part of a love triangle
53 Hole number
55 Friend of Pooh
56 Monument of lexicography, for short
57 Poem of Sappho
58 Hint to the starts of 20-, 27- and 50-Across
64 Innocent ones
66 Mock words of understanding
67 Appear to be
68 Bridge bid, briefly
69 Skirt to twirl in
70 Opposite of "Out!"
71 Rustic
72 Louisiana, e.g., in Orléans
73 "Vissi d'___"

DOWN

1 Pitched too low
2 Rolling in dough
3 Prefix with science
4 Attacks
5 Mile High City team
6 Arcing shots
7 Cut out
8 Philippine peninsula
9 Old, to a car buff
10 Leave speechless
11 Toward the mouth
12 Like krypton
13 Alley cat, perhaps
21 "Bus Stop" playwright
22 Place for some polish
27 "Lou Grant" paper, with "The"
28 One who saves the day
29 His questions are answers
30 Western treaty grp.
31 Deep-six
32 Loser to R.M.N., 1968
36 Author Ferber
37 Meg of "In the Cut"
39 P.T.A. meeting place: Abbr.
41 Inn take
44 Deodorant type
45 Crucifix
47 Resolve, as differences
48 Wasn't in the black
51 So far
52 Black Sea port
53 N'awlins sandwich
54 Hersey's bell town
59 Seal up
60 "The Thin Man" dog
61 Within reach
62 Like a pickpocket's fingers
63 "Peter Pan" pirate
65 Hydrocarbon suffix

by Harvey Estes

ACROSS

1 "Huckleberry Finn" character and others
5 Jaws
9 In short supply
14 Trial balloon, e.g.
15 Twistable treat
16 Misanthrope, e.g.
17 V.I.P. accompanier
19 Journal submission
20 Product-pitching cow
21 Weigh down
23 One of a matched pair
24 Pro-Second Amendment grp.
26 Put on
28 Alcohol misuser
32 Cheer in Juárez
33 Meditative sect
34 Throws high in the sky
38 Wrongdoing
41 Take air in and out
43 Like 101 courses
44 X-X-X part
45 Ambulance chaser's advice
46 Wedding figure
51 Knock the socks off
54 Olympics chant
55 Toast topper
56 —— Eleanor Roosevelt
58 Golfer's set
62 Monroe's successor
64 What 17-, 28- and 46-Across are always willing to do
66 Exodus mount
67 Actress Falco
68 Yeats's home
69 Checks out
70 Successful solver's cry
71 Paint layer

DOWN

1 Be in accord
2 Temple image
3 Pills, slangily
4 "That's life!," e.g.
5 One of us?
6 49-Down's —— Sea
7 Protein in hair and nails
8 Soaking wet
9 "—— loves me . . ."
10 Tobacco or cotton
11 Befuddled
12 Closes in on
13 A private eye might videotape one
18 Richard of "Primal Fear"
22 Fraternal fellow
25 Timber-shaping tool
27 Slippery sorts
28 Screen flop
29 Skater Kulik
30 1987 Costner role
31 —— alert
35 Angle
36 Line up
37 Tarot card user
39 Tactful one
40 Back talk?
41 Fix, in a way
42 Hose shade
44 Early scene in "The Wizard of Oz"
47 They grow when fertilized
48 Camped out
49 See 6-Down
50 Astronomical distance
51 Act the blowhard
52 Almost any doo-wop song
53 Trains to the cup, say
57 Related
59 Canton's home
60 Asta's mistress
61 Margin notation
63 A sib
65 Fat foot spec

by Michael Doran

ACROSS

1 False god
5 Overly hasty
9 Huge ice chunks
14 Nervously irritable
15 Comic Sandler
16 Mrs. Bush
17 Despot Idi ___
18 String tie
19 Houston baseballer
20 Gentle/not gentle
23 Stops from yo-yoing
24 Conqueror of 1066 England
28 The "I" of T.G.I.F.
29 Old what's-___-name
30 Relative of beer
31 1960's radical Hoffman
35 Interval
36 Assert
37 Former pupil/present pupil
41 Stitch's cartoon pal
42 Closemouthed
43 Twinges
44 Serious drug cases, for short
45 "Man's best friend"
46 Fortune 500 listings: Abbr.
48 Firearm, e.g.
50 Loving touches
55 Furious/not furious
57 Fire starter
60 Inch or teaspoon
61 Measure (out)
62 Having a close resemblance
63 Longtime Yugoslav leader
64 Sign to interpret
65 The present
66 Harry Potter's lightning bolt
67 Rome's fifth emperor

DOWN

1 Grins widely
2 Let in
3 Nimble
4 ___ Carter, who played Wonder Woman
5 Cottontail
6 Loves to pieces
7 Casa parts
8 Group insurance grps.
9 Taste sensation
10 Light in a light show
11 Not at home
12 Say 2 + 2 = 5, say
13 ___ Paulo, Brazil
21 Parisian goodbye
22 Bumbling
25 Expert
26 "I knew it all ___!"
27 Bright salamanders
29 Consumes
31 Luminous
32 One who says 34-Down
33 Model builder's wood
34 Wedding declaration
35 Precious stone
36 Org. for cavity fillers
38 In the middle of
39 Harbor boat
40 Unexpected sports outcome
45 Democratic Party symbol
46 Per ___ (each)
47 Lincoln, e.g., at Gettysburg
49 Arctic jacket
50 Sour sort
51 ___ Says (child's game)
52 "If they could ___ now . . ."
53 Start, as school
54 Shorthand taker
56 Boring routines
57 Was in session
58 Mahmoud Abbas's grp.
59 Pitch in for

by Norma Steinberg

ACROSS

1 Insubstantial stuff
6 "Show Boat" novelist Ferber
10 Regarding
14 Cowpoke competition
15 Wiener schnitzel meat
16 Mix together
17 "That is to say . . ."
18 Eliel Saarinen's son
19 Huff and puff
20 Words following an oath, sometimes
23 Writer Roald
24 Take care of
25 Roman god of love
28 Like Easter eggs
31 Govt. code breakers
32 Peace of mind
34 Womanizer
36 Gullible one
39 Avoid technobabble
42 Something some people return from vacation with
43 WWW addresses
44 Paid attention to
45 "Casablanca" pianist
47 Conductor Klemperer
49 Afternoon socials
50 Russian plain
53 Cashmere, e.g.
55 "I didn't understand a thing you said"
60 The good life
61 "Roseanne" star
62 Sees the sights
64 Grandson of Adam
65 Plumbing problem
66 Blue book filler
67 Flat payment
68 Professional charges
69 Catches one's breath

DOWN

1 Work wk. ender, for most
2 Cakewalk
3 Old music halls
4 Pendant gem shape
5 Accord maker
6 Without highs and lows
7 Consider
8 —— a soul
9 Up in the air
10 Trembling trees
11 Get out of the way
12 Touch of color
13 Garden products brand
21 Words of a worrier
22 Weasel out (on)
25 Unable to move, after "in"
26 City near Phoenix
27 Legal hunting period
29 Dadaism pioneer Max
30 Buck's partner
33 Batting woes
35 Release, as a chain
37 Out of port
38 Highest degrees
40 Worldwide workers' grp.
41 Went wild
46 Most appropriate
48 Pipsqueaks
50 Have the helm
51 Macbeth's title
52 Treble clef lines
54 Aquatic mammal
56 Nearly unique in the world
57 Canal of song
58 Rumple
59 Word after quod
63 Method: Abbr.

by Nancy Salomon

ACROSS

1 Abrupt transitions
6 Guitarist Hendrix
10 Go-___
14 Tunesmith's org.
15 Midmonth day
16 Borodin prince
17 See 39-Across
19 Highchair feature
20 Good name for a trial lawyer?
21 Fat unit
22 Sulky pullers
24 Put into memory
25 Maximally swank
26 Clunky shoes
29 Hawkins of Dogpatch
30 1847 Melville work
31 Catch a glimpse of
33 Garden decoration
37 Is an angel to
39 Word defined by 17- and 59-Across and 10- and 24-Down
40 Phileas Fogg portrayer, 1956
41 Stick it to
42 Tavern offerings
44 Without wrinkles
45 Moves like sludge
47 Jim ___, "Mission: Impossible" role
49 Angels leader
52 A-line line
53 More capacious
54 Brand, in a way
55 Frank McCourt memoir
58 Gung-ho about
59 See 39-Across
62 Wrap for leftovers
63 It may go down a tube
64 Sealy competitor
65 Headed for overtime
66 "Great" detective of kid lit
67 Young pigeon

DOWN

1 Child-friendly dogs, informally
2 Jacob's twin
3 1/40 of "the back 40"
4 Scorecard figure
5 Water source
6 War against infidels
7 Footnote word
8 Mal de ___
9 14-legged crustacean
10 See 39-Across
11 Feel the same
12 Rolling-in-the-aisles sounds
13 Event in "The Merry Wives of Windsor"
18 Completely demagnetize, say
23 "It's ___ of the times"
24 See 39-Across
25 Stewart of golf
26 Sounds after a tragedy
27 Eastern nanny
28 ___ Grande, Fla.
29 Neuters
32 Mall binge
34 Frame shape
35 "Beam ___, Scotty!"
36 Tolkien creatures
38 Walked quietly
43 Pickle unit
46 December stone
48 Hound
49 "From Here to Eternity" co-star, 1953
50 1970's bombing locale
51 "The Sopranos" restaurateur
52 Terse summons
54 Contents of some plain brown wrappers
55 Drive-___
56 Minute amount
57 Wild guess
60 Gardner of "Mogambo"
61 Et ___ (footnote abbr.)

by Allan E. Parrish

ACROSS

1 Vice President Spiro
6 Many miles away
10 The "T" of S.A.T.
14 Colonial newscaster
15 In ___ straits
16 Prefix with sphere
17 Suffer a serious blow
20 180° from NNW
21 Words repeated in "___ or not ___"
22 Noble's home
23 Withered
24 Bit of butter
25 Old film comic Sparks
26 Boxer Sonny
29 Uncovers
31 Thomas Paine's "The ___ Reason"
32 Dampens
33 "What Child Is ___?"
37 Out, so to speak
40 Sea eagle
41 President's prerogative
42 Boxing venue
43 Noisy fight
45 Fancy, as clothes
46 Number before "Liftoff!"
49 6:00, 7:00, 8:00, etc.: Abbr.
50 Products of Hammond
51 Sore
53 Roof overhang
54 Sault ___ Marie
57 Give up
60 God of love
61 Shower affection (on)
62 ___ and Novak (old news partnership)
63 Mysterious letter
64 Always
65 "Divine Comedy" writer

DOWN

1 ___ of the Apostles
2 Mardi ___
3 New Balance competitor
4 Wide shoe spec
5 Cancellation of a debt
6 Hacienda material
7 & 8 Museum material
9 Practice a part
10 Savoir-faire
11 Revolutionary War hero ___ Allen
12 Strike, in the Bible
13 Quieted, with "down"
18 Shredded
19 Villa d'___
23 Jagger's group, informally, with "the"
24 Medical prefix with logical
26 Put on board
27 Dr. Frankenstein's assistant
28 Mended
29 Singer Midler
30 Mall units
32 Small songbirds
34 Shades
35 Lodges
36 "Don't leave!"
38 Nullify, as a 41-Across
39 Covered, as a floor
44 Masticate
45 Host Letterman, for short
46 Water-loving animal
47 India's first P.M.
48 Company in a 2002 scandal
50 Bill formerly of "Politically Incorrect"
52 Amount of medicine
53 Suffix with major
54 Bird on a lake
55 Campsite sight
56 Additional
58 Oct. follower
59 Lab eggs

by Robert Dillman

66

ACROSS

1 Internet hookup, for many
6 Storybook elephant
11 Piece worn under a blouse
14 Martian or Venusian
15 Utensil with many holes
16 Stadium cheer
17 Arboreal rodent
19 Spanish eye
20 Rich-voiced
21 Mine car carrier
23 Any of the Great Smokies: Abbr.
24 News bit
26 Washer cycle
27 To's partner
28 "___ making myself clear?"
30 Aid in crime
33 Walk leisurely
36 "Later!"
37 Bone-dry
38 17- and 60-Across and 11- and 35-Down
41 PC "brains"
42 Lee's men, for short
43 Bogs down
44 Golfer's bagful
45 Victorian ___
46 Rambler mfr.
47 Telegram
49 Highly energetic
51 Nutritionist's fig.
54 Fixes at the cobbler shop
57 Was philanthropic
59 One of the Gershwins
60 Western raptor
62 Up to, in ads
63 Be of use to
64 Mill output
65 26th of 26
66 Like a pool table, ideally
67 Hardly wordy

DOWN

1 Billiards bounce
2 Red flag
3 Try for, at auction
4 For fear that
5 The National ___ (tabloid)
6 Other half of a hit 45
7 Make public
8 Ernie's Muppet pal
9 Strong dislike
10 Pass again, in a race
11 Grizzly, e.g.
12 Indian prince
13 Sailor's hail
18 "Do ___ others . . ."
22 Full of foul vapors
25 Postal carrier's tote
27 One of the Bobbseys
29 "Serpico" author Peter
31 Writer ___ Stanley Gardner
32 "___ of the D'Urbervilles"
33 Depositor's holding: Abbr.
34 Act gloomy
35 Earth's largest mammal
36 Prompt giver
39 1960's mantra
40 Full of oneself
46 Opposed to, in dialect
48 Kingly
50 Children's author Scott
51 Radioer's "Got it!"
52 Metes (out)
53 Dance partner for Fred
54 Cracker brand
55 Toledo's lake
56 Serb or Croat
58 Stadium receipts
61 Become extinct

by David Bunker

ACROSS

1 Lab containers
6 Stay away from
10 Rapscallions
14 Fool
15 Flying prefix
16 A two-piece?
17 Publisher Zuckerman's book about weapons negotiations?
19 "Beetle Bailey" pooch
20 It usually pops up
21 Purification aid
23 "So there!"
26 With not much vermouth
27 After-game meeting place
28 Lead ___
29 Language of the Koran
31 Harmless
33 Put on again
34 Actress Derek's book about port facilities?
37 ___ Zone (bar and restaurant chain)
38 Street-smart
39 Pronoun in a Hemingway title
40 First baseman Vaughn's book about bad pitching?
42 Night sound
43 Egyptian underworld god
44 Put to rest, in a way
45 Normandy negative
47 QB Dawson
48 Spongy ground
49 Erie Canal mule
50 Swallow up
52 On the way out
54 Pope with an appropriate-sounding name
55 Singer Charles's book about healthy eating?
60 Teen worry
61 The shady bunch?
62 Drink garnish
63 Reduced by
64 All-star game side
65 Brought down to earth?

DOWN

1 Pep
2 Wedding declaration
3 Word with strike or ball
4 Trent of the Senate
5 Substituted (for)
6 Smart-alecky
7 Cooking direction
8 www.yahoo.com, e.g.
9 "I don't appreciate the humor"
10 Any Beatle, once
11 Comic strip character's book about butchers' cuts?
12 Fizzle, with "out"
13 Squirrel away
18 One who monitors traffic
22 Footnote abbr.
23 Spouses of a sultan
24 "You ___ right!"
25 A Marx brother's book about shooting?
27 Lowly workers
30 Wedding proclamation
31 Hits on the head
32 Prom apparel
34 Ina in films
35 Split country
36 Ammonia, e.g.
38 Happy-go-lucky
41 Something read in many a murder mystery
42 Confirm the receipt of
44 Finish off
45 It abuts Tibet
46 Chilling
48 Shot in the arm
51 Employs
52 B-ball sites
53 Arizona river
56 Carte start
57 Show ___
58 "Who's That Girl?" rapper
59 Carrot-top's nickname

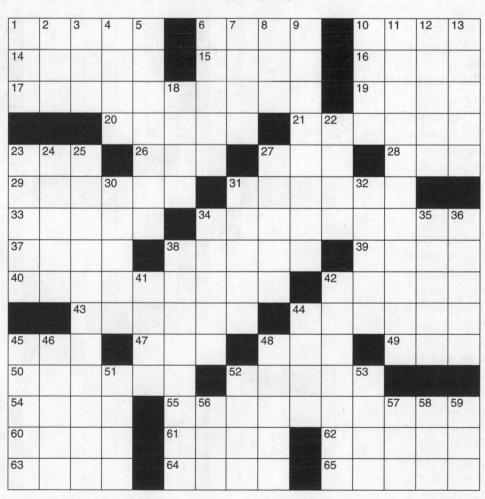

by Joe DiPietro

ACROSS

1 "The World According to ___"
5 Peach ___ (dessert)
10 Nobleman
14 Cake decorator
15 Brainstorms
16 Opera highlight
17 Mysterious writing
18 Doc
19 See 24-Across
20 Where actors put costumes on
23 Took care of
24 With 19-Across, where to get on a freeway
28 Buffoons
31 Sounds like a donkey
32 Take steps
35 1950's girl's fashion
39 Make ready, briefly
41 In progress
42 Swing around
43 Witty banquet figure
46 Opposite NNW
47 1964 Olympics city
48 "Time ___ the essence"
50 In the movies
54 "___ my case"
58 Thanksgiving decoration
61 Mongolian desert
64 Czar or king
65 Cozy spot
66 One who might have a prime corner office
67 Obliterate
68 Answer's opposite
69 Scrutinizes
70 Jobs for repair shops
71 Porkpies and panamas

DOWN

1 Strengthens
2 Integra maker, formerly
3 Keep one's subscription going
4 Cousin of "Abracadabra!"
5 Food critic Sheraton
6 Idyllic garden
7 Shelf
8 Scottish child
9 Fancy tie
10 Special features
11 Coach Parseghian
12 Perimeter
13 Once around the track
21 Afternoon TV fare
22 Planets
25 Manicurists' targets
26 Secretary of State Vance
27 Cosmetician Lauder
29 Lather
30 Upholstered piece
32 Is ___ (probably will)
33 Sing softly
34 Trees used in shipbuilding
36 MS-___
37 French novelist Pierre
38 Summers on the Riviera
40 Mediums
44 Matador charger
45 Muddy up
49 Word that can precede the start of 20-, 35-, 43- or 58-Across
51 Flubbed
52 Accustom
53 Pitcher Ryan
55 ___ Gay (W.W. II plane)
56 Not exactly svelte
57 Kiddies
59 Holiday suffix
60 J.F.K. or Dubya
61 "Gosh!"
62 Prefix with acetylene
63 Quilting party

by Alison Donald

ACROSS
1 Replaceable shoe part
5 Construction girder
10 $ dispensers
14 Morales of "La Bamba"
15 Paul of "Hollywood Squares"
16 Hatchery sound
17 Two, to four
19 Yes-___ question
20 ___-Rooter
21 George Meany's org.
23 Like some risers
26 Holiday dinner insert, perhaps
29 ". . . ___ saw Elba"
30 Next in line?
31 Guys' partners
32 Easy-to-prepare, as cheesecake
34 Gambling mecca
36 Troupe member's "closet"
41 "Livin' la Vida ___"
42 On the decline
44 Country singer Tucker
48 One taking tel. messages
50 Honoree's spot
51 Medulla's place
53 Hostess Perle
54 Daniel of Nicaragua
55 Sharif of film
57 Amer. counterpart
58 Where 10-Across may be found
64 Changed locks?
65 Nine: Prefix
66 Reason for an R rating
67 Independence achievers of 1991: Abbr.
68 Orchestra group
69 Old Harper's Bazaar illustrator

DOWN
1 Cock and bull
2 Atty.'s title
3 ___ de vie
4 1997 Jim Carrey film
5 "___ a song go out . . ."
6 How times tables are learned
7 Brian of ambient music
8 Commotion
9 Rock genre, informally
10 Classic Harlem theater
11 Bygone Toyota model
12 Like a McJob
13 "S.N.L." skits, e.g.
18 Cowboy Rogers
22 Felt topper
23 Velvet finish?
24 Get one's ducks in ___
25 Country's McEntire
27 Flyboy's place
28 Jane's role in "Klute"
30 Deli product
33 Frequent duettist with Tony Bennett
35 Food package amt.
37 One-___ (old ball game)
38 Bounceable?
39 Vardalos and Peeples
40 Make a sweater
43 Fed. property manager
44 Some gov't issues
45 Lines up neatly
46 Yak, yak, yak
47 Rates of return
49 Utterly defeated, in slang
52 Rattled weapon?
53 Scratch
56 New corp. hires
59 Suffix with meth- or eth-
60 Vane dir.
61 Fish/fowl connector
62 PC hookup
63 Bray starter

by Sarah Keller

70

ACROSS

1 Mold-y food?
6 Gathering clouds, say
10 Picnic racer's gear
14 Fuzzy 66-Across
15 Whatever she wants, she gets, in song
16 Shrek, e.g.
17 Betting odds, for example
18 Speaker's place
19 Overwhelm with humor
20 Start of a quip
23 Like a churl
24 Way of the East
25 Hitched, so to speak
26 Notable time
29 Do a salt's job
31 Caterer's vessel
33 Something to pick?
35 Matinee —
37 Full of substance
41 Part 2 of the quip
44 Con game
45 Be oversentimental
46 Dig for
47 Part of a dish's name
49 Be anxious
51 Salon supply
52 Noshed
55 One with pointy-toed shoes
57 Nationals, again
59 End of the quip
64 Prefix with crat
65 Have coming
66 Some produce
68 Floored it
69 Little dent
70 Journalist Ellerbee
71 White knight
72 Substitute spread
73 Beaverlike?

DOWN

1 Kind of financing
2 Political prize
3 It's trodden
4 Not so congenial
5 Repeated part
6 Ancient Mariner, e.g.
7 Complain
8 "The Sacred Wood" essayist, 1920
9 Bahamian capital
10 Just O.K.
11 Lit up
12 The Hula Hoop, once
13 Excited, with "up"
21 Buzz Aldrin's birth name
22 Bellini opera
26 Falls back
27 Lopsided win
28 Prefix with lock or knock
30 Extra $$$
32 Lepidopterists' gear
34 Europe's highest volcano
36 Title happening in a much-discussed 1973 film
38 Dumbfounded
39 Unnamed ones
40 Farm link
42 Makes eyes at
43 Brashness
48 Reflecting power of a planet
50 Iron product
52 Up to one's ears
53 Hosiery shade
54 Script direction
56 Hardly robust
58 A Shriver
60 Fuss
61 Fish-eating raptor
62 Like some telegrams
63 Cause of shore erosion
67 Blacken

by Lyell Rodieck

ACROSS

1 Tiny bit of land in the sea
6 Courtroom event
11 Weather London is famous for
14 Thick-skinned critter
15 Vietnam's capital
16 ___ Perón, former Argentine first lady
17 Assault
19 Lobe site
20 Fraction of a joule
21 Danish money
22 Friend in war
23 ___ volente (God willing)
24 Shooting marble
25 Shows approval, as a crowd
28 Citation
32 Big party
35 Batman and Robin, e.g.
36 Scotch whiskey drink
37 Measures (out)
39 Econ. datum
41 Carpenter famous in the 1970's
42 Get situated
44 Critical hosp. areas
46 Nasdaq competitor
47 Affirmed
50 Like Desi Arnaz, by birth
51 Keg opening
52 Greyhound vehicle
55 Kind of speed, in "Star Trek"
57 Scratch-off ticket game
59 I
60 Second letter before iota
61 Rare event in horseracing
64 Show ___
65 Indian title
66 Harassed, as in a fraternity
67 Hog's home
68 Formally change
69 Outbuildings

DOWN

1 Annoyed
2 English county
3 Specialized talk
4 Maze goal
5 Began to like
6 Small floor covering
7 Flooding cause
8 Makes a deduction
9 Yahoo! competitor
10 Tell falsehoods
11 Regret
12 Racetrack shape
13 "The Far Side" cartoonist Larson
18 Illegal activity
22 A black one may be worn at a funeral
26 Not just my or your
27 Berserk
28 "Things aren't so bad!"
29 Photocopier need
30 Turndowns
31 "Auld Lang ___"
32 Popular coll. guy
33 Prefix with dynamic
34 1980 Wilder/Pryor comedy
38 One with a turned-up nose
40 Went on and on and on and . . .
43 Sched. "question mark"
45 The "S" of M.S.U.
48 Surfing the Net, say
49 Long times
52 Hooch
53 Still single
54 Dispatches
55 Spiders' creations
56 Working away
58 Forthright
61 ___-la-la
62 Computer capacity
63 "Go team!"

by Tyler Hinman

ACROSS

1 Waikiki greeting
6 Speed demon
11 Charlie Chaplin's brother
14 Léhar's "The Merry ___"
15 Dog on "Frasier"
16 Weeding tool
17 Do embroidery
19 River curve
20 Electees
21 Cry repeated in aerobics class
22 ___-ski
24 Bloodhound feature
26 Old TV show that featured "bachelorettes," with "The"
29 Understand
31 Carson's successor
32 Rouse
33 Newborn Newfoundland
35 E.P.A. subj.
37 Giant Mel
38 & 41 Question associated with the last words of 17-, 26-, 55- and 64-Across
43 ID information
44 Stuffed shell
46 Stately tree
47 Dad
49 Catches
51 Duck down
55 Classic toy for budding engineers
58 Fare carrier
59 About
60 Golfer's vehicle
62 Wood finish ingredient
63 Bank book abbr.
64 It can't light just anywhere
68 Part of NATO: Abbr.

69 Movie star Kevin
70 Play to the back row and then some
71 Myrna of the movies
72 Deep-___ (threw away)
73 Spanish girls

DOWN

1 Shade maker
2 Legal claim holder
3 Black Sea resort
4 Mason's need
5 Cobblers' tools
6 The 21st Amendment, e.g.
7 One taken under another's wing
8 Roman 401
9 German one
10 Put a new price on
11 Popular hotel chain
12 California hikers' mecca
13 A sweet finish
18 Airport schedule abbr.
23 Some movie ratings
25 Cable channel owned by ABC
27 Ancient Peruvian
28 Not a soul
30 Fourth down option
34 Grand or baby grand
36 Grammy winner Lovett
38 Viciously attack
39 In a proficient manner
40 Identifying mark
42 Pass over
43 One-time TV showing
45 Bawdy
48 N.C. State grp.
50 No longer standing
52 007 player
53 Two-horse bet
54 Wealth
56 Work assignments
57 Attempt
61 Some govt. agents
65 Will Smith title role
66 Pickle
67 Overseas friend

by Gary Steinmehl

ACROSS

1 Term of affection for 37-Across
5 Arborist's concern
9 Daily delivery
13 "Beowulf" and "Paradise Lost"
15 Optimistic
16 Deutsche article
17 Office of 37-Across
19 Recommended amount
20 Indefatigable
21 Persian Gulf ship
22 Football gains or losses: Abbr.
23 Home for 37-Across
26 Ocean's bottom
27 Feel remorse for
28 Adolescent's outbreak
31 Former Israeli P.M.
37 Leader elected in 2005
40 Budget director under Jimmy Carter
41 "Quickly!"
42 Sch. in Tulsa
43 Really bad coffee
45 Title for 37-Across
51 ___ au vin
54 Good way to go out
55 Subject to sanctions, maybe
57 Party of the first part?
58 Predecessor of 37-Across
60 Stir up
61 View from Toledo
62 Ice cream unit
63 Tyne of "Judging Amy"
64 Kind of blocker
65 Coastal raptors

DOWN

1 Small-minded
2 Sap sucker
3 Landing places
4 Sleep preventer
5 Secret engagement
6 Martini's partner
7 Nice-to-Rome dir.
8 Storm part
9 Battlefield shout
10 Garlicky spread
11 Atlas enlargement
12 Distrustful
14 Figure out
18 ___ poisoning
21 Last non-A.D. year
24 Boorish
25 BMW competitor
26 Red shade
28 Police alert, for short
29 Miler Sebastian
30 "Morning Edition" airer
31 Tedium
32 "___ Ramsey," 1970's TV western
33 Just slightly
34 Dr.'s orders
35 Frank's wife before Mia
36 Laotian money
38 Hit to short right, say
39 ___ of Sandwich
43 No. on a new-car sticker
44 "___ directed"
45 Squirrel away
46 Home to more than a billion
47 Hold off
48 Comfortable
49 Like seven Nolan Ryan games
50 Nine: Prefix
51 Amber or umber
52 Belted sky formation
53 Canal cleaners?
56 Purple shade
58 One of the Bushes
59 Miner matter

by Victor Fleming

74

ACROSS

1 Shutterbug's setting
6 Playful aquatic mammal
11 S, to a frat guy
14 Scarlett —— of "Gone With the Wind"
15 Khaki cotton
16 Opposite of vertical: Abbr.
17 Shrinking Arctic mass
19 Singleton
20 Full range, as of colors
21 Hotshot
23 Fibber
24 Run-down joint
25 Lands' End competitor
28 Tends
29 Production from a well
30 Soda bottle unit
32 Salty drops
35 Heavy burden
37 Sub finder
39 Carefully pack (away)
40 A real mouthful?
42 Off-the-cuff
44 "Uncle Tom's Cabin" girl
45 College entrance exams
47 Broccoli piece
49 Naps
51 Baseball's Felipe
52 Washington zoo attractions
53 Ultimate
57 L.B.J.'s successor
58 Competition on an indoor rink
60 Wide shoe spec
61 Gloomy, in verse
62 Painter's stand
63 Archaic verb ending
64 Poker-faced
65 Each has two senators

DOWN

1 Fancy dressers
2 Machinist's workplace
3 Hard-to-believe story
4 Revealer of the future
5 Incomplete
6 Happen
7 The people over there
8 —— Tacs (breath mints)
9 Allow
10 Most fibrous
11 Very large ham
12 Part of ancient Asia Minor
13 —— Shorthand course
18 Tehran natives
22 Bill of Microsoft
24 Untamed
25 Stolen goods
26 Queue
27 Texas' official flower
28 Transmits
31 Relatives of frogs
33 Wander about
34 Try to hit, as a housefly
36 Prepared to sing the national anthem
38 One going through papers in a safe, say
41 Sand traps, in golf
43 Ones who "have more fun"
46 Vacation destination
48 Consume more than
49 Shopping jag
50 Directory contents
51 Big maker of office supplies
53 Great flair
54 —— Major (constellation)
55 Assist in crime
56 Singer Lovett
59 Zodiac lion

by Jim Hyres

ACROSS

1 Fix firmly
6 April fools
10 With 69-Across, split
14 Top-notch
15 ___ Bator, Mongolia
16 "Je t'___" (French words of endearment)
17 Adventurer ___ Polo
18 Beatles' meter maid
19 Itsy-bitsy biter
20 Split
23 Cop's badge
25 Regret bitterly
26 Always, in verse
27 Sweetie
28 Perfect plots
31 Engine hums
33 Et ___ (and others)
35 ___ alai
36 Fuel additive
37 Split
43 A little freedom?
44 Darjeeling or oolong
45 Not having a thing out of place
46 Lou Grant portrayer
49 Gift of the Magi
51 Alias preceder
52 Sporty Pontiac
53 Give it a go
55 Penny metal
57 Split
61 Writer Rice
62 Zeus' spouse
63 Soft leather
66 ___-Ball (arcade game)
67 Like Death Valley
68 Eye opener
69 See 10-Across
70 Head honcho
71 Takes a chance

DOWN

1 Tach letters
2 Far-sighted investment, for short
3 Old Dominion
4 Mike holder
5 Play the piccolo
6 Wise guy
7 Set down
8 Crocs' kin
9 Major miscue
10 Pudding starch
11 More benevolent
12 Photocopier, e.g.
13 Dies (out)
21 Work for a jack-of-all-trades
22 Third dimension
23 Persian potentate
24 Pocket problem
29 Musical gift
30 ___-gritty
32 Words before "arms" or "the air"
34 Indolent
36 Frisk
38 Scottish inlet
39 The Zombies' "Tell ___ No"
40 2000, for one
41 Water-skiing locale
42 Headliner
46 Thunderstruck
47 Three sheets to the wind
48 Secondhand
49 "You're a lifesaver!"
50 "What a pity!"
54 Recovery center
56 Newswoman Zahn
58 New driver, usually
59 Tennessee's state flower
60 Wanders aimlessly
64 Rap's Dr. ___
65 Dash widths

by Nancy Salomon

ACROSS
1 Go wide of, say
5 Seven-time Wimbledon champ of the 1980's and 90's
9 Celeb's way around town
13 Be a brat
15 Down time
16 From the top
17 Georgian's question before a fight?
20 Curry of "Today"
21 Gad about
22 Siouan speakers
23 Archipelago part
24 Artist Alex, leader of modern realism
26 Montanan's comeback?
33 Cortés victim
34 Hang in there
35 Neighbor of Bulg.
36 Charles of "Hill Street Blues"
37 Places to find dates?
39 Attend
40 Tolkien beast
41 Air
42 Vinegar holder
43 New Yorker's dare?
47 Pump sign in Canada
48 Aid's partner
49 "___ to every purpose . . ."
52 Start to flutter one's eyes, say
53 From Okla. City to Mobile
56 Alaskan's sorry cry after a fight?
60 Like most bathroom graffiti: Abbr.
61 Table leveler
62 Moose's place
63 Sari-clad royal
64 Traditional snake dancer
65 Boston suburb

DOWN
1 Early Yucatán people
2 Smiley face, e.g.
3 Send reeling
4 Cartesian "I am"
5 Danny of "The Color Purple"
6 Bit of writing on the wall?
7 TV E.T.
8 Winter bug
9 Taoism founder
10 The skinny
11 Same: Fr.
12 Is in the red
14 3.26 light-years
18 Fizzy drink
19 ___ a long shot
23 Really steamed
24 Shakespeare's shrew, informally
25 [Sigh]
26 Google competitor
27 ___ Mountains
28 City on the Mohawk
29 Piece in The New Republic
30 Rainbow ___
31 Clan emblem
32 Overdo a scene
37 What we have
38 Suffix with buck
39 Stick-to-it-iveness
41 Tahiti-bound, perhaps
42 Actress Ladd
44 Sana'a citizen
45 Japanese mat
46 "In memoriam" item
49 Nearly closed
50 Sandwich filler
51 Privy to
52 FedEx, say
53 Countercurrent
54 Gemini, for one
55 Scene of a fall
57 Show theatergoers to their seats, informally
58 "___ cares?"
59 MSN competitor

by Kumar Balani and Lou Sabin

ACROSS

1 "Tubby" musical instrument
5 What a soldier goes out on
11 Hit on the head
14 On
15 Printed mistakes
16 Suffix with chlor
17 Dr. Zhivago's love
18 April to October, for baseball
19 Understood
20 Inquire about the leaving time?
23 "___ Rebel" (1962 #1 hit)
24 Way in
25 Comfortable to stay in
28 "The Republic" writer
31 Perfect tennis serve
32 Actress Brennan
35 Ingenuity
39 Endure a comedy routine?
42 Sport with mallets
43 Dinosaur remnant
44 It's dialed before a long-distance number
45 Stew seasoning
47 Earl in Shakespearean England
49 Texas shrine, with "the"
52 The "A" of I.R.A.: Abbr.
54 Substitute for a jittery pilot?
61 "It's c-c-cold!"
62 More diminutive
63 Worsted fabric
64 In the past
65 Draw out
66 Book before Nehemiah
67 Hankering

68 Like rooms on TV's "Trading Spaces"
69 Shallow's opposite

DOWN

1 Fine powder
2 One of the Four Corners states
3 Make yawn
4 Military helicopter named for an Indian tribe
5 Mexican coins
6 Stadium
7 ___ II (razor brand)
8 Hotheaded
9 Siouan tribe
10 Surgeon's tool
11 Intolerant person

12 Scent, in England
13 Small-minded
21 Excited, with "up"
22 Widely recognized
25 Padlock holder
26 Eight: Prefix
27 Breakfast, lunch or dinner
28 Intrinsically
29 Minus
30 Pro's opposite
33 Uncertain
34 Weaving machine
36 Wedding vows
37 Melody
38 X-ray ___ (kids' goggles)
40 "I'm innocent!"
41 Smart ___ (wise guy)

46 Owl, by nature
48 More than tipsy
49 Cornered
50 The "L" of XXL
51 Ohio city
52 Dined at home
53 À la ___ (way to order)
55 Loathsome
56 Lady of Arthurian romance
57 Puerto ___
58 Stuff that seeps
59 Golfer's shout
60 Noisy to-do

by Marc J. Gameroff

ACROSS

1 Fend (off)
5 Puts on
9 Threshold
14 Nerve impulse transmitter
15 Smart-alecky
16 Lefty of 1920's–30's baseball
17 First trick
20 San Jose-to-Fresno dir.
21 ThinkPad, e.g.
22 Otherwise
23 Čapek play
24 Neuter
26 Uninspired reactions
27 Middle part
31 Hard up
33 Second trick
36 Pitts of "Life With Father"
37 Domain of the Hapsburgs, once: Abbr.
38 Like many college dorms
42 Third trick
47 Statistic
49 Eagles on the wing
50 Fall guy
51 Seine feeder
54 They keep "Q" from "U"
55 Samoan port
57 Agassi and Maginot
59 Motherly ministering, for short
62 Trickster's comment, after 17-, 33- or 42-Across
65 Open, as a bottle
66 Suffix with million
67 Twist the arm of
68 Jury composition
69 Place for a bouncing baby
70 Reactions to dirty tricks

DOWN

1 Go in with rolled-up pants?
2 Main line
3 Stood up
4 Crime lab stuff
5 Hat and coat, e.g.
6 Bottomless
7 Mild oaths
8 Razor sharpener
9 Mezzo-soprano Frederica ___ Stade
10 Head start
11 Muddied the waters
12 Cautious
13 Actress Sommer et al.
18 Perpendicular
19 "The smile of beauty" toothpaste
23 Full-bodied
25 "I agree"
27 Cutting tool
28 Top of the lingerie line
29 Criticize, slangily
30 NuGrape competitor
32 Police car with a flashing light, maybe
34 Unhappy response
35 "Sure, why don't we?!"
39 See red?
40 Always, poetically
41 A.M.A. members
43 Status ___
44 Eskimo boat
45 Anticipate
46 Cow catcher
47 Love object of Apollo
48 Each
50 Paid attention, so to speak
52 Move under cover
53 Reagan attorney general ___ Meese
56 Open a bit
58 Pretty pink
59 New kid on the block
60 Nike's swoosh, e.g.
61 Pool sticks
63 Photo ___
64 Gist

by Sherry O. Blackard

ACROSS

1 Juggler's perch, perhaps
6 Shooters
10 Completely
14 Scout master?
15 Perched on
16 It may be supernatural
17 "Big news!"
19 Graph line
20 Peace, in Pravda
21 Move furtively
22 Sportscaster Musburger
23 F.D.R.'s Fala, for one
25 Dance version of a song, maybe
27 Fred Sanford player, on TV
29 Shoebox marking
32 Batter or bruise
35 Fair-hiring letters
36 U.S.N. rank
37 Flip decision?
38 U.S.N. rank
39 Golf gimme
40 "Horrors!"
41 Sew up
42 Directed at
43 Chart type
44 Like some menus
46 Valued violin, for short
48 With one's sweetie, say
52 Monteverdi opera
54 Reactor parts
56 Debussy subject
57 60's happening
58 Photocopier "ink"
60 "Need You Tonight" band, 1987
61 Hateful group
62 Commercial prefix with lodge
63 Old German duchy
64 Vogue rival
65 Fragrant oil

DOWN

1 Florists' cuttings
2 Like some industrial waste
3 Opening bars
4 U.S.P.S. delivery
5 Diner devices
6 Got ready for takeoff
7 Envelope abbr.
8 Office or studio
9 Place to find sweaters
10 Donkey Kong company
11 Like some bonds
12 Actress Lena
13 Gusto
18 Say "li'l," say
22 Stunt biker's bike
24 Jerry Marcus comic strip
26 River of Devon
28 One way to ship
30 Microsoft Word option
31 Puzzlemaker Rubik
32 Blue-roofed eatery
33 "M*A*S*H" soft drink
34 "The Complete Book of Running" author
36 Flogged
38 Kind of battery
39 Oil, slangily
41 Glass of public radio
42 Nasal spray brand
44 Links figure
45 As an example
47 Wound up
49 Playground retort
50 Brandon —— (Hilary Swank Oscar-winning role)
51 Overthrow, say
52 Kimono sashes
53 Sofer of "Blind Justice"
55 Said
58 Classic Jaguar
59 Apple-picking mo.

by Brendan Emmett Quigley

ACROSS

1 Stogie
6 "Remember the ___!"
11 ___-la-la
14 Place to study, in France
15 Some jazz
16 1975 musical with a Yellow Brick Road, with "The"
17 Mole
19 Place for post-op patients, for short
20 Involves
21 Remover of hides
23 Household power: Abbr.
25 Reagan attorney general Edwin
26 Salad leaf
30 Acquire
33 Terse note from a boss
34 ___ Lee Corp. (Fortune 500 company)
35 End-of-week cry
38 Progresso product
39 Sent, as a letter, by phone line
40 Bring on, as an employee
41 Fairy tale starter
42 Suffered from a cut
43 Prison-related
44 More nervously irritable
46 Sublet
47 Confused
49 Soothsayer
51 More matronly in dress
54 Most adroit
59 ___ Baba
60 Romantic dinner reservation
62 Thick drain-cleaning option
63 Bottled water brand
64 Aired again
65 Takeoff guesstimate: Abbr.
66 Silence markers, in music
67 Track events

DOWN

1 Hand over
2 Computer symbol
3 Joint inflammation
4 ___ Longa, birthplace of Romulus and Remus
5 Substitute for, as a pitcher
6 Humiliate
7 Journey segment
8 Lincoln and others, informally
9 Man in a robe
10 Popular charge card
11 Small plane
12 Reduces to bits
13 Blue shade
18 She, in Cherbourg
22 Nor's partner
24 Persuaders
26 Old U.S. gasoline
27 Gas light
28 Poker variation
29 Blocked
31 Born's partner
32 Itsy bit
34 After-Christmas event
36 Persia, now
37 Hat fabric
39 Secretive org.
43 Play
45 Shoe style
46 Coral formation
47 Saying
48 Sign in a boardinghouse window
50 Perfect places
52 Overhang
53 Sluggers' stats
55 Peach or beech
56 Raison d'___
57 ___ team (police group)
58 Heaps
61 Counterpart of long.

by Robert Dillman

ACROSS

1 Off one's trolley
5 Predatory sort
10 Motorists' citations: Abbr.
14 Plot unit
15 "Not a chance"
16 — avis
17 Never
20 Big Apple daily, briefly
21 Source of government revenue
22 Mossy side of a tree
24 Reunion group
25 Fodder storers
28 Late actor Davis
31 Cause of a wince
32 Prevents, legally
34 Reporter's question
37 Sometimes
40 "For shame!"
41 Continued ahead
42 Burn soother
43 Excused oneself, with "out"
44 Jazz phrases
45 Wash gently against
48 Cervantes's land
51 Retiree's title
54 Search, as at a sale
58 Always
60 Monied one
61 Chinese "bear"
62 Uncool sort
63 Looks over
64 Some Art Deco pieces
65 Plays for a sap

DOWN

1 Eos' domain
2 Stiff and sore
3 Fingerboard ridge
4 Like a multipurpose tool, perhaps
5 Look of contempt
6 "The Planets" composer Gustav
7 Piercing tool
8 Huck Finn's conveyance
9 Actress Sedgwick
10 High in pitch
11 Internet music-sharing service
12 Lock of hair
13 MS. enclosures
18 Med. care providers
19 Cut out
23 Busy places
25 Catch a glimpse of
26 Fleming and Paisley
27 Beat soundly
29 Go it alone
30 Made, as a web
32 Sufficient, old-style
33 All there
34 Alarmist's cry, in a fable
35 Dance, slangily
36 Small bills
38 Fly ball fielder's shout
39 Primary computer list
43 — & Noble
44 Just misses, as a putt
45 River in Hades
46 Home products seller
47 Really annoy
49 Priggish one
50 Saintly glows
52 Pound a keyboard
53 Out there
55 N.Y.C.'s 5th and 7th, e.g.
56 Richard of "Chicago"
57 They may be tight or loose
59 Windsor's prov.

by Mike Torch

ACROSS

1 Bring in
5 Get moving
9 Mudville whiffer
14 Dutch ___ (uncommon sights nowadays)
15 Item in a frame
16 One way to look
17 Hamburger center
19 Sheets and stuff
20 Galley mover
21 Niagara River source
22 One of Chekhov's "Three Sisters"
23 Makes one
25 Sore throat soother
29 Antiarms slogan
31 Ryder rental
32 Public image, briefly
33 "Nuthin' But a 'G' Thang" rapper
34 Forbidden fruit site
36 Word that can follow either half of 17-, 25-, 37-, 52- or 62-Across
37 Chinese bowlful
40 What 17-, 25-, 37-, 52- and 62-Across are, themewise
43 Computer adventure game
44 Shoptalk
48 "The Gold Bug" author's inits.
49 ___ Tomé and Príncipe
50 This person or that
52 Sweet appetizer
55 Waterproof again
56 "Superman" role
57 What mobsters pack
59 Cardinal's letters
60 Public relations person
62 Steaming mugful
64 Crazed
65 Bibliog. space saver
66 Surf sound
67 Spiel
68 Get set for a shot
69 Some airport data: Abbr.

DOWN

1 Echo
2 1930's–40's first lady
3 Cree, e.g.
4 Pressure meas.
5 Thinly spread
6 Jacques of "Mon Oncle"
7 Chip giant
8 Juan Carlos, e.g.
9 Visit
10 Set straight
11 Bobbysoxer idol
12 Garden party?
13 Kyoto capital
18 Cheater, perhaps
22 Yemeni's neighbor
24 Gang territories
26 Turns inside out
27 Surprised shriek
28 Big bruiser
30 "Later"
35 Driller's deg.
36 Daughter of Saturn
38 Apples that can't be eaten
39 Snapped out of it
40 Cool, in slang
41 Former Mideast inits.
42 Ever so lavish
45 Likes a lot
46 Running wild
47 Check cashers
49 Knit or purl
51 Delphic seer
53 Charged, in a way
54 Snap
58 Greek H's
60 Band equipment
61 Moo goo ___ pan
62 Not squaresville
63 Lobster ___ Diavolo

by Nancy Salomon

ACROSS

1 Chasm
6 Grassy clump
9 Pond organism
13 Provide comfort to
15 Crazy eights spinoff
16 Competed
17 Stuff oneself
18 Enter quickly
20 Response to an insult
21 Angry audience reaction
23 Low point
24 Detail in a builder's plan
26 Infuse with oxygen
27 Store for future use
32 Cleanse totally
33 In a snit
34 Sharp turn
37 Parade spoiler
38 Pasture
39 Continental coin
40 Football distances: Abbr.
41 Spree
42 Home in the Arctic
43 Spend time playfully
45 Have ambitions
48 Wax-coated cheese
49 "One of ___ days, Alice . . ."
50 Sensible
52 Taj Mahal city
56 Devour quickly
58 Pay what's due
60 Planning to vote no
61 Bowling target
62 Not quite a homer
63 Breather
64 "___ the season . . ."
65 Centers of operation

DOWN

1 Nile slitherers
2 Seethe
3 Spiritual exercise
4 Reason to hit the brakes
5 Moo ___ pork
6 Lather
7 Burden
8 Med school grad
9 House that's for the birds
10 Singer Ronstadt
11 Be in on the joke
12 Idolize
14 Potent anesthetic
19 Bread machine cycle
22 Skater's hangout
25 Prefix with schooler
26 Thinking "Gee whiz!"
27 Nimble
28 Campus area
29 Leon ___, who wrote "Mila 18"
30 Feudal lord
31 Spellbound
34 South African native
35 What spinach is rich in
36 Dandy
38 Dandy
39 Extreme self-centeredness
41 Ready for a change
42 S. & L. holding
43 Fish out of water
44 Highly capable
45 Fighting
46 Gleamed
47 Animal hides
50 What V-J Day ended
51 Rustic retreats
53 Swindles
54 Hold sway
55 Pals of Tarzan
57 Decide
59 Sun or moon

by Lynn Lempel

ACROSS

1 Warhead weapon, briefly
5 Like the kiddie rides at a park, relatively speaking
11 —— Paulo, Brazil
14 "Encore!"
15 Not dismissive of, as suggestions
16 Smidge
17 Beach community near LAX
19 Khan who wed Rita Hayworth
20 "It'd be my pleasure"
21 "Norma ——"
22 Bikini parts
23 Like a bump on a log
24 Outermost strata
26 Lengthy lurkers of the deep
27 Like Bo Peep's sheep
28 Beetle Bailey superior
29 Foxy
30 Air force?
31 2004 Liam Neeson film
32 & 33 Anagrams and puns (or parts hidden in 17-, 24-, 44- and 51-Across)
34 "Never on Sunday" star —— Mercouri
37 Hammer part
38 Dipstick wipe, often
41 Sans friends
42 Philosopher Descartes
43 Psychologist Jung
44 Soldier's reassignment papers
46 Backyard party spot
47 Who-knows-how-long
48 Tempe sch.
49 Main arteries
50 Surfacing stuff
51 Duel (with)
53 Pittsburgh-to-Boston dir.
54 Multicar accident
55 Highway division
56 Takeoff stat: Abbr.
57 Guitarist Segovia
58 Went like the wind

DOWN

1 Hints at
2 Cavalry V.I.P.
3 With courage
4 Ari of "Kate & Allie"
5 Heading on a list of errands
6 King Kong, e.g.
7 "Place" name on TV
8 Wholly absorbed
9 Girder material
10 Cracker Jack bonus
11 People around a 54-Across, typically
12 Egg carton spec
13 Amazing adventure
18 QB's pass, whether completed or not: Abbr.
22 —— means possible
24 Ratted
25 Iraqi or Thai
27 "Tomb raider" Croft
30 One who's done for
31 Swiss artist Paul
32 Skid row sights
33 Confident solvers' supply
34 Animal on a Florida license plate
35 Tastefully beautiful
36 Revised downward
37 Reader
38 Seedy stopover
39 She helped Theseus escape the labyrinth
40 Smoothed (over)
42 Auctioned again
43 Holiday music
45 "Splish Splash" singer, 1958
46 Impact sound
49 Nile snakes
51 Tax prep. expert
52 "So —— me!"

by Merl Reagle

ACROSS

1 Purchases at nurseries and hardware stores
6 "I ___ the opinion . . ."
10 Basics
14 "You're ___ and don't even know it"
15 Calamitous
16 Model Banks
17 Yogi's language
18 First word of "The Raven"
19 Capital of Samoa
20 Totally harmless
23 Not just laugh
25 Cast items
26 Good fortune, informally
30 You can put them on
31 Eyelid woes
32 Vane dir.
33 Apt title for this puzzle
36 Mahmoud Abbas's grp.
39 Oscar nominee for "A Beautiful Mind"
40 Carpet layer's calculation
41 Classic interrogatory ad slogan
45 Actor Delon
47 They generate lots of interest
48 Advice after a bad golf shot
52 Not kosher
53 Spicy cuisine
54 Cleans up, in a way
57 Burglar's take
58 Place for a pump
59 Spanish babies
60 Take notice of
61 Either of two N.T. books
62 Gardening tool

DOWN

1 "Phooey!"
2 News org.
3 ___ Square (Times Square, once)
4 Adorns
5 Bombed
6 Newspaperman Ochs
7 Go for the gold?
8 Danger of the deep
9 Users' costs
10 Completely mystified
11 Secondary route
12 Part of "C.S.I."
13 Swedish imports
21 King in 1922 news
22 "___ to a Kill" (1985 Bond film)
23 Tartan sporters
24 Completely botch
27 Sibilant sounds
28 Onetime telecom giant
29 Alternative to whole wheat
33 "The Faerie Queene" character
34 Easter's start?
35 Blow away
36 Getting dolled up
37 Goatish glance
38 Bungling sorts
39 In the main
40 Wore down
41 "Pay attention!"
42 Certain 1-Across, in time
43 Fu-___ (legendary Chinese sage)
44 City south of Salem
45 "Casey ___ Bat"
46 "___ Theme" ("Doctor Zhivago" tune)
49 ___ Helens
50 "Naw"
51 Weak, as an effort
55 Kind of time
56 Old map abbr.

by Nick Grivas

ACROSS

1 Blackguard
4 Coin with Monticello on its back
10 Mlle. from Acapulco
14 Sport —— (all-purpose vehicle)
15 Tennis champ Goolagong
16 His and ——
17 Automated device in a bowling alley
19 Give off
20 Epic that ends with Hector's funeral
21 Grand Prix, e.g.
23 Nail on a paw
24 Garden item cut up for a salad
26 Grope
28 Historical time
29 Berlin maidens
34 Naked —— jaybird
37 Legislative act that imposes punishment without a trial
41 Little troublemaker
42 Example of excellence
43 Cry loudly
46 Part of a tied tie
47 Cotton menace
52 Expensively elegant
56 What a lumberjack holds
57 River of oblivion
58 Tilt
59 1988 Kevin Costner movie
62 Pioneering computer game
63 Important parts of dairy cows
64 "Green Acres" star Gabor
65 Nays' opposites
66 "Brace yourself!"
67 —— and Stimpy (cartoon duo)

DOWN

1 Three-dimensional
2 To any degree
3 Shepherdess in Virgil's "Eclogues"
4 Dweeb
5 "—— Got the World on a String"
6 Army bed
7 Small knob
8 Become a member
9 Delaware tribe
10 Himalayan mountain guide
11 Chart again
12 Instant
13 Fall bloom
18 Within the rules
22 German "the"
24 Steak or ground round
25 Inventor Howe
27 Jeff Lynne's rock grp.
29 J. Edgar Hoover's org.
30 Place for a basketball net
31 Mont Blanc, e.g.
32 To the —— degree
33 Popular vodka, informally
34 Ending with Gator or orange
35 Instant
36 "Where —— you?"
38 Base truant
39 Wall Street event: Abbr.
40 RCA dog
43 Biases
44 Hold the rights to
45 Nighttime biter
47 Touched in the head
48 Common daisy
49 —— apso (dog)
50 Get away from
51 African terrain
53 "None of the above"
54 Use a razor
55 One with big biceps
57 Insatiable desire
60 "—— Misérables"
61 Rap's Dr. ——

by Raymond Hamel

ACROSS

1 Wet snowball sound
6 Radio choice
10 Hair goops
14 ——-Roman wrestling
15 1971 Cy Young Award winner —— Blue
16 Not written
17 Stuffed animals
19 Festive
20 Business V.I.P.
21 Jeer
23 Like meat thrown to a lion
26 Stuffed headrests
30 Pinza of "South Pacific"
32 Went yachting
33 Stuffed appetizers
35 Contents of a big bowl
40 "Am not!" response
41 Most of Libya
42 Cuban bills
43 Stuffed mailers
46 College graduate's goal
48 Furnace's output
49 Stuffed polling receptacles
54 Sun spot?
55 Momentarily
56 Teacher's grp.
58 Lemon-lime malt brand
59 Stuffed diners
66 Coup d'——
67 With no help
68 Dewey, to Truman
69 Cold war news service
70 Either half of Gemini
71 Community workout spots, for short

DOWN

1 Police dept. rank
2 Relative of ante-
3 Headed
4 Kind of converter
5 Trifled (with)
6 Greeting on the Appian Way
7 "Mamma ——!"
8 T.V.A. promoter
9 Number 5 iron
10 "Dead Souls" novelist Nikolai
11 Poet's Muse
12 Early Steven Bochco series
13 Blind parts
18 Miscue
22 Buddy from way back
23 Plot again
24 Shade of blue
25 Smartens (up)
27 Try to win
28 60's war zone, briefly
29 Scoreboard fig.
31 "—— be in England"
34 Pistol, slangily
36 "Now we're in for it!"
37 Puppy pickup places
38 Haunted house sound
39 Like many a retreat
41 Calm
43 Tarzan creator's monogram
44 Prefix with natal
45 Irk
47 Even less than wholesale
49 "Carmen" composer
50 Author Loos
51 Holy Tibetans
52 Exams before some postgrad. studies
53 Serta alternative
57 Positron's place
60 Solemn pledge
61 Yalie
62 1980's White House nickname
63 Top left PC key
64 Stephen of "Still Crazy"
65 Soon-to-be-alumni: Abbr.

by Lee Glickstein and Nancy Salomon

88

ACROSS

1 Winter Palace ruler
5 Convinced
9 "Let me demonstrate . . ."
14 Winter coating
15 Manitoba native
16 Attu dweller
17 Black cat, to some
18 Iranian cash
19 Wild guesses
20 Futile search
23 Actor Wallach
24 Go for a seat
25 Applicant for a civil union, maybe
26 Old hand
28 Draw support from
30 Delta rival: Abbr.
31 "Any day now"
32 Cultured fare?
34 "Ask!"
35 Activity with a list
38 Actor Keach
39 Use again, as a Ziploc
40 Dismantled ship
41 Brown of renown
42 Fire breather
46 Brian of ambient music
47 Sushi selection
48 Vane dir.
49 Beryl, e.g.
50 Game with pies
54 Miss by ___
55 Famous Amos
56 It may thicken
57 Usher, perhaps
58 Go to work on Time?
59 Sleeper ___
60 Atlas feature
61 Univ. offerings
62 Suit to ___

DOWN

1 Mason's tool
2 "Sick as a dog," for instance
3 ___ Island, Fla.
4 Tear apart
5 Dumpster-dive, say
6 Hunter of myth
7 Places to graze
8 Primary selections
9 Wishy-___
10 Utah ski resort
11 Small dosage amount
12 2, to 8
13 Elevs.
21 "Cool!"
22 "Silent" prez
27 Minn. neighbor
29 Hudson River town
30 Impulses
31 Legendary grid coach Don
33 Like bush pigs and guinea pigs
34 Generous one
35 Daring stand-ins
36 Food label figure
37 Hearts and diamonds
38 "___ Loves Me"
41 Wahine wear
43 Lancelot player in "Camelot"
44 American League bird
45 Irritate
47 Javelin, e.g.
48 Mistletoe bit
51 "Would ___?"
52 49-Across source
53 Humane org.
54 "___ see it . . ."

by Richard Chisholm

ACROSS

1 Tams
5 Wood that repels moths
10 "Ali ___ and the 40 Thieves"
14 Natural burn medication
15 Speechify
16 Dutch cheese
17 Rod at a pig roast
18 United Nations' goal
20 Sweetie pie
21 Termite, e.g.
22 "Wait a sec!"
23 Romanov ruler
25 Study of plants: Abbr.
26 Terminus
27 Bubbly drink mixer
32 Black-and-white cookie
33 Roald who wrote "Charlie and the Chocolate Factory"
34 Katmandu's land
38 Thpeakth like thith
40 Vietnamese holiday
41 Like old bread
42 Come after
43 Part of the eye
45 Length × width, for a rectangle
46 Musician's asset
49 Boom box abbr.
52 Bashful
53 With proficiency
54 Slowly, in music
56 Giants great Willie
58 Chem class
61 Something caught near the end of a race?
63 Word that can follow the end of 18-, 27-, 46- or 61-Across
64 "Off for now, love"
65 Soother
66 Change for a five
67 Narrow opening
68 Ostentatious
69 Words

DOWN

1 An A.T.M. dispenses it
2 Brand for Fido
3 Futile
4 Harden
5 Cringed
6 Deity with a bow and arrow
7 Feathered missile
8 Capital of Ga.
9 Making the mouth burn
10 "___ here long?"
11 Maxim
12 Breakfast strip
13 Revise
19 Communion plates
21 La ___, Bolivia
24 Plug, as a hole
25 Purple Monopoly avenue
27 Shoe bottom
28 Land o' blarney
29 Confirm with a vote
30 Question in a geography quiz
31 Sell in stores
35 Political platform
36 Knighted Guinness
37 Wife of Jacob
39 Meets, greets and seats
44 Keep out of the rain
47 Colossus of ___ (one of the Seven Wonders)
48 "Sesame Street" network
49 Sail holders
50 Perfect
51 Desert plants
55 Animal with a beard
56 ___ soup (sushi starter)
57 From square one
59 Top spot
60 Top spot
62 Baby's bawl
63 Place to put bets

by Earl W. Reed

90

ACROSS

1 The Righteous Brothers and the Everly Brothers
5 Wall St. letters
9 Actors Robert and Alan
14 Other, in Oaxaca
15 "The Clan of the Cave Bear" author Jean
16 Athletic events
17 —— riot (very funny skit)
18 Bruins' sch.
19 Picture with a posse
20 After 29-Down, a movie starring Diane Lane
23 Stir-fry vegetable
24 Athletic sites
28 Cry said while pointing
29 Samovar
31 Singer who definitely has her own dressing room
32 Chicago airport
35 South American range
37 ——-Mex cuisine
38 After 29-Down, a James Grippando thriller
41 Prefix with sac or duct
42 Some Art Deco works
43 Life line
44 Cry for attention
46 Swiss river
47 Call letters?
48 Storyteller Hemingway
50 Thinks
54 After 29-Down, a Drifters hit
57 Like whitecaps
60 Shot, for short
61 Song that may include some high notes
62 Swashbuckler Flynn
63 Actress Osterwald

64 Brand of smokes
65 Teary-eyed
66 Keep —— (persevere)
67 Roughly computed: Abbr.

DOWN

1 Boneheads
2 Salt Lake City native
3 Monteverdi opera
4 Computer programs
5 Deep disgust
6 State flower of New Mexico
7 Ward of "Once and Again"
8 Verve
9 Love in Lyon
10 Wasn't quite a ringer
11 Police rank: Abbr.
12 Had a bite
13 Lith., once
21 "Psst! In the balcony!"
22 More clear-headed
25 Warmer and sunnier
26 Sailor's "halt!"
27 Latin dance
29 See 20-, 38- and 54-Across
30 Suggestions on food labels: Abbr.
32 Carol starter
33 What helicopters do
34 Par —— (by air)
35 Popular shaving lotion
36 Did figure eights
39 Pontificate
40 Asleep

45 Floor cleaner's implement
47 Skillful
49 In a bashful manner
50 Metrical feet
51 Tropical roots
52 Writer George or T. S.
53 Bard of old
55 —— Wawa, role for Gilda Radner
56 Leave out
57 Not very many
58 Assayer's stuff
59 "—— we there yet?"

by Sarah Keller

ACROSS

1 Friars Club offering
5 Great time
10 Surgery aftermath
14 J __ judge
15 Abu Dhabi deity
16 Southern dish
17 A question of timing
18 Fraternal fellow
19 Part of xoxox
20 Successfully defended in court by Melvin?
23 16½ feet
24 Big name in cosmetics
25 Southwestern gully
29 Quench
32 Mutual fund fee
33 Electron tube
34 Gretna Green beret
37 Donates a small bird on behalf of actor Jacques?
41 Cask serving
42 Draw a bead on
43 Occasion for proctors
44 Sovereign
45 What to do at a turning point
47 "Wake of the Ferry" painter
50 Have miseries
51 What Cassius Clay said starting in 1964?
59 Learning method
60 It comes from the heart
61 Hawkish Olympian
62 Software buyer
63 Sound from the fold
64 Abundant
65 Walkers, for short
66 Get goggle-eyed
67 Like the White Rabbit

DOWN

1 Blockbuster movie of 1975
2 Dept. of Labor division
3 Capital of Ukraine
4 Feminine suffix
5 Shoots to eat
6 "Safety Last" star Harold __
7 Heaps
8 Pane holder
9 What you used to be
10 Field of activity
11 "You __ say that"
12 Special approach
13 Amber material
21 Teetotaling
22 Apron wearer
25 Aquarium growth
26 Muddy up
27 Carry on
28 Dedicated lines
29 "Norwegian Wood" instrument
30 Room at the top
31 Flap
33 Stopping place?
34 Hack
35 Not much
36 Performer in whiteface
38 Hot spot
39 "Open __ midnight"
40 Private eye
44 Derby entries
45 Swell
46 Shady street
47 Sundae topping
48 One way to hang
49 Exposed
50 Nuptial site
52 Makes a collar
53 Farm newborn
54 Side by side?
55 __ of Essex
56 Oratorio highlight
57 Sailor's port
58 Conversational filler

by Richard Silvestri

ACROSS

1 Younger brothers, stereotypically
6 Char
10 Exploding star
14 Betray à la a snitch
15 Miss from Marseille: Abbr.
16 Greek war god
17 Classic Charles Darwin work
20 Game at the corner store
21 Globe
22 Card that wins lots of tricks
24 Web site address starter
27 Sharpens
28 Sheraton or Ritz-Carlton
31 Terre ___, Ind.
33 N.F.L. scores
34 Sketcher's eraser
36 Stomach soother, for short
38 What the love of money is, they say
42 Pumps and clogs
43 Go looking for, as business
45 Driver's lic. and company badge
48 Decree
50 Not in short supply
51 Indian stringed instrument
53 Dark film genre, for short
55 Home for Ger. and the U.K.
56 Scents
58 More pleasant
61 The Big Bang, to a physicist
66 Yale students
67 Slender woodwind
68 Broadcasting
69 Soapmaking substances
70 Mercedes competitors
71 Seasons, in a way

DOWN

1 Old hand
2 "Lent" body part
3 Short dagger
4 Like takeout orders
5 Pique
6 Like satin to the touch
7 North Pole worker
8 Gore and Sharpton
9 Salespeople, in brief
10 Cheese-covered chip
11 Cathay and environs, with "the"
12 Swerved
13 Impose, as a tax
18 Utmost
19 Short-lived things
22 "So that's it!"
23 Not wrong: Abbr.
25 Tangy hot sauce
26 Knit and ___
29 They're sometimes inflated
30 Certain Protestant
32 Snitched
35 Atmosphere
37 Egg cell
39 Ireland's Sinn ___
40 Magnificent
41 Lollapalooza
44 The "p" in r.p.m.
45 Santa ___, one of the Solomon Islands
46 With ominousness
47 "Smoke" to chew on
49 Traces of color
52 Wrongly
54 Brazilian vacation spot, informally
57 One whose nose is in the air
59 Corp. money managers
60 Sicilian volcano
62 Hewlett-Packard rival: Abbr.
63 At once
64 Sch. near Harvard
65 Hosp. areas

by Alison Donald

ACROSS

1 Set-to
6 Carpet type
10 Meat on a kabob, maybe
14 Cute "bear"
15 Contented sound
16 Decorative pitcher
17 Bear and Berra
18 One opposed
19 Big do
20 One liable to get hurt
23 Ally of America
27 It may need massaging
28 Sodium hydroxide
29 Provision for late-arriving spectators
33 Prayer start
34 Potato bud
35 Star in the constellation Cygnus
39 Declare
40 Like hilly beaches
43 Be the master of
44 French mothers
46 The last King Richard of England
47 Abstraction
48 Insect that's well-camouflaged on a tree
52 Grow old
55 China's Chiang ___-shek
56 Atlas features
57 Co-nominee
61 Keen on
62 Paint unskillfully
63 Originator of the phrase "Familiarity breeds contempt"
68 Barely gets, with "out"
69 Other than
70 Maker of Seven Seas salad dressing
71 Ancient harp
72 Losing proposition?
73 Busybody

DOWN

1 Poseidon : sea :: Uranus : ___
2 Avian sound
3 Cleaning cloth, often
4 MacGraw of "The Getaway"
5 Said "no thanks"
6 Set-to
7 Event for hounds
8 More pretentious
9 "Old ___" (1989 Jane Fonda film)
10 Show the way
11 Just terrible
12 Something asked of the 33-Across
13 Out of money
21 Fibber's words
22 "Well done!"
23 Belief of 4½ million Americans
24 Griddle locale
25 Harder to find
26 Fergie's ex
30 Big Apple educ. institution
31 They may be rubbed out
32 Is worthy of
36 Skin flick
37 Vote in
38 Woodpeckers' peckers
41 German article
42 Finger or toe
45 "The Square Egg" writer
49 Got, as a job
50 Capital of Rwanda
51 Underhanded
52 Sharon of 23-Across
53 Gooey
54 Keyboard key
58 Sniffer
59 Inspiration source
60 Help in a heist
64 Before, before
65 ___ Andreas fault
66 Frequently
67 Mom-and-pop org.?

by Nancy Kavanaugh

ACROSS

1 Beats it
6 Doo-___
9 Many an attic
13 Big name in siding
14 Bagel stuffer
15 River of Florence
16 1952 Best Actor for 37- and 38-Across
18 Per ___
19 Pentathlon weapon
20 Lorre's "Casablanca" role
22 Web video gear
23 With 49-Across, theme song of 37- and 38-Across
26 High ball
29 Sgt., e.g.
30 Hydroxyl compound
31 Helped to escape, maybe
33 Architects' output
37 & 38 Subject of this puzzle
39 Clear up
43 Was suspicious
46 Bugs or Daffy
47 Litmus bluer: Abbr.
48 Anonymous John or Jane
49 See 23-Across
54 Weisshorn or Nadelhorn
55 Monkey bread tree
56 Clinched
60 The same, in footnotes
62 16-Across's co-star in 37- and 38-Across
64 Abysmal grade
65 Are, in Ávila
66 Caesar boast starter
67 Big times
68 Make out
69 Audition C.D.'s

DOWN

1 Herb in stuffing
2 Keep time, in a way
3 Farm measure
4 Trifled
5 Old U.S.A.F. org.
6 Tom of "The Dukes of Hazzard"
7 Stuffed to the gills
8 Saga start
9 Like a wet hen
10 Author Jong
11 ___ preview
12 1916 battle site
14 Rotten to the core
17 Prevention measure?
21 Lustful god
24 Que. neighbor
25 Arm support
26 Co-star of Bolger and Haley
27 Award bestowed by the Village Voice
28 Tries for change?
32 Egyptian god of wisdom
34 Prod
35 De ___ (again)
36 Snick's partner
40 Bausch & ___ (lens maker)
41 Ocean crossings
42 Stand behind
43 One of a percussive pair
44 "Well, ___!"
45 Runner, of sorts
49 Yellow shade
50 Patriarch
51 "Martha" or "Norma"
52 Let up
53 Bridget Fonda, to Jane
57 Silent one
58 Adm. Zumwalt
59 Blackens, perhaps
61 Criminals' ways, briefly
63 Josh

by Verna Suit

ACROSS

1 Smile
5 Body of water in Italy
9 Alternative to U.P.S.
14 City for a quickie marriage or divorce
15 Push up against
16 Fred's dancing partner
17 Aide: Abbr.
18 Filet of ___
19 Stirs up
20 Choice at a supermarket checkout
23 Ram's mate
24 Sculptures and oils
25 52, in old Rome
26 Choice offered at an electronic payment machine
33 Man's name that's an alphabetic string
34 Actress Gardner
35 Group of 100 in Washington
36 Singer Sedaka
37 Squeeze (out)
39 Cap and gown wearer
40 Single-celled creature
43 Finish
45 Pipe bend
46 Choice at an airplane ticket counter
49 Neither's partner
50 ___ tai (drink)
51 Singer Sumac
54 Choice at a coffee bar
59 Runs across the field
60 Hatcher of "Desperate Housewives"
61 Actress Anderson
62 Dress style
63 Sporting blade
64 ___ Rabbit
65 Religious offshoots
66 Grass clumps
67 The "a" in a.m.

DOWN

1 Vineyard fruit
2 Cut again
3 State auto requirement
4 Middle C, e.g.
5 Longtime Dodger manager Tommy
6 Cut short, as an attempt
7 Big swallow
8 Verdi's Moor
9 Gary Larson comic, with "The"
10 Rewrite
11 Meat slicer locale
12 It's A.C. or D.C.
13 Crosses (out)
21 "Norma ___"
22 Shows, as programs
27 Governed
28 Giver's opposite
29 TV actress Georgia
30 Malt liquor base
31 Slanted, as type: Abbr.
32 Excellent adventurer with Bill
33 18-wheeler
36 No, slangily
38 Smitten
41 Job rewards
42 Illegally off base
44 Journals
47 Speechifies
48 Half-brother of Tom Sawyer
52 "A Bar at the Folies-Bergère" painter
53 In flames
54 Actor's part
55 Movie best seen on a wide screen
56 Lady's man
57 Used auto, perhaps
58 Isle of exile for Napoleon
59 ___ Cruces, N.M.

by Kurt Mengel and Jan-Michele Gianette

ACROSS

1 Wagering sites, for short
5 Rosary component
9 Big name in kitchen foil
14 When shadows are short
15 "___ want for Christmas . . ."
16 Elementary school door sign
17 Breakfast order
20 Lend ___ (listen)
21 Lug
22 Last of 26
23 "Wild Kingdom" host Marlin
26 What apartment dwellers have to pay
28 Actress Verdugo
30 Summer, in Somme
31 Lucky charms
38 Astronaut Grissom
39 Rock's ___ Fighters
40 Kind of instinct
41 U.S. senator's salary, e.g.
48 Crazy eights cousin
49 Jazz pianist Blake
50 House wrecker
54 Place for a Ping-Pong table
58 Inventor Whitney
59 Absorbs, with "up"
61 Redhead's helper
62 Bygone music collection
66 1008 on a monument
67 Jai ___
68 NBC's peacock, e.g.
69 Passover feast
70 Stampeders
71 ___ Smith, who won the 1972 Wimbledon

DOWN

1 Like draft beer
2 Oscar-winning screenwriter Robert
3 One voicing displeasure
4 Air Jordan, for one
5 Groceries holder
6 Chicago transports
7 Tons
8 Duffer's gouge
9 Go along with
10 Tell a "story"
11 Mania
12 Showbiz twin Mary-Kate or Ashley
13 So far
18 Give the third degree
19 Lucy and Ricky's landlady
24 Once known as
25 Big mess
27 Person of the cloth, for short
29 Prior to, old-style
31 N.F.L. 3-pointers
32 French affirmative
33 Fortune 500 steelmaker
34 ___ d'Alene, Idaho
35 It may be stroked
36 Bacardi, e.g.
37 Sault ___ Marie
42 Jocularity
43 Agitated
44 Classic Becket play, informally
45 "May ___ of service?"
46 Not, in Nuremberg
47 Kix and Trix
50 Abounds
51 Popeye's love
52 Unbending
53 Where Dr. Phil got famous
55 High, in a way
56 Russia's Lake ___
57 Building subcontractor
60 Sign that attracts crowds
63 Step on it
64 Cougar or Jaguar
65 Tease

by Jim Hyres

ACROSS

1 Defrosts
6 Jazz player
9 Set as a price
14 Leonardo da ——
15 Leave speechless
16 Amtrak's "bullet train"
17 Home for an 11-Down
19 Castle dweller
20 Following behind
21 Stunt man, perhaps
22 Need Bengay
25 Hit head-on
27 Was able to
29 Time line divisions
30 Gullible sorts
33 Andean flier
35 Dull as dishwater
37 Actress —— Dawn Chong
38 Withdraws
40 Potter's pedal
42 "The Crying Game" actor
43 C.E.O.'s degs.
45 Pokémon and pet rocks, e.g.
46 Early Bond foe
48 Outback avians
50 It's grand at the Grand Canyon
51 Hive male
54 Dish served with a big spoon
55 Nationals living abroad, informally
57 Marathoner Waitz
59 Bloodletter's need
60 Emulate a veteran 11-Down
64 "I give!"
65 Overacting actor
66 One-eighty
67 Magic Johnson was one
68 Golfer Ernie
69 Mailings to record execs

DOWN

1 Dam-building agcy.
2 —— Master's Voice
3 "Go on . . ."
4 "The Bank Dick" actor
5 Speak manually
6 Sweet-talk
7 Klutzy
8 Rolodex no.
9 Baseball record-setter of 4/8/74
10 Expert knot tiers
11 Person of letters?
12 Flier to Ben-Gurion
13 Chip's cartoon chum
18 Elevs.
21 Render harmless
22 Honda model
23 Rock's Alice ——
24 Emulate a rookie 11-Down
26 Place to trade
28 Banish to Hades
31 Winetaster's asset
32 Plaything for two
34 Flemish painter
36 Wally's sitcom bro
39 Easy to manage
41 Licorice-flavored cordial
44 Intermediate target
47 Delphic prophet
49 Medical fluids
52 Catchall category
53 Common Market inits.
55 End of the Jewish calendar
56 Lucy Lawless role
58 Fall heavily
60 Everyday article
61 "Deee-lish!"
62 What a star athlete may turn
63 U.S.N.A. grad.

by David Liben-Nowell

98

ACROSS

1 President before Jefferson
6 Couch
10 "Picnic" Pulitzer-winner William
14 Performing poorly in
15 Knocks for a loop
16 Gas in advertising lights
17 With 59-Across, lyric from "America, the Beautiful"
20 Bro's counterpart
21 U.N. working-conditions agcy.
22 Molecule part
23 Guinness suffix
24 Dict. info
26 For adults, as films
30 Lyric from "The Star-Spangled Banner"
33 Numbskull
34 Perlman of "Cheers"
35 Society newcomer
36 These break the silence of the lambs
39 Derisive laugh
40 Huff and puff
41 Prints, pastels and such
42 Hollywood's Ken or Lena
44 Nasdaq debut: Abbr.
46 Lyric from "America"
51 Lunatic
52 Japanese wrestling
53 Smallish batteries
55 Thick slice
57 Band booking
58 Air conditioner meas.
59 See 17-Across
64 "Garfield" dog
65 Talk wildly
66 Etc. and ibid., e.g.
67 Magician's stick
68 Jazz singer James
69 Unlike a rolling stone?

DOWN

1 Humiliate
2 Breakfast roll
3 Extends
4 Apple computer, for short
5 Large steps
6 Took to the airport, say
7 Confess, with "up"
8 Greek salad cheese
9 Wood source for a baseball bat
10 Director Bergman
11 Newcomer, briefly
12 Moo —— gai pan
13 Finish up
18 Bread spreads
19 —— Linda, Calif.
25 Leaves in the lurch
27 "Look what I did!"
28 Fifty-fifty
29 Borrower's burden
31 Apron wearers, traditionally
32 L.B.J.'s veep
36 Soothing ointment
37 Neck of the woods
38 Env. notation
39 Get a move on, quaintly
40 Luau paste
42 Toothbrush brand
43 Spy novelist John
44 Shooting marble
45 Write computer instructions
47 Dropped a line in the water
48 Should, informally
49 Bigwigs
50 Swamp swimmers
54 Like dishwater
56 Dinghy or dory
59 "I'm impressed!"
60 Rhoda's TV mom
61 10th-anniversary metal
62 Blasting stuff
63 "The Sopranos" network

by Nancy Salomon

ACROSS

1 Tough trips
6 Poster holder
10 Shi'ites, e.g.
14 Two under, on the links
15 Double-reeded woodwind
16 Pertaining to
17 Tee off
18 Elbow/hand connector
19 Marked, as a box on a test
20 Noted actor's writing implements?
23 "Nope"
25 Actress Hatcher
26 Candidate's concern
27 Instruction to a woman in labor
30 Get-up-and-go
32 Danger signal
33 Yo-Yo Ma's instrument
34 Rodeo wear, often
36 Noted actor's sons?
41 Farmer's spring purchase
42 Orderly grouping
44 Dear old —
47 Headlight setting
48 Public face
50 "Wheel of Fortune" purchases
52 Huge-screen film format
54 Church perch
55 Noted actor's underarms?
59 Shopper stopper
60 Fiddle sticks
61 California/Nevada lake
64 Keep — (persist)
65 A couple of chips in the pot, maybe
66 Tempest
67 Perfect Olympic scores
68 Makes calls
69 "Breaking Away" director Peter

DOWN

1 Lipton product
2 Made haste
3 Shade of white
4 Swiss artist Paul
5 Word repeated after "Que" in song
6 Rug with nothing swept under it?
7 More competent
8 Plotted
9 9/11 commission chairman Thomas
10 Rush-hour hr.
11 Win over
12 Shrink in fear
13 Made tight, as muscles
21 Highest degree
22 Analogous
23 "The West Wing" network, originally
24 Plane measure
28 Resigned remark
29 Cut down on the flab
31 Electees
34 Dentist's deg.
35 Neighbor of Earth
37 Floral necklace
38 Movie ticket mandate
39 Finesse stroke in tennis
40 With it, mentally
43 Not fly absolutely straight
44 Blots lightly
45 Supply with oxygen
46 Join a teleconference
48 Written permissions
49 Abbr. before a date on a pkg.
51 "Golden Boy" playwright
53 Workweek letters
56 Construction beam
57 Wee
58 "See ya!"
62 Miner's find
63 German spa

by Beth Hinshaw

ACROSS

1 Kindergarten instruction
5 Modern music holder
9 Next-to-last Italian queen
14 Soften, as chocolate
15 Draft-board classification
16 Puts a top on
17 Follow
18 Cereal box figure with a hat
20 Eucalyptus muncher
22 "To happiness!," e.g.
23 Group forcing men into military service
26 Young troublemakers
30 "Go away!"
31 Product of dehydration
33 Years ___
36 Disney goldfish
38 Pang
39 Popular family dog, familiarly
40 Emergency military operation
43 Hells Canyon locale: Abbr.
44 Shooter
46 Raison d'___
47 Inquire
48 Classic novel banned in the U.S. until 1933
51 Was present
53 Word on a biblical wall
54 Enhancing undergarment
58 Sucker
60 Stylish Ford, briefly
62 Orange snack item
67 Russian choreographer Moiseyev
68 Gather
69 Dairy case item
70 It may be wrinkled
71 Body of art?
72 Deep in thought
73 Got larger

DOWN

1 One way to run
2 Fast-tempoed jazz
3 Free from confusion
4 Does salon work
5 ___ Martens (casual shoes)
6 Pig ___ poke
7 Dividing membranes
8 Church bylaws
9 Blunders
10 Stupid and ill-mannered
11 String of periods
12 Super Bowl winner more than 50% of the time: Abbr.
13 Hair color
19 Where to put an old newspaper, maybe
21 Trash bins
24 Songs for one
25 Suffix with theater
27 Julie Andrews role in "The Sound of Music"
28 Trudges
29 Porterhouse, e.g.
32 Essay
33 Music holder
34 House feature
35 Delivery specialist, for short?
37 Grand ___ Opry
41 Nagging desire
42 Lady of the Haus
45 Of no value
49 Olympics blade
50 Assistance
52 Subsiding
55 Longtime Dolphins coach
56 Stiffness
57 Popped up
59 Classic gas
61 Attracted
62 Cool ___
63 Patient care grp.
64 Pitcher part
65 Workout unit
66 Parking site

by Raymond Hamel

ACROSS

1 Swiss peaks
5 Bit of dust
10 It holds a bunch
14 Blood fluids
15 Cather who wrote "My Ántonia"
16 Personal flair
17 Greeting for Julius
19 In position, as a cornerstone
20 One who proffers an arm
21 Destructive beetles
23 Dictation taker
24 Number of zodiac signs
26 Words to live by
28 Rand McNally product
32 24-hour conveniences, for short
36 Fund for old age: Abbr.
37 One under one
38 Bit of bridal attire
39 Giant
41 Catch ___ (start to understand)
42 Rationalization
44 Humble home
45 Struggle for air
46 Cash in a cache, e.g.
47 Fruit whose seeds are spit out
49 Sand trap, for one
51 Following
56 Oscar winner for "Kramer vs. Kramer"
59 Star, in Paris
60 Org. that defends individual rights
61 Title song of a Prince film
64 Baseball's Musial
65 Duos
66 Gait between walk and canter
67 Duck's home
68 "Tiny Alice" playwright Edward
69 Diner sign

DOWN

1 Fireplace remnants
2 "That's the ___ I can do"
3 Three for a dollar, e.g.
4 Hairdresser's shop
5 Big baseball hit
6 Cobbler
7 Raised railways
8 Mauled, as by a bear
9 Čapek who wrote "R.U.R."
10 Mel Torme's sobriquet, with "the"
11 Jai ___
12 Mast item
13 Means justifiers, some say
18 Relative of a gator
22 Hoosier senator Bayh
24 Actress Garr
25 This puzzle's theme
27 Ceremony
29 Actress Turner
30 Kitchen pests
31 Cease
32 Madison and Fifth, in N.Y.C.
33 What's read
34 Isinglass
35 Illicit reserve
37 Mad about
40 "___ Lang Syne"
43 Fraud
47 Alternative to automatic
48 Archibald of the N.B.A.
50 Frank of the Mothers of Invention
52 Strong point
53 Queen's headgear
54 Author T. S. ___
55 Income for Fred and Ethel Mertz
56 Trunk closer
57 Eight: Prefix
58 Sweet Spanish dessert
59 Otherwise
62 Kid
63 Before: Prefix

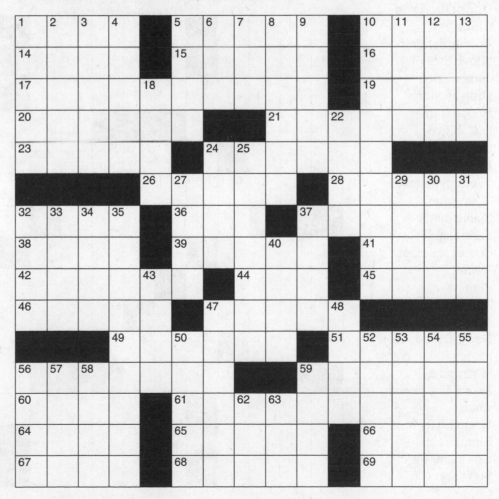

by Janice M. Putney

ACROSS

1 Nurses' workmates
5 Leave clueless
10 Headliner
14 Russia's ___ Mountains
15 Lack of laxness
16 Kent State's state
17 "I'm game"
19 On guard
20 Jane of "Klute"
21 Had in mind
23 "Telephone Line" rock grp.
24 Pretend to sing
28 Star Wars mil. project
31 "I'm game"
33 One of the Twin Cities
35 Cold-relief brand
37 "Love Story" author Erich
38 Drop anchor
41 Hedge former
43 D.C. bigwigs
44 Out of kilter
46 Letter lines
48 "Tommy" rockers
50 "I'm game"
54 Stable diet?
55 Fashionable
57 Soccer standout Hamm
58 Plug
60 They leave marks on the road
62 New Mexico resort town
64 "I'm game"
68 Like a G.I. peeling spuds
69 Susan Lucci's Emmy role
70 Don Juan, for one
71 Sight seers
72 Got up
73 Cultural doings

DOWN

1 ___ bag (camper's tote)
2 Baltimore ballplayer
3 Defeatist's word
4 Musher's transport
5 Hindu honorific
6 Small songbird
7 "Gross!"
8 Daddy's counterpart
9 Fixes feathers
10 Scattered, as seed
11 "I'm game"
12 Go public with
13 "Crying" singer Orbison
18 Hider in kids' books
22 Does something
25 Electrified particles
26 Cores
27 Ogle
29 Twofold
30 Sorry situations
32 You may make its head turn
34 Coke competitor
36 One of the Three Stooges
38 Trig, e.g.
39 Govt. workplace watchdog
40 "I'm game"
42 One, for one
45 Passing fancy
47 Mouthing off
49 Unwelcome obligations
51 Key with two flats
52 Lay low
53 Has a bite
56 Brief burst
59 Cairo cobras
61 Actress Sedgwick
62 Bunion's place
63 Whatever
65 Brazilian hot spot, briefly
66 System starter?
67 Roll of dough

by Nancy Salomon

ACROSS

1 Op-Ed piece
6 "Huh?"
10 Something to haggle over
14 India's first P.M.
15 Plotter in a play
16 Call from the nursery
17 No longer carry Folgers or Maxwell House?
20 "Uncle Tom's Cabin" girl
21 Aid and ___
22 Giving off light
23 X out
25 Soup base
27 Prisoner's tally on a cell wall
29 ___-la-la
30 Belly muscles
33 True
36 Baby kangaroo's nickname for mom's pouch?
39 Ditch
40 Four for the road
41 Old Italian money
42 How a high-pitched weasel goes?
44 Squalid
45 Uranus' domain
46 Address starting http://
47 Provider of the first bone transplant?
49 Varieties
51 Rebuttal to "No, you're not"
55 Eyed food
58 Cogitate, with "on"
60 Overmodest
61 Oasis store?
64 In ___ (where found)
65 Govt. disaster relief org.
66 Mowed path
67 Tugboat sound
68 Opening in Vegas
69 Home of the Lyndon B. Johnson Space Center

DOWN

1 Over
2 Wait on
3 Underwater sandbank
4 Dadaist Jean
5 Seat of ancient Mayan civilization
6 Lois, to Hi
7 Sword handles
8 Time of one's life
9 Jumps on the ice
10 Great big kiss
11 Aftermath
12 "So be it"
13 Result of hairsplitting?
18 What a hypnotist may tell you to do
19 A lot of, slangily
24 Outer limits
26 City in a classic railroad name
28 Safeguard
30 Similar (to)
31 Shipping hazard
32 Corset stiffener
33 Skiers' paradise
34 "Hey, over here!"
35 Cosby/Culp TV series
37 ___ pro nobis
38 Simoleons
40 Freeway exits
43 Andean capital
44 Life jacket
48 Turned blue, maybe
49 Not working
50 Dolt
52 Mountaineer's tool
53 View in an angiogram
54 Old stories
55 "Hey, over here!"
56 Buckeye State
57 Emerald City visitor
59 Incubate
62 ___ Aviv
63 Neighbor of Norw.

by Manny Nosowsky

104

ACROSS

1 Swine
5 "Money __ everything"
9 Northern Scandinavians
14 Toward shelter, nautically
15 Burn the surface of
16 Devoured quickly
17 Soft light
18 Give new décor
19 Desmond of "Sunset Blvd."
20 Lungful
21 1976 Hoffman/Olivier film
23 Music from Jamaica
25 Dover fish
26 Coward's color
29 Portugal's capital
33 It may be acute or obtuse
35 Master hand
37 The woman of Lennon's "Woman"
38 Dik Browne's "Hi and __"
39 Strikingly bright
40 Habeas corpus, e.g.
41 Make a boo-boo
42 2005 Christo display in New York City, with "the"
43 Social class
44 Got quiet, with "down"
46 Take back, as one's story
48 Draft status
50 Hold back
53 Character who debuted in All Star Comics, December 1941
58 August 1 sign
59 April 1 sign
60 Word said before opening the eyes
61 Cain's victim
62 & 63 First two names of Guy de Maupassant
64 Inlet

65 Advances of money
66 Conclusions
67 Looks at

DOWN

1 Dik Browne's "__ the Horrible"
2 Stan's partner in old comedy
3 Title song of a 1966 hit movie
4 Darn, as socks
5 Tel Aviv's land
6 Prophet
7 Nothin'
8 Brings (out)
9 Lipstick ingredient
10 Makes up (for)
11 Salon job, informally
12 Cougar
13 Bridge
21 Stag party attender
22 __ up (hid out)
24 Hair goops
27 Fail to mention
28 Be unsteady
30 Brendan Behan book
31 Step __ (hurry)
32 Observe
33 Actor Guinness
34 Nick Charles's wife
36 Workshop gripper
39 Darth __ of "Star Wars"
40 Kind of ad
42 Book before Exodus
43 Normandy city
45 One of the M's in MoMA
47 Construction site machines
49 Cognizant
51 Christopher of "Superman"
52 Bob and Elizabeth of politics
53 Actor Ken of TV's "Wiseguy"
54 Creme cookie
55 Ship of Columbus
56 What a prophet reads
57 Darn, as socks
61 High card

by Randy Sowell

ACROSS

1 Electric guitar hookup
4 Johnny of "Edward Scissorhands"
8 Kind of hose
13 Corner piece
15 One in the red
16 Island greeting
17 Nay
19 Advice to a sleepyhead
20 Yea
21 Physical, e.g.
22 Maltese money
23 Big gobblers
25 SuperStation initials
27 Schoolroom fixture
28 Elephantine
30 El ___, Tex.
31 Aykroyd et al.
32 Gas purchase
34 Culpable
38 Holiday team leader
39 Kind of eyes
40 Lower California
41 River in Spain
42 Some escapist literature
44 One teaching econ or psych, e.g.
48 Fahrenheit figure: Abbr.
49 Vigorous dance
50 "___ Jacques"
51 Transfusion fluids
53 Nay
56 Jest
57 Yea
58 Spring (from)
59 Kennel features
60 Art subject
61 Fictional rabbit
62 Whirl
63 One way to stand

DOWN

1 First name in action films
2 Former Met Wilson
3 Propels
4 Martial arts school
5 Cuddly "Star Wars" creature
6 Jack, in Spain
7 Victimize
8 Beeper calls
9 "Potent Potables for 200, ___"
10 Nay
11 Yea
12 Mouth, slangily
14 Olympic vehicle
18 Fabric measure: Abbr.
24 Sight from Tokyo
26 Frosh, next year
28 Oxford protector?
29 Abbr. on a bank statement
30 Arafat grp.
31 Batman and Robin, e.g.
33 Eddie Cantor sweetheart
34 Like good wine
35 Yea
36 Nay
37 In the past
38 1941 film "A Yank in the ___"
40 Filled with awe
43 Buffet tidbit
44 Primp
45 Excites
46 Frozen foods brand
47 Black-footed critter
49 More sensible
50 Small fish
52 Late Kennedy matriarch
54 Work in the bleachers
55 "Calm down"
56 Soft diet

by Mark Diehl

106

ACROSS

1 Courtyards
6 ___ d'état
10 Part of a gateway
14 Middays
15 Facilitate
16 Denver's home: Abbr.
17 Disoriented
20 Dancers Fred and Adele
21 ___-Japanese War
22 Actor Sparks
23 ___ end (very last part)
25 Prime-time hour
26 Soviet labor camp
30 Party to a defense pact
31 Spirited horse
32 Prophet who anointed Saul
34 Mimic
37 Disoriented
40 Jet to Heathrow
41 Vigorous
42 Actress Spelling
43 Operatic prince
44 Dead, as an engine
45 Had been
48 Guinness Book suffix
49 One of the Gershwins
51 Once more
53 Captain Picard series
58 Disoriented
61 State south of Ky.
62 Kind of smasher
63 Sharp as ___
64 Chair
65 They hold hymnals
66 Where Seoul is

DOWN

1 Paul who sang "Having My Baby"
2 Shipping units
3 Cheer (for)
4 Andean of old
5 Inquiring
6 Relinquished
7 Schmoes
8 G.I. entertainers
9 Each
10 Rights protection grp.
11 Chicken house
12 In the ball park
13 Board, as a trolley
18 "Able was I ___ . . ."
19 Historic county of Scotland
23 Botches
24 Native Alaskan
26 Wanders (about)
27 "Exodus" author
28 Endure
29 Roseanne's network
30 Love, in Lourdes
32 Urban woes
33 Monastery V.I.P.
34 Over
35 Where the Amazon originates
36 Make a change for the verse?
38 China and environs, with "the"
39 One ___ time
44 Noted site of Egyptian ruins
45 Floats gently
46 Be of one mind
47 Finnish bath
49 News paragraphs
50 "Far out"
52 "Money ___ everything!"
53 Pack
54 Dog in Oz
55 Bring up
56 Suffix with exist
57 America's first commercial radio station
59 Séance sound
60 Dined

by Sidney L. Robbins

ACROSS
1 Rushes (along)
5 Amassed
10 They cover Highland heads
14 Neglect
15 Mes numero uno
16 "In a cowslip's bell ___": "The Tempest"
17 One nourished by daydreams?
19 Rotten to the ___
20 One of "Them!" things
21 Author O'Brien
22 Ready for framing
24 Genealogical chart
25 New Rochelle college
26 One who counts calories?
32 Perspiration perforations
33 Alternative to a watering can
34 Khan married to Rita Hayworth
35 Detective Charlie
36 Dress style
38 Classic art subject
39 Elephant's weight, maybe
40 Israeli Abba
41 "For ___ sake!"
42 One with a high-iron diet?
46 Hollywood giants?
47 Jemima, for one
48 Farm trough
51 ___ .45
52 Dallas school, for short
55 Strip of wood
56 One fond of dining on tongue?
59 Florence's river
60 Destroy
61 Motion supporters
62 High schooler's test, briefly
63 Went out with
64 Key letter

DOWN
1 "J'accuse" author
2 Springsteen's "___ Fire"
3 English P.M. called "The Great Commoner"
4 Alphabet trio
5 Carolina river
6 More ridiculous
7 "I ___ Song Go Out of My Heart"
8 Before, to a poet
9 Member of Alice's tea party
10 Popular breath mint
11 Loads
12 Slough
13 Burpee's bit
18 Some Bosnians
23 ___ Morrow Lindbergh
24 Feds
25 Clothes presser
26 Not at all
27 Heavens: Prefix
28 Tableware
29 ___ cuisine
30 Presbyter
31 Deli loaves
32 Election numbers: Abbr.
36 Sucked up
37 Statutes
38 Its eye is needed in a "Macbeth" recipe
40 Slight advantage
41 Sophia's Carlo
43 Boiling mad
44 "Tao Te Ching" author
45 Quieted
48 Part of an envelope
49 Auricles
50 Lab burner
51 Layer
52 Hebrides island
53 Make the acquaintance of
54 Twinkling bear
57 Man-mouse link
58 Taxi

by Jonathan Schmalzbach

ACROSS

1 Catch-22
5 Nimble
9 Paul of "American Graffiti"
14 Where pirates moor
15 Queen of scat
16 Khomeini, for one
17 Ugandan tyrant
18 Carpenters' work?
19 Frankie or Cleo
20 "Citizen Kane" spoiler
23 First-class service
24 Diamonds, to hoods
25 Scattered
29 Oversized
31 —— and Span (cleaner brand)
35 Poi ingredients
36 Bring in
37 Roxy Music co-founder Brian
38 "Planet of the Apes" spoiler
42 Cartoon dog
43 Provides machine maintenance
44 Venusian, for one
45 Lobster pot
47 In high spirits
48 Bells and whistles
49 Kind of shore
51 Afflict
52 "The Crying Game" spoiler
61 Salad bar implement
62 Unpleasant person
63 Roast beef request
64 Hello in Hilo
65 Concept of Descartes
66 Deck hands
67 Snappish
68 Copper
69 Vehemence

DOWN

1 Lasting impression?
2 Pitcher Hideo
3 Budget alternative
4 Kind of pool
5 Figure out
6 Give the slip
7 Whipped along
8 "Toodle-oo!"
9 Violet shade
10 Gets the lead out
11 Knights' garb
12 Actress Jeffreys
13 Bound
21 Opera villain, often
22 Autographs
25 Kick off
26 Times or Post
27 Games site
28 Donnybrook
29 In the worst way
30 Spring flower
32 Hidden rocks, to a ship
33 Microchip giant
34 Lawyer Roy and family
36 Hollywood's Kazan
39 "I read you"
40 Baseball's Wynn
41 Champion of 10/30/74
46 Pickle
48 Choice cut
50 School assignment
51 #1 Green Mountain Boy
52 G.D.P., for one
53 Swimming ——
54 Hazzard County deputy
55 "War and Peace," e.g.
56 One who takes messages
57 Military parade passageway
58 Dam
59 Rug figure
60 First name on Capitol Hill

by John D. Leavy

ACROSS

1 Poverty
5 Mutual of ___
10 Track tipster
14 Neighborhood
15 Artist Bonheur and others
16 Like Solomon
17 Watch face
18 Whitney's partner in airplanes
19 Pizazz
20 1970's New York Knick's nickname
23 Western alliance: Abbr.
24 Sidestep
28 Grotto
32 20- and 51-Across, e.g.
35 States firmly
36 To ___ (precisely)
37 "___ the season to be jolly"
38 Hank Ketcham comic strip
42 Purpose
43 Harrow's rival
44 Dog: Fr.
45 When American elections are held
48 Rio ___ (border river)
49 Take care of, as duties
50 Nearly worthless coin
51 1960–66 N.B.A. scoring leader, informally
59 Jellystone Park bear
62 "I don't give ___!"
63 Scent
64 G.I. addresses
65 Jazz singer Vaughan
66 Burn soother
67 Didn't part with
68 Pickpocketed
69 Physics unit

DOWN

1 Walk in the baby pool
2 La Scala solo
3 Not distant
4 Six-foot or more
5 Annie, e.g., in the comics
6 Folkways
7 "Rush!"
8 Abhor
9 30's movie dog
10 Midnight
11 Source of Rockefeller money
12 Red, white and blue initials
13 Hamilton's bill
21 Trunks
22 Seminary subj.
25 Reach
26 Cleared, as a winter windshield
27 Ancient Palestinian
28 West Pointers
29 Boulevard
30 Buyer
31 Suffix with east or west
32 One of the Three Musketeers
33 MTV's target viewer
34 Haw's partner
36 Bar member: Abbr.
39 Poseidon's realm
40 Pale colors
41 Shelter grp.
46 Double curve, as in yarn
47 "How ___ love thee? Let me . . ."
48 "Faust" dramatist
50 Sand bar
52 Sweetheart
53 "Anything but ___!"
54 Bullfight bull
55 "The Wind in the Willows" character
56 Without thought
57 Diving bird
58 Chestnut or walnut
59 Talk, talk, talk
60 Unlock, in poetry
61 Republicans, collectively

by Gregory E. Paul

ACROSS

1 Pitchers
6 Take to the dump
11 Say "pretty please"
14 Republican politico Alexander
15 Skip the big wedding
16 Genetic letters
17 1978 Faye Dunaway film
20 I.B.M. or 3M, e.g.: Abbr.
21 In this place
22 Taboos
23 —— of war
24 Luxuriate, as in the sun
25 Tone down
26 Incredible bargain
28 Boeing product
29 The "I" in T.G.I.F.
30 G.H.W. Bush's home
34 Peer Gynt's mother
35 1932 Will Rogers film
37 Tofu source
38 Late singer named for a Dickens character
39 Midmorning
40 Douglas ——
41 Adagio and allegro
45 Pennsylvania, for one
47 Food inspection inits.
50 Suffix with convention
51 Kind of closet
52 Italian princely family name
53 Mata ——
54 1948 Ava Gardner film
57 N.Y.C. subway operator
58 Olympic judge
59 Come up

60 Prodigy competitor, for short
61 Used colorful language
62 40- and 51-Across, e.g.

DOWN

1 Puts into office
2 Exit
3 Come out
4 Bronchitis symptom
5 Full house sign
6 Tennis's Monica
7 Co-worker of Lois and Jimmy
8 Libertine
9 30-day mo.
10 Subject for George Washington Carver
11 Wave, as a weapon
12 Along the way
13 Helium and neon, e.g.
18 Mortgage agcy.
19 Teeming group
24 Hard punch
25 French assembly
27 On-board greeting
28 Bishop of old TV
31 Loosen, as laces
32 Recipe directive
33 "Long" or "short" amount
34 "Don't look —— like that!"
35 Fait accompli
36 Singer Coolidge

37 53 minutes past the hour
39 Puget Sound city
40 Frenzies
42 Villain
43 Look over
44 Record-setting van Gogh canvas
46 —— King Cole
47 Fallen house of literature
48 Squirrel away
49 Rock's —— Leppard
52 Outside: Prefix
53 München Mr.
55 Detroit labor grp.
56 Grape masher's work site

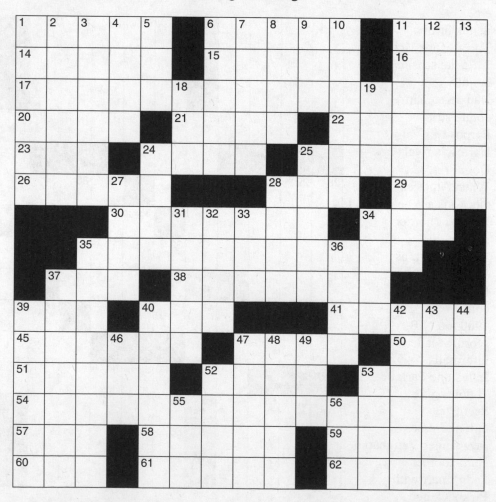

by Elizabeth C. Gorski

ACROSS

1 Conspiracy
6 Thundering
11 Quipster
14 Diminish
15 Stir up, in a way
16 Billy Joel's "___ to Extremes"
17 Limited group?
19 Oriental absolute
20 Kind of steel
21 Astronaut in 1996 news
23 Undercover operative
24 "Frasier" character
25 Communion dishes
28 Like TV's Jaime Sommers
30 Nile bird
31 Academy student
32 Prearrange
35 Suede feature
36 Straw hats
38 Part of a name on a menu
39 Surprising "gift"
40 This comes in as March goes out
41 Quite some distance off
42 Gofer's assignment
44 Joan of Arc, e.g.
46 Salon treatment
48 Figures
49 Gentle as ___
50 Unexpected
55 Malaysian export
56 Vein
58 "The Island of the Day Before" author
59 Broadcast
60 Bristles
61 Consult
62 Unkempt
63 Discernment

DOWN

1 Stadium souvenirs
2 Blind as ___
3 Theda the vamp
4 Now and then
5 Inaugural Rock and Roll Hall of Fame inductee
6 Jibe
7 Flagwoman?
8 Circus cries
9 Elvis's "A Fool Such ___"
10 Moves in the garden
11 Sorcery
12 "Not ___!"
13 Former Philly mayor Wilson ___
18 Right-angle joints
22 News inits.
24 Activist
25 Loblolly, e.g.
26 Down with: Fr.
27 Harrison sobriquet
28 Like some breath
29 Time to beware
31 "The Postman Always Rings Twice" author
33 "Now ___ me down . . ."
34 Actress who played Tootsie's tootsie
36 One whom Pilate pardoned
37 Kind of history
41 Uzbek lake
43 Hoops target
44 Sportscaster Albert
45 Bear witness
46 Clotho and Lachesis
47 Author Walker
48 To whom "my heart belongs"
50 Resentful
51 Pigeon-___
52 Political suffixes
53 Spiffy
54 Jubilation
57 Golfer's concern

by Chet Currier

112

ACROSS

1 Garb for Superman
5 Ice cream dessert
10 Work detail, for short
14 Singer Guthrie
15 Ness of "The Untouchables"
16 ___ Strauss (jeans maker)
17 What a ghost may give you
19 Coup d'___
20 Boundary
21 Meat cuts
22 Stockholmer
23 Wise one
24 Pay no attention
26 Georgia city where Little Richard was born
29 Western hero
31 Keeps away from
33 "Whose Life ___ Anyway?" (1981 movie)
34 Suffix with cash
37 Factory on a stream
38 Department at an auto shop
40 Fairy tale starter
41 Tally (up)
42 Bundled cotton
43 "Well said!"
45 Honkers
48 A Musketeer
49 Pass ___ (make the grade)
50 Poll amts.
52 Bar for a bird
53 California lake resort
55 Notwithstanding, briefly
58 Actress Chase
59 With feet pointing in
61 Above, in Berlin
62 Not moving
63 Singer Fitzgerald
64 Articulates
65 Go along (with)
66 Enemy's opposite

DOWN

1 Hamster's home
2 "East of Eden" brother
3 Slog (through)
4 Dawn goddess
5 Obscure
6 Hardy and North
7 Bearing
8 Most domineering
9 Numerical ending
10 Quite a few, after "a"
11 "Network" co-star
12 Dodge, as a question
13 Commend
18 African antelope
22 Perturbed state
23 Loam
25 Grain for grinding
26 Baby doll's cry
27 Enthusiastic
28 One way to quit
30 Personnel person
32 Outpouring
35 Reverberate
36 "Cheers" actor Roger
39 Emulating Paul Revere
40 Inning parts
42 This and that
44 Granola-like
46 Katharine Hepburn has four
47 Globe
49 Opera star Nellie
51 "Veddy" British actor Robert
52 Papal name
54 Finish for teen or golden
55 Auto commuter's bane
56 "War is ___"
57 Singer Anita
59 Actress Zadora
60 Wonderland drink

by Stephanie Spadaccini

113

ACROSS
1 Poland's Walesa
5 Fine violin
10 With 39-Across, featured boxing match
14 "As Long — Needs Me" ("Oliver!" song)
15 Two-door
16 Capital on a fjord
17 Gallows reprieve
18 Quite healthy
20 Eternally, to poets
21 Downwind
22 "We — the World"
23 Not firsthand
25 Biting
29 Patisserie employee
30 Application information
31 Downhill runner
33 Amusement park features
35 Uncles and others
36 Around
38 "— Ruled the World" (1965 hit)
39 See 10-Across
41 Rope-a-dope exponent
42 Angers
45 Angers
46 Rural way
48 Comes to the rescue
50 Teaches the A B C's
51 Self-defense art
54 Like some humor
55 Kind of chop
56 Kovic of "Born on the Fourth of July"
57 "Designing Women" co-star
61 Pinochle combo
62 Food bar
63 An archangel
64 Baseball's Rose
65 Talon
66 Litigants
67 Hullabaloo

DOWN
1 Light in a light show
2 Lauder of cosmetics
3 "The Most Beautiful Girl" singer
4 "Yo!"
5 Tackle box gizmos
6 "And so —"
7 Hold sway over
8 Imitate
9 Spectacular failure
10 Part of MoMA
11 "Unaccustomed — am . . ."
12 Spot in the mer
13 Visual O.K.
19 To avoid the alternative
21 Parliamentary stand
24 Current status
25 Tax filer's dread
26 1978 Gerry Rafferty hit
27 Ammonia-derived compound
28 Parts of dollars
30 Played a flute in a march
31 Temporary protectors
32 New Hampshire's state flower
34 Actress Bonet and others
37 Colorado city
40 "I saw," Caesar-style
43 Oedipus' foster father
44 Marine fishes
47 Servilely defer (to)
49 H-L connectors
51 Wild card
52 Conductor Georg
53 Secondary to
55 —-dieu (pew part)
57 Medic
58 Angled annex
59 Pasture
60 It neighbors Braz.
61 AWOL hunters

by Thomas W. Schier

ACROSS

1 Theme of this puzzle
5 Odorless gas
11 Finger-paint
14 Body of troops
15 The general Pelopidas, for one
16 Toothpullers' grp.
17 Coffee-loving "Star Wars" character?
19 Singing syllables
20 Unlock, in poetry
21 First ___
22 Muslim leaders
24 Actor who demands frothy coffee on the set?
28 Granny Smiths
31 1953 A.L. M.V.P. Al
32 Boors
33 Like "Aida"
37 Aldrich Ames, for one
38 Subsided
40 Japanese soup
41 Endorsement
43 More rational
44 Parry
45 Football ploy
46 50's comedienne with a taste for flavored coffee?
50 Imposing residence
51 Small dog, for short
52 Veteran
55 Graffiti, to some
56 Vaudevillian fond of coffee with milk?
61 Actress Scala
62 Patron
63 Lacey on "Cagney & Lacey"
64 Telesthesia
65 Factors in conjugation
66 Underworld river

DOWN

1 Stephen King thriller
2 Take ___ (rest)
3 Take ___ (rest)
4 Schedule abbr.
5 Moral principles
6 1971 courtroom drama
7 Chuckle sound
8 ___ Dhabi (Mideast capital)
9 Slave Turner
10 Lorelei
11 ___ Lama
12 Rhett's last words
13 One who sings the part of Mefistofele
18 Yarns
23 60's Defense Secretary
24 Sidekick
25 Stumper
26 Vicar of Christ
27 Worn
28 ___ mater
29 Gossip
30 Juicer refuse
34 Antler point
35 "Amazing Grace" ending
36 Moonshine ingredient
38 "The Blackboard Jungle" author Hunter
39 Invited
42 Ham it up
43 Jerk
45 ___ Bluff National Monument
46 Mind's-eye view
47 One of the Yankees' M&M sluggers
48 Coming up
49 Suppose
52 H.S. exam
53 Depend (on)
54 Kind of marble
57 Small: Suffix
58 Chinese author ___ Yutang
59 Loser to D.D.E.
60 Mormons: Abbr.

by Jonathan Schmalzbach

ACROSS

1 Desert plants
6 Swap
11 Stomach muscles, for short
14 Extraterrestrial
15 King or queen
16 Do some soft-shoe
17 Big name in video rentals
19 Kimono accessory
20 Musical partner of Crosby and Stills
21 Madison Avenue worker
23 Big monkeys
27 French artist Henri
29 Adjusts to fit
30 Extreme cruelty
31 Religious factions
32 Top floor
33 Rainbow shape
36 Lodge members
37 Air raid alert
38 Words of comprehension
39 Tiny bit, as of cream
40 Asia's —— Peninsula
41 Bus station posting: Abbr.
42 Mickey of "National Velvet"
44 Word said to a photographer
45 Split with a hatchet
47 Scorched
48 Contract with a car dealer
49 Limerick, e.g.
50 Bic filler
51 Yegg
58 "We're number ——!"
59 Eskimo boat
60 Lariat's end
61 Neighbor of Isr.
62 Little finger
63 Soaked

DOWN

1 Quick way around town
2 The whole shooting match
3 A.F.L.'s partner
4 Gumshoe
5 Tied up
6 Supporting beam
7 "High priority!"
8 Supermodel Carol
9 Ruby or Sandra
10 Unpredictable
11 Cyclotron
12 Rum cakes
13 Vertebra locale
18 Prohibits
22 Malign, in slang
23 Established
24 Writer —— Rogers St. Johns
25 Exhausting task
26 Chooses
27 Chum, to a Brit
28 Tennis score
30 Homeless animal
32 Felt crummy
34 Pee Wee of Ebbets Field
35 Yielded
37 Having one's marbles
38 Cake finisher
40 Advances
41 Tribal healers
43 Western treaty grp.
44 Sonny's ex
45 Advertising awards
46 Comedian Bruce
47 Overly self-confident
49 Mountain
52 "—— Blue?" (1929 #1 hit)
53 Five smackeroos
54 Dove sound
55 Keystone character
56 Sixth sense, for short
57 Juan Carlos, e.g.

by Fred Piscop

116

ACROSS
1 Anesthetize, in a way
4 Some chain clothing stores
8 Video game hub
14 Play the part
15 Zone
16 Stops the tape temporarily
17 "Little" extraterrestrials
19 Passé
20 Had a bug
21 Inspirationalist Norman Vincent ___
23 Before, in verse
24 Home on the Black Sea
26 Smart-alecky
28 Pop duo with the album "Swamp Ophelia"
34 Reply to a masher
38 Satellite ___
39 Bunk
40 Actress Anderson
41 Newton or Stern
43 Actress Thurman and others
44 Small choir
46 Outfielder's cry
47 Oct. precursor
48 Drinks with gin, Cointreau and lemon juice
51 Greeting at sea
52 Undignified landing
56 Hardly Mr. Right
59 Facilitates
62 Unpaid factory worker
64 "All ___!"
66 Some Gainsborough forgeries
68 Ice cream parlor order
69 Two-wheeler
70 Sometime theater funder: Abbr.
71 Be at
72 French holy women: Abbr.
73 Blow it

DOWN
1 Crazy (over)
2 Pungent
3 Inscribed column
4 Leader called Mahatma
5 Tattoo place
6 Coop sound
7 Psychologically all there
8 Noted Harlem hot spot, with "The"
9 Durham's twin city
10 Bossy's chew
11 Connors opponent
12 ___ John
13 Isabella d'___ (Titian subject)
18 Continental trading org.
22 Khyber Pass traveler
25 1941 Glenn Miller chart topper "You ___"
27 Reverent
29 Lets down
30 "Let me repeat . . ."
31 Where the Vatican is
32 Giant hop
33 Method: Abbr.
34 Leisurely
35 Ness, for one
36 One doing a con job?
37 Michelangelo masterpiece
42 So-so grades
45 Iran's capital
49 Stinking rich
50 Shopping binges
53 Defensive tennis shot
54 Have ___ to pick
55 One who's not playing seriously
56 Home for la familia
57 Go up against
58 Word of warning
60 Drops off
61 Cut
63 Pre-1917 ruler
65 Fruit juice
67 Hawaiian music maker

by Elizabeth C. Gorski

ACROSS

1 Picket line pariah
5 Singer McEntire
9 Laissez-___
14 "Winnie ___ Pu"
15 Hagman TV co-star
16 Clinker
17 Café au ___
18 Très ___
19 Air Jordans
20 Patriotic cheer for the tricolor
23 Chocolate on a hotel pillow, e.g.
24 Sycophant
28 "Bravo!"
29 Bother
31 Bother
32 Central courts
35 Boxers, derogatorily
36 Dennis the Menace, at times
37 Advice in solving some mysteries
40 Communications prefix
41 Like mud
42 Rest stops
43 Actress Hagen
44 Scrawny
45 Bearded beast
46 Finally makes good on a debt
48 Was successful, slangily
52 Phrase of resignation
55 Neck
58 Numbskull
59 Window part
60 Forbidden
61 Spy in a 1962 exchange
62 Plane, e.g.
63 Sends forth
64 Change the decor
65 Sicilian province or its capital

DOWN

1 Forest, to Fabius
2 Prospector's filing
3 Still with us
4 Bugbear
5 Sales lure
6 Enlighten
7 Suds
8 Actress Magnani
9 1987 Tony-winning play
10 Zodiac start
11 Perturb
12 Caviar
13 Hems and haws
21 Pale purple
22 Sour gum tree
25 Schoolteachers of old
26 "There Is Nothin' Like ___"
27 Observes
29 Unclear
30 Nasty
32 Misbehave
33 It's between eta and iota
34 Kind of station
35 Menial
36 Noble act
38 Basketball, informally
39 Melted cheese dish
44 Like the Aires of Argentina
45 Male escort
47 Go quickly
48 Bewildered
49 Heavenly hunter
50 Acrylic fiber
51 Street on TV
53 Skiers' aid
54 Ear part
55 Jeanne d'Arc, e.g.: Abbr.
56 Popular cooking spray
57 Sash

by Richard Hughes

118

ACROSS

1 Ravioli base
6 Numbered hwys.
10 Nicholas was one
14 Sour
15 The Emerald Isle
16 "What's — you?"
17 18-wheelers
18 Communication means for computer-phobes
20 Grotesque imitation
22 Eat like a rabbit
23 Trees with cones
24 Tries again
25 Cornell's home
27 Passover event
28 Spanish gold
29 Moral principle
31 Convened again
35 Eggheady sort
37 "Cheers!" in Cherbourg
39 Dumb — (scatterbrain)
40 Length of yarn
42 Spud
44 Q-U link
45 Agrees (with)
47 Bang and buzz, e.g.
49 Graphed
52 "Lorna —" (1869 romance)
53 Reddish brown
54 Comes to light
57 Communication means at the office
59 Eat away
60 Once, once
61 Blue-pencil
62 "The Thinker" creator
63 Henna and others
64 Old newspaper section
65 Sugary

DOWN

1 Auld lang syne, with "the"
2 Perfect server
3 Communication means at sea
4 "Jeopardy!" staple
5 "— makes the heart . . ."
6 Takes five
7 Minuscule
8 Period of history
9 Trawled
10 Having trees
11 Knifes
12 Like Pisa's tower
13 Parts
19 Pepsi bottle size
21 Train reservations
24 Split the cards again
25 Charged particles
26 "Star —"
27 "— Marner"
30 More than disliked
32 Communication means for emergencies
33 Language spoken in Dingwall
34 Does lacework
36 Upsets
38 José Carreras, for one
41 British fertilizer
43 Ones at the top of their business?
46 Stapleton Airport site
48 Lined up
49 Pent up
50 "Faster!"
51 Belittle
52 Because of
54 Tizzy
55 Actress McClurg
56 Faxed
58 Bachelor's last words

by Mary E. Brindamour

ACROSS

1 Pickle container
4 Motionless
9 Fashion
14 Matriarch of all matriarchs
15 Actor Romero
16 Boiling
17 Weighed in
20 Light lunches
21 To any extent
22 List-ending abbr.
23 Moo juice container
25 Grp. overseeing toxic cleanups
28 Perfect rating
29 Most prudent
31 Become raveled
32 Painful spots
33 Carroll adventuress
34 Caused disharmony
38 Napping spots
39 Magazine exhortation
40 Break in relations
41 Out of business
43 Compaq products
46 —— Miss
47 Engulfs in amusement
48 Cream ingredient
49 Tear to shreds
51 Part of MoMA
53 Blabbed
57 —— pedis (athlete's foot)
58 Take to the stump
59 Certain shirt
60 Anxiety
61 Wanderer
62 Japanese honorific

DOWN

1 High-fliers
2 Fly
3 Change tactics
4 Like an eclair
5 Composer Rorem and others
6 Superlative ending
7 Short cheer
8 Firestone features
9 Clergyman
10 Kind of surgery
11 Indoor court
12 Indian with a bear dance
13 Some M.I.T. grads
18 Chum
19 Leave be
23 Wielded
24 Partner of search
26 Warsaw ——
27 Word of assent
29 Canton cookware
30 Land west of Eng.
31 Current
32 Sing "shooby-doo"
33 Out for the night
34 Aggravate
35 Part of a church service
36 Piano-playing Dame
37 Ariz.-to-Kan. dir.
38 Sign of stage success
41 Professor Plum's game
42 Pomeranian, for one
43 Stitched folds
44 Window of an eye
45 Breath mint brand
47 Sloppy-landing sound
48 Suffix with stock
50 France's —— de Glenans
51 Queens team
52 Follow the code
53 —— Puf fabric softener
54 Wrestler's goal
55 Have a go at
56 Gen. Arnold of W.W. II fame

by Gerald R. Ferguson

120

ACROSS
1 Response to a pass?
5 Green-skinned pear
10 Plug of tobacco
14 Glazier's sheet
15 Master
16 ___ avis
17 Italian wine region
18 Alberta national park
19 Fair
20 "Skeletons From the Closet" group
23 Prefix with second
24 Antique car
25 Get into trouble, in a way
28 Scant
30 Watch pocket
33 Food for a ladybug
34 Japanese plane of W.W. II
35 Don Juan
36 Lehar work, with "The"
39 Crackerjacks
40 Grays
41 Words to an audience
42 Philly-to-Norfolk dir.
43 ___ Minor
44 Happy hour perch
45 ___ Lanka
46 "That is so funny"
48 #1 song of 1973 and 1996
56 I-79 terminus
57 When to celebrate el año nuevo
58 ___ Minor
59 Genuine Risk, for one
60 Squelched
61 Echelon
62 Prep exam, for short
63 Comic Arnold
64 Gets on the nerves of

DOWN
1 Flap
2 Pirate's punishment
3 Upfront money
4 Apres-bain gowns
5 Composer Berg
6 Nifty, in the 50's
7 Primer girl
8 German composer Carl
9 Straighten, as a brow
10 Belief
11 Be afflicted with
12 Environs
13 Prop for Doug Henning
21 Lustful
22 Wilderness Campaign general
25 Parking garage features
26 Copycats
27 Kind of pillow
28 Euripedes tragedy
29 Valentine's Day visitor
30 Page number
31 Surpass
32 Rim that holds a gem
34 Sharp turns
35 Early name of Haile Selassie
37 Suspicious quality
38 California Indian
43 Geller with paranormal powers
45 February forecast
46 Shore bird
47 "With ___ in My Heart"
48 Dole's 1996 running mate
49 They may be rolled over
50 Italy's capital
51 Small annoyance
52 "I ___ man who wasn't there"
53 Figure in a Rimsky-Korsakov opera
54 Join
55 Shaggy oxen

by Jonathan Schmalzbach

ACROSS

1 Not fiction
5 Prefix with legal or chute
9 Fire starter
14 Hand lotion ingredient
15 At any time
16 Macho dude
17 Author Fleming and others
18 Extinct bird not known for its intelligence
19 Sky-blue
20 Louisa May Alcott classic
23 Envision
24 Deli loaves
25 Participants in a debate
27 World's fastest sport, with 2-Down
29 Footfall
32 Sounds of satisfaction
33 Thomas —— Edison
35 "Woe is me!"
37 Walkway
41 Nightgown wearer of children's rhyme
44 Four-door
45 It has a keystone
46 Lass
47 "Now —— seen everything!"
49 Store, as a ship's cargo
51 Aye's opposite
52 Woven cloth or fabric
56 Not able to hear
58 "—— Believer" (Monkees hit)
59 Don Ho standard
64 Sprite
66 Destroy
67 —— one's time
68 It's a piece of cake

69 Atlanta arena, with "the"
70 "What's —— for me?"
71 Affirmatives
72 Endure
73 Kett of the comics

DOWN

1 Flunk
2 See 27-Across
3 Artificial
4 Irritable and impatient
5 Place for a statue or a hero
6 Affirm
7 Give a makeover
8 Fragrance
9 Major Chinese seaport
10 Candy that comes in a dispenser
11 Tickle the funny bone
12 Harder to find
13 Strike zone's lower boundary
21 "—— Misérables"
22 Memorable time
26 Taking advantage of
27 Shark tale
28 Sheltered from the wind
30 First name in scat
31 Couples
34 Watch for
36 Religious splinter group
38 Miser

39 Trevi Fountain coin
40 Slippery
42 People asked to parties
43 Murder mystery
48 Yale grad
50 World Wide ——
52 A bit blotto
53 Writer Zola
54 The line y=0, in math
55 Register, as a student
57 60's protest leader Hoffman
60 City in Arizona
61 Storage containers
62 Do magazine work
63 —— high standard
65 Skating surface

by Shannon Burns

122

ACROSS

1 Some sports cars, for short
5 Foundation
10 Yield
14 Grimm villain
15 Novelist Jong
16 Jump at the Ice Capades
17 British heavy metal group
19 Canned meat brand
20 Disney's Dwarfs, e.g.
21 Printings
23 Support for Tiger Woods?
24 Pop singer Peeples
26 Prepares leather
27 Do a few odd jobs
32 —— Ababa
35 Cape Cod resort town
36 Acuff of the Country Music Hall of Fame
37 Androcles' friend
38 Headgear for Hardy
39 Celebration
40 Worshiper's seat
41 Bruce Wayne's home, for one
42 Valentine's Day gift
43 Inexpert motorist
46 Klondike strike
47 Org. that advises the N.S.C.
48 Computer key abbr.
51 One who works for a spell?
55 Sauteed shrimp dish
57 Not this
58 Huck Finn portrayer, 1993
60 Bring to ruin
61 As a companion
62 To be, in Tours
63 Afrikaner
64 London length
65 Fortuneteller

DOWN

1 Ceiling supporter
2 Conform (with)
3 Search blindly
4 E-mailed
5 "Hit the bricks!"
6 Jackie's second
7 Pro or con
8 Chilled the Chablis
9 Hygienic
10 Dealer's employer
11 Film box datum
12 Cain of "Lois & Clark"
13 Stately shaders
18 Luncheonette lists
22 Tropical root
25 Look after, with "to"
27 Wrestler's goal
28 Diamond flaw?
29 Decorative heading
30 Bit of marginalia
31 Changes color, in a way
32 European chain
33 The Almighty, in Alsace
34 Reduce in rank
38 Class distraction
39 On behalf of
41 Having a Y chromosome
42 Boxer's stat
44 Alter deceptively
45 Countenance
48 Overplay onstage
49 Fern fruit
50 Autumn beverage
51 Hit, as the toe
52 "You gotta be kidding!"
53 Model Macpherson
54 Very funny fellow
56 Makes one's jaw drop
59 Dad's namesake: Abbr.

by Patrick Jordan

123

ACROSS

1 Wingding
5 Commoner
9 Rabbit
14 "What have you been ___?"
15 Hideout
16 "Home ___"
17 Rabbit's title
18 1 for H, or 2 for He
19 Poet who wrote "The Sonnets to Orpheus"
20 Line from a Copland "Portrait"
23 Darrow of "King Kong"
24 Pilot's heading: Abbr.
25 Plains Indian
26 Political suffix
27 "Looky here!"
28 Hydroelectric project
31 Line from a Copland "Portrait"
37 Versifier Nash
38 Teachers' grp.
39 McDowall of "Planet of the Apes"
40 Line from a Copland "Portrait"
43 Married
44 "My mama done ___ me"
45 Eggs
46 Year Justinian II regained the throne
48 Clothing size: Abbr.
49 Certain brain size
52 Subject of Copland's "Portrait"
56 "Go ahead and ask"
57 Sound system brand
58 Over
59 Kind of boom
60 Writer Bombeck
61 Site of the fabled forges of the Cyclopes
62 "Christina's World" painter
63 Navy diver
64 Close

DOWN

1 Good ole boy
2 It keeps a cook tied up
3 Rudder's locale
4 Telephone, slangily
5 Outlined
6 Potato pancake
7 "___ kleine Nachtmusik"
8 Kind of tube
9 Lash of old westerns
10 "A Town Like ___" (Nevil Shute novel)
11 11th President
12 Like an octopus's defense
13 Bio word
21 Have in view
22 1982 cyberfilm
26 "Uh-huh"
27 Newsman Roger
28 Carpenter's groove
29 Como's "___ Love You So"
30 Baseball's "Say Hey Kid"
31 Hershey candy
32 Not fer
33 "If I Knew You Were Comin' ___ Baked a Cake"
34 Pioneers
35 Motivated
36 Suburban New York college
41 Hankering
42 Like Mr. Spock's answers
46 French right
47 Fisherman's take-home
48 Cousin of a camel
49 Florence's ___ Vecchio
50 Actress Verdugo
51 Egypt's Sadat
52 Tar hail
53 Archeological find
54 A ___ bagatelle
55 Normandy city
56 24-Across's opposite

by Mark Elliot Skolsky

124

ACROSS

1 Sandwich shop
5 Fitzgerald and others
10 "We're looking for ___ good men"
14 North Carolina college
15 Gettysburg victor
16 Pepsi, for one
17 41339
20 Sweet liqueur
21 Gallic girlfriends
22 Ascot
23 ___-Coburg-Gotha (British royal house)
25 62060
33 Affixed with heat, as a patch
34 ___ number on (mess up)
35 Campground letters
36 20's gangster Bugs ___
37 Each of the numbers in this puzzle's theme
38 Being a copycat
40 They: Fr.
41 ___ Tse-tung
42 Tone deafness
43 49236
47 "Horrors!"
48 Hawaiian wreath
49 Companionless
52 They're handy by phones
57 97352
60 I in "The King and I"
61 Heathen
62 Glow
63 Cheer (for)
64 Lodge member
65 Reading light

DOWN

1 "It was ___ vu all over again"
2 Enthusiasm
3 Graph points
4 Signs, as a contract
5 Sentiment
6 Of the pre-Easter season
7 TV's Ricki
8 Summer refresher
9 Thurmond, e.g.: Abbr.
10 Shrewdness
11 Points of convergence
12 Actress Sommer
13 Streets and avenues
18 Places atop
19 Metered vehicle
23 Ladled-out food
24 Pie ___ mode
25 Copycat
26 On ___ (proceeding successfully)
27 Back: Prefix
28 Pig ___ poke
29 Dialect
30 Approving
31 Ancient Aegean land
32 Late astronomer Carl
37 Like the Marx Brothers
38 More pale
39 Taro dish
41 "Hi ___!" (fan's message)
42 Common solvent
44 Like many diet products
45 Quaker pronoun
46 Actress Massey et al.
49 Slightly open
50 Late-night host
51 ___ consequence (insignificant)
52 Canceled
53 Bells' sound
54 Water, to Joaquin
55 College student's home
56 Rice Krispies sound
58 Engine speed, for short
59 ___ Paulo, Brazil

by Richard Hughes

ACROSS

1 Elbowroom
6 One of the 3 B's
10 Kellogg Foods brand
14 Plant in Flanders fields
15 Double-reed woodwind
16 Prod
17 Mac maker
18 Start of a quip
20 I-95, e.g.: Abbr.
21 Fritter away
23 Kind of down
24 "One —— customer"
25 Actress Alicia
26 Two-toned horses
28 Quip, part 2
33 Sighs of distress
34 A lot of a drill sergeant's drill
35 Hoo-ha
36 Take a chance on
39 It may help you "catch up"
40 Fret
41 Shade of blond
42 Modern summons
44 Genetic letters
46 Quip, part 3
52 Boated, maybe
53 Chop down
54 Maiden name preceder
55 Actress Gaynor
57 Matrix
59 How the Des Moines R. flows
60 End of the quip
62 A lot
64 Big —— elephant
65 Result of venting?
66 Part of a spur
67 Five-time Wimbledon champ
68 Session with an M.D.
69 Nuts

DOWN

1 Side in the Peloponnesian War
2 Beer opener
3 Telethon, e.g.
4 Pfc.'s boss
5 Baloney
6 Potted tree
7 Help with the heist
8 Whitewashes
9 Giggling sound
10 Prodding
11 Spot overlooking center court, say
12 Way in
13 Fungus byproduct
19 Brings up
22 Aardvark fare
27 Passé
29 "All systems go"
30 Guys
31 Wordsworth work
32 "Get going!"
36 Wet behind the ears
37 —— Kabibble
38 Have a good day on the links
39 Can't wait to have
40 Word with whip or rip
42 Kind of acid
43 Snake charmee
44 Mother of Hera
45 The Big Apple
47 Lounging around
48 There may be a catch in it
49 Powerful combination
50 Look for again
51 With vigor
55 Ancient kingdom east of the Dead Sea
56 In that case
58 Invitation letters
61 Chicken —— king
63 Rock's —— Fighters

by Nancy Salomon

126

ACROSS

1 Promise
5 Lowers, as the lights
9 Biblical queen's home
14 Peculiar: Prefix
15 Olympics event since 1900
16 Ached (for)
17 Emulated the sirens
18 "Alas!"
19 End of a Pindar poem
20 Mythological sculptor who really loved his work
22 Church niches
23 "Shake ___!"
24 Round, full do
26 Court matter
29 Scott of antebellum legal fame
31 Crooked
35 Gladiator's place
37 Require
39 Vintage designation
40 "Nana" author
41 Nasal passage
42 38-Down, for example
43 German river
44 Disable
45 With glee
46 Deliver, in a way
48 Middle: Prefix
50 Slalom curve
51 Mineral suffixes
53 Emulates Xanthippe
55 Defeat
58 Athenian princess who was turned into a nightingale
63 Ouzo flavoring
64 Mother of Helen of Troy
65 Gen. Bradley
66 Arboreal animal
67 Ticked off
68 Fork prong
69 Snake, to Medusa?
70 Prepare 49-Down
71 Generations

DOWN

1 Thin strand
2 Singer Anita
3 Cabal
4 Inflexible teaching
5 Narc's collar
6 Daughter of Agamemnon and Clytemnestra
7 Office note
8 ". . . like you've ___ ghost!"
9 Weapons for the Myrmidons
10 Queen of the Amazons
11 Son of Seth
12 Eliot hero
13 Lime coolers
21 "Everyone Says I Love You" actor
25 Hula hoops and such
26 Chin smoother
27 Wear away
28 Graf rival
30 Casual cotton
32 Eagle's home
33 Things to be filed
34 Classical-sounding cities in New York and Michigan
36 Youth who fell in love with his reflection
38 Another name for the Furies
41 Bob Hoskins's role in "Hook"
45 Kind of dancer
47 Pronounces
49 Some lunches
52 Divvy up
54 Slew
55 Creator of Mickey and Goofy
56 Lollapalooza
57 Frost
59 Leander's lover
60 Nabob of the Near East
61 One of Artie's exes
62 Greek war god

by D. J. DeChristopher

ACROSS

1 Org. that guarantees bank holdings
5 Poets
10 Egyptian snakes
14 Moon goddess
15 German sub
16 Patricia who co-starred in "The Fountainhead"
17 Late newsman Sevareid
18 Waken
19 The Supremes, e.g.
20 1989 Spike Lee film
23 French school
24 Weights
25 Letter before beth
28 Kapow!
30 Top 3 hit of 1963 and 1977
34 Mont Blanc is one
37 "Play it ___ lays"
38 Studio sign
39 Light bulb, in cartoons
40 Happened upon
41 Moonshine
43 Camp beds
44 Suns
45 ___-Kettering Institute
48 Chilled meat garnish
51 Unwelcome sight in the mail
57 In the past
58 Finger-pointer
59 Cake finisher
60 Backside
61 States
62 Jasmine or morning glory
63 Commits a sin
64 Present, for example, in English class
65 Mini-whirlpool

DOWN

1 Vamoosed
2 Five-peseta coin
3 Any part of J.F.K.: Abbr.
4 Ornamental container in a flower shop
5 Grand Canyon transport
6 Irate
7 Cheek cosmetic
8 Elan
9 Proofer's mark
10 "La Marseillaise," e.g.
11 Printing flourish
12 Benjamin Moore product
13 Trudges (through)
21 Classical nymph who spoke only by repetition
22 Holier-___-thou
25 Economist Smith
26 Emit coherent light
27 Perform copy desk work
28 Formal order
29 Wedding dance
31 Eradicate, with "out"
32 Burden
33 One of the Bobbsey twins
34 Appends
35 Onion relative
36 Bears' hands
39 Like some volcanoes
41 "___ Lisa"
42 Wading bird
43 Supplies the food for
45 Plant reproductive part
46 Unsocial sort
47 Award for "Braveheart"
48 Saatchi & Saatchi employees
49 Litigators
50 Intrinsically
52 Tiny pest
53 Roof overhang
54 Battery fluid
55 Repair
56 Wolves, for wolfhounds

by Derek Allen

128

ACROSS

1 Cobblers
5 City near Phoenix
10 "Half-Breed" singer
14 Med. sch. course
15 All possible
16 Part of A.P.R.
17 Nimble
18 Dancer Jeanmaire
19 Persia, today
20 The Boy King
21 Sculpture in the Louvre
23 Madalyn O'Hair, e.g.
25 "Norma ___"
26 Deborah's role in "The King and I"
27 Reason for a small craft advisory
32 Paris newspaper, with "Le"
34 Blow one's top
35 Circle segment
36 Baker's dozen
37 Sign of spring
38 Headliner
39 What Dorian Gray didn't do
40 "___ Irish Rose"
41 Computer device
42 Dogpatch dweller
44 Author John Dickson ___
45 Bill's partner
46 Costa Rican export
49 Former Ford offering
54 Org. that sticks to its guns
55 Bread spread
56 Memorable ship
57 Count calories
58 Gen. Bradley
59 Modify
60 ___ Domini
61 Precious metal
62 Lascivious looks
63 He was a "Giant" star

DOWN

1 Naples noodles
2 Enter, as data
3 1955 hit for the Penguins
4 Pig's digs
5 Mother ___
6 The Super Bowl, e.g.
7 Diner's card
8 Nov. electee
9 Tears?
10 "___ and Misdemeanors"
11 Mata ___
12 Useful Latin abbr.
13 Gambler's mecca
21 Ivy plant
22 It may be Far or Near
24 Brings to a close
27 Town ___ (early newsman)
28 Regrets
29 Apollo mission
30 Intervals of history
31 Farm measure
32 Repast
33 Today, in Turin
34 Southernmost Great Lake
37 Irregular
38 Carolina rail
40 "___ Ben Adhem" (Leigh Hunt poem)
41 Tailless cat
43 International agreement
44 Wickerworkers
46 Sketch comic John
47 Sports center
48 Squelched
49 Synthesizer man
50 "Tickle Me" doll
51 Genuine
52 Where Bill met Hillary
53 Lo-fat
57 Father figure

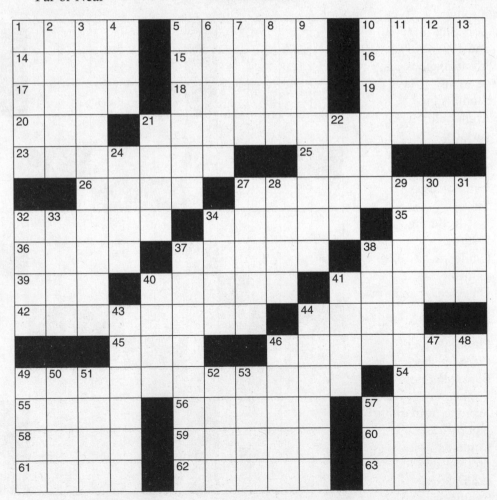

by Gregory E. Paul

129

ACROSS

1 Two out of two
5 Holy war
10 Take illegally
14 Ambience
15 Writer St. Johns
16 Part of A.D.
17 Anne Morrow Lindbergh book
20 How two hearts may beat
21 Gluck and Mahler
22 Corp. honcho
23 Hill dweller
25 Furtive fellow
27 Superior
32 Actor Depardieu
35 Netanyahu's land: Abbr.
36 Cap feature
38 Double-reed instrument
39 Michael Landon portrayal
43 "Dies ___"
44 Tijuana title
45 Sky sight
46 Tie up
49 Banter
51 Rigs
53 Compass point
54 Actress Thurman
56 Chou of China
59 Fill with joy
63 1941 Disney film, with "The"
66 Women, condescendingly
67 To have, in Le Havre
68 Twine
69 "Born Free" lioness
70 Comic Bruce
71 Clashing forces?

DOWN

1 Rum-soaked cake
2 Sharers' word
3 Jazz combo, often
4 Political theorist Arendt
5 Preserves
6 Bright thought
7 Get better
8 Grads
9 Vietnamese seaport
10 Anatomical pouch
11 Loaf
12 Concerning
13 Not stereo
18 John Calvin's city
19 Words of understanding
24 H.S. math
26 Lined up
27 Command to the band
28 Rhone tributary
29 Montana's second-largest city
30 Takes advantage of
31 Megalomaniac's desire
33 John who married Pocahontas
34 Moll Flanders's creator
37 Russo of "Tin Cup"
40 Radar's soft drink
41 Lariat
42 Desk item
47 Board member
48 Video store transaction
50 Tie up again
52 Drudge
54 Push
55 Ground grain
57 Auth. unknown
58 Pack ___ (give up)
60 Popeyed
61 Mower maker
62 Aims
64 "Born in the ___"
65 Not sweet

by Glenn E. Sykes

ACROSS

1 Poet Sandburg
5 Sand bar
10 Jemima, e.g.
14 Guy with an Irish Rose
15 "College Bowl" host Robert
16 Chew (on)
17 Off-color
19 New York theater award
20 Escalator alternative
21 Boat propellers
23 "___ Maria"
24 Tear-jerker in the kitchen
26 "Bald" baby bird
28 Big toe woe
30 Patsy's pal on TV's "Absolutely Fabulous"
31 Dapper fellow
32 Foe
34 Numbskull
37 Catch sight of
39 Saccharine
41 Garbage boat
42 Chartres chapeau
44 "Deutschland uber ___"
46 High season, on the Riviera
47 Before the due date
49 African antelopes
51 Actress Loren
53 Four-time Gold Glove winner Garvey
54 Chicken ___ king
55 ___ platter (Polynesian menu choice)
57 Bug's antenna
61 What not to yell in a crowded theater
63 Off-key
65 Tied, as a score

66 Revolutionary patriot Allen
67 Lo-cal
68 Funnyman Foxx
69 Horned zoo beast
70 Son of Seth

DOWN

1 Elliot of the Mamas and the Papas
2 Be next to
3 Latvia's capital
4 French Foreign ___
5 Rap or jam periods
6 Stetson, e.g.
7 Betelgeuse's constellation
8 Thomas Edison's middle name
9 Looked lecherously
10 In the past
11 Off-center
12 Innocent
13 Sound from an aviary
18 Sgt. Bilko
22 Stated
25 Street sign with an arrow
27 Wildebeests
28 Pedestal
29 Off-guard
30 Embroidered hole
31 Cotillion V.I.P.
33 Director Brooks
35 Bunkhouse beds
36 Female sheep
38 "You bet!"
40 It's used for a call in Madrid
43 Excursion
45 Lifeguard, sometimes
48 Giver of compliments
50 Thread's partner
51 Morley of "60 Minutes"
52 Martini garnish
53 Japanese dish
56 ___ helmet (safari wear)
58 Reclined
59 Inner: Prefix
60 1 and 66, e.g.: Abbr.
62 Finis
64 Campbell's container

by Stephanie Spadaccini

ACROSS

1 "Let's go!"
5 Miss Cinders of old comics
9 Stravinsky's "Le ___ du printemps"
14 It's pulled on a pulley
15 Music for two
16 Farm units
17 Once more
18 Schooner part
19 Signified
20 Hit NBC comedy of the '90s
23 Passing grade
24 Director Howard
25 X's in bowling
27 It's behind home plate
32 Sugar source
33 "___ American Cousin" (1859 comedy)
34 Results of big hits?
36 "Gandhi" setting
39 Mecca resident
41 1997 has two
43 Brothers and sisters
44 Flattens
46 Plains home
48 Tam-o'-shanter
49 Yin's counterpart
51 Not the subs
53 Liberace wore them
56 A.F.L.'s partner
57 Tempe sch.
58 Novelty timepiece
64 Cinnamon unit
66 ___-Seltzer
67 First name in supermodeldom
68 Actress Berry
69 Alice doesn't work here anymore
70 Campus authority
71 Buzzing
72 Organic fuel
73 Klutz's utterance

DOWN

1 Pack in
2 "___ Lisa"
3 Like a William Safire piece
4 Alternative to J.F.K. and La Guardia
5 Oilers' home
6 Molokai meal
7 For fear that
8 Esqs.
9 Belushi character on "S.N.L."
10 Expert
11 Bartender's supply
12 "Walk Away ___" (1966 hit)
13 ___ Park, Colo.
21 Pear type
22 Like some stocks, for short
26 Lodges
27 Part of an old English Christmas feast
28 Atmosphere
29 Hodgepodge
30 Cross out
31 Glazier's items
35 Back-to-school time: Abbr.
37 Building support
38 Egyptian threats
40 Romeo
42 Maine's is rocky
45 Tee-hee
47 Psychiatrist Berne
50 Bearded creature
52 "Holy ___!"
53 Russian-born violinist Schneider, informally
54 These, in Madrid
55 Rascal
59 "Twittering Machine" artist
60 Neighbor of Kan.
61 Nondairy spread
62 Bit of thunder
63 Dolls since 1961
65 Cato's 151

by Elizabeth C. Gorski

132

ACROSS

1 "Stat!"
5 Grow dim
9 Stop ___
14 "___ Barry Turns 40" (1990 best seller)
15 Oak variety
16 Begot
17 Mark left by Zorro?
18 Ring site
19 1954 Oscar-winning composer
20 "Anatomy of a Murder": Defense
23 Singer with the 1991 #1 hit "Rush, Rush"
26 Pupils' spots
27 "Anatomy of a Murder": Prosecution
32 Affectedly creative
33 Stadium since 1964
34 ___ Club (retail chain)
38 ___ du Diable
39 Because
41 Chance
42 Rebuilder of Rome
44 Plenty
45 Zhivago's love
46 "Inherit the Wind": Prosecution
50 Classic work by Montaigne
53 Extra
54 "Inherit the Wind": Defense
59 The Law of Moses
60 Ages
61 Unhinged
65 Missouri river
66 Players
67 "Whoops!"
68 Not as bright
69 MoMA artist
70 Risqué

DOWN

1 Pitches
2 Animal pouch
3 A Gardner
4 Swearing falsely
5 Medium of this puzzle's theme
6 ___ vera
7 Presidential candidate who campaigned from prison
8 They've split
9 Maintain
10 Dolts
11 ___ dust
12 Category
13 "Golden Boy" playwright
21 High school subj.
22 Uncle Jose
23 Once more
24 Tuesday night fixture on early NBC
25 Adoring one
28 Double curve
29 Tot
30 Gent from Argentina
31 Chollas
35 "___ Day's Night"
36 ___ Island, Fla.
37 Hall-of-Fame pitcher Warren
40 Computer key
43 At the point in one's life
45 Word repeated in a children's rhyme
47 Higher in fuel-to-air ratio
48 Vane dir.
49 Big ___
50 Prevent legally
51 Bride, in Brescia
52 Pertaining to ecological stages
55 Torture device
56 Small duck
57 A Kennedy
58 Pot starter
62 "I see!"
63 Big gobbler
64 Short

by Michael S. Maurer

ACROSS

1 "Too bad!"
5 Sen. Lott
10 Hardly colorful
14 Parks who wouldn't take discrimination sitting down
15 12-inch stick
16 Superb
17 Water conduit
18 China's Zhou ___
19 Do, re or mi, e.g.
20 "Little Orphan Annie" character
23 "There ___ young . . ." (common limerick start)
24 WNW's reverse
25 Plant dripping
28 ___ Kippur
31 Newsman Pyle
35 Puts up
37 Spigot
39 Switch positions
40 Santa Claus
44 Cousin ___ of "The Addams Family"
45 Great Lakes cargo
46 C_2H_6
47 Sweetie
50 1040 grp.
52 Last name in cosmetics
53 Photo ___ (media events)
55 Supreme Court Justice Black
57 Nobel author, informally
63 Pack (down)
64 To no ___ (worthless)
65 Snake eyes
67 Lemon go-with
68 Menu at Chez Jacques
69 One of the corners at Four Corners Monument
70 Blockhead
71 Gouged sneakily
72 Akron product

DOWN

1 It may be slung in a sling
2 Dumptruckful
3 Where China is
4 B.L.T., e.g.
5 Deuce toppers
6 Takeoff site
7 Actress Raines
8 Not distant
9 Cree or Crow
10 Martha Graham, e.g.
11 Castle, in chess
12 Orkin targets
13 Quilting party
21 "The Divine Comedy" poet
22 Take advantage of
25 Install to new specifications
26 Poet's Muse
27 Brawl
29 Partner for this and that, with "the"
30 Spoil
32 Wanderer
33 Absurd
34 Ruhr Valley city
36 Box-office letters
38 Bit of Trivial Pursuit equipment
41 Dernier ___
42 Coach Amos Alonzo ___
43 Discard
48 Went one better than
49 Place for a little R and R
51 Devout Iranian
54 Rough cabin
56 Proceeding independently
57 Item for Jack and Jill
58 Bullets and such
59 Writer Hunter
60 Stallion's mate
61 The "A" in ABM
62 Vintage
63 Special attention, for short
66 "___ Drives Me Crazy" (1989 #1 hit)

by Gregory E. Paul

134

ACROSS

1 Certain drapes
6 Atlantic food fish
10 Gator's kin
14 Cop ___ (confess for a lighter sentence)
15 White-tailed flier
16 Deli offering
17 Colt 45, e.g.
19 List member
20 "That's a lie!"
21 Household
23 70's–80's robotic rock group
25 The United States, metaphorically
27 Uris hero
28 Dance, in Dijon
29 Member of the 500 HR club
30 Rock impresario Brian
31 Surgical fabric
33 Ant, in dialect
35 "Texaco Star Theater" host
39 Cut down
40 Brilliance
43 High dudgeon
46 Mai ___
47 Go on to say
49 "Bravo!"
50 It once settled near Pompeii
53 Part of a whole
54 Kangaroo movements
55 Hayfield activity
57 Prefix with China
58 Kind of cereal
62 Shade of red
63 Conception
64 Bizarre
65 Brontë heroine
66 Pre-1821 Missouri, e.g.: Abbr.
67 He had Scarlett fever

DOWN

1 Uncle of note
2 New Deal prog.
3 Stream deposit
4 "I can't ___" (Stones refrain)
5 Morton product
6 "Rocky II," e.g.
7 Diabolical
8 Due halved
9 Words of assistance
10 "I ___" (ancient Chinese text)
11 Record again
12 Where to find Eugene
13 Awaken
18 Early Shirley role
22 Signed up for
23 U.N.'s Hammarskjöld
24 Former polit. cause
26 ___ of the Unknowns
28 Like some greeting cards
32 Nine-digit number, maybe
33 Ultimate point
34 R.N.'s offering
36 Send
37 Trompe l'___
38 Stretch
41 He KO'd Quarry, 10/26/70
42 Asian holiday
43 Tipple
44 "Didja ever wonder . . . ?" humorist
45 Successful escapee
47 Incarnation
48 Spanish Surrealist
51 Certain investment, informally
52 More competent
53 Jesse who lost to Ronald Reagan in 1970
56 Composer Stravinsky
59 Ending with quiet
60 N.Y.C. subway
61 Modern information source, with "the"

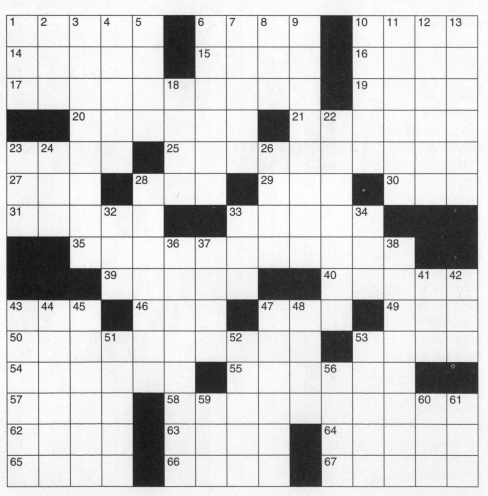

by Alan Arbesfeld

ACROSS

1 Cookbook phrase
4 You can't control it
9 Ramadan observance
13 Beaujolais, say
14 Rock band named for an inventor
15 Mr. T group
17 Fraternity letter
18 Hunter of myth
19 A masked man
20 Looking through photo albums, perhaps?
23 Baseball's Sandberg
24 Reactor part
25 Posed
26 Place to lose oneself
27 Emasculate
30 "Now I see!"
31 Supped
32 Like some eligibles, once
33 Eponymous physicist
35 Party item
41 Weed
42 Caps Lock neighbor, on a computer
43 Something to shoot for
44 Zeppo, for one
47 Where the buffalo roam
49 Label info
50 ___ pro nobis
51 Bilko's rank: Abbr.
52 57-Down measurement
53 #1 movie of 1985
59 Singer Cara
60 Composer Copland
61 "Interview With the Vampire" co-star
62 Debussy work
63 Post-toast sound
64 "Independence Day" villains

65 High schooler
66 Some cigarettes
67 Like a wallflower

DOWN

1 Declare as fact
2 Highbrows
3 One critically examining
4 Hot spot
5 Prefix with scope or meter
6 "Q ___ queen"
7 Work hard
8 Repeated word
9 Disconcerted
10 Over
11 Hoverer near God's throne
12 Human ankle
16 Words on a coat of arms
21 Suffix with Alp
22 Center of a roast
26 Queen described by Mercutio
27 Experience
28 Cultural org.
29 Pyramid builder
30 Wake-up times: Abbr.
32 Surprised cry
34 "Just hold everything!"
36 "___ 1138" (1971 sci-fi film)
37 U.P.S. cargo: Abbr.
38 Connoisseurs
39 Home of Mary and Joseph
40 Italian numero
44 Shell competitor
45 Genesis mount
46 Flower part
48 Go at
49 Wait
51 Unaccommodating
52 Street toughs
54 Baby-bouncing locale
55 Vigorous
56 Land of poetry
57 Printer's choice
58 Accommodating

by Brendan Emmett Quigley

136

ACROSS

1 Pre-entree dish
6 Sit in the sun
10 Cozy home
14 Reflection
15 Opposing
16 Go ___ (exceed)
17 The "N" of U.S.N.A.
18 "Forever"
19 "Get going!"
20 Go
23 Withdraw from the Union
26 Those going 80, say
27 Med. cost-saving plan
28 And so on
30 Historical period
31 Teen woe
33 It makes an auto go
35 ___ latte
40 Go
44 Intuit
45 Hankering
46 Castle's protection
47 Chef's measure: Abbr.
50 Something to go to a bakery for
52 Wash. neighbor
53 Delivered a sermon
58 Comments to the audience
60 Go
62 Milky-white gem
63 Sacred Egyptian bird
64 War story, Greek-style
68 Chant at a fraternity party
69 Swiss painter Paul
70 The brainy bunch
71 George Washington bills
72 Arid
73 Cousin of a Golden Globe

DOWN

1 Transgression
2 Doc's org.
3 Restroom, informally
4 Wide-open
5 Deceive
6 False god
7 Black cattle breed
8 Treeless plain
9 Mouth, to Ralph Kramden
10 One always on the go
11 Call forth
12 Cut off
13 Lock of hair
21 "Take your hands off me!"
22 Instruct
23 Pre-Ayatollah rulers
24 Host
25 Sir Arthur ___ Doyle
29 Saturn, for one
32 Mag workers
34 Pigpen
36 Order between ready and fire
37 Result of a bank failure?
38 Distress signal
39 ___ Park, Colo.
41 "Go get it, Fido!"
42 Jitterbug's "cool"
43 First digital computer
48 Arab leaders
49 Little rock
51 Inuit
53 Kind of ID
54 Wisconsin college
55 Story, in France
56 Ayn Rand's "___ Shrugged"
57 Less moist
59 South Sea getaways
61 Words of comprehension
65 Business abbr.
66 Simile's middle
67 ___ es Salaam

by Stephanie Spadaccini

ACROSS

1 Smart
5 Diminished by
10 E, in Morse code
13 Nimbus
14 Makes amends (for)
16 Morn's opposite
17 Part of B.P.O.E.
18 Like some regions
19 Levy
20 No middle ground, successwise
23 Corn serving
24 Mornings, for short
25 Like some history
28 "Beau ___"
31 Not guzzle
32 ___ firma
33 Sounds from the stands
34 Approximately
36 Trial judge Lance
37 Dad's mate
38 Bit of hope
39 Turndowns
40 Words before taking the plunge
43 Certain breakout
44 Channels
45 Married
46 Newspapers
47 At bats, e.g.
48 Eternal queen, of book and film
49 Former Mideast merger: Abbr.
50 Eventually
56 Hawaiian necklace
58 ___ to go (eager)
59 The Clintons' alma mater
60 Possess
61 Pindar's country
62 Class with a Paul Samuelson text
63 Entreat
64 Pothook shapes
65 1958 Presley #1 hit

DOWN

1 One whose work causes a stir?
2 Robust
3 Actress Chase
4 Pampers
5 Estate home
6 Anatomical passage
7 Foul
8 Free
9 Appears
10 Hoped-for effect of having a big military
11 Eggs
12 Cowhand's nickname
15 ___ Lanka
21 ___ kwon do
22 Christmas carol
26 Cases for insurance detectives
27 Maidens
28 Operates, as a hand organ
29 Patronize restaurants
30 Highlighting
31 In an undetermined place, in dialect
32 Attempt
34 Back-to-work time: Abbr.
35 Paddle
37 ___ Olson (ad character)
41 Director Preminger
42 Eastern thrushes
43 In formation
46 Buddy
48 Trap
49 Prods
51 Assoc.
52 A long time ago
53 Sandwich with fixin's
54 Carolina college
55 1996 Tony musical
56 High return
57 Farm mother

by John R. Conrad

ACROSS

1 ___ center
4 Protection against chills
9 Biting
14 Listening device
15 Shire of "For Richer, For Poorer"
16 Paint ingredient
17 Saddam Hussein's former title
20 Playful water animal
21 "Speed" name
22 Popular N.B.A. nickname
23 They avail themselves of Vail
26 ___ Canals
29 "The Joy Luck Club" author
30 A & W rival
31 Con job
32 This is one for the books
33 Dwellers along the Volga
35 Informative dialogues
38 Not moving
39 Resell at inflated prices
40 Run amok
41 Marquee names
42 %: Abbr.
45 Computer's "guts," for short
46 Bomb tryouts
48 Prefix with space or stat
49 Title for Cervantes
51 Persian Gulf nation
52 Most typewriters have them
57 Spine-tingling
58 Freeze
59 "Hold On Tight" rock group
60 Office furniture
61 Part of a spool
62 "___ Misérables"

DOWN

1 Send another E-mail message
2 Actress Kitt
3 Canea resident
4 Move a muscle
5 "It ___ to Be You"
6 Pintful, perhaps
7 Take the gold
8 Potato pancakes
9 Code words for "A"
10 He went east of Eden
11 Ancient Italian
12 Stephen of "The Crying Game"
13 Diagonal chess capture
18 Et ___ (and the following)
19 "The Star-Spangled Banner" preposition
23 1978 Peace Prize winner
24 Actor Kristofferson
25 Mensa hurdles
27 Galley items
28 Meditation syllables
30 Signs of winter's end
31 Word in an octagon
32 Work without ___ (risk injury)
33 Some Romanovs
34 Suffers
35 Common swab
36 Firebrands
37 Imitate Mel Torme
38 Pinball path
41 Pianist Rudolf
42 "Stormy" sea bird
43 Hold protectively
44 Some sculptures
46 Poker payments
47 Slinky or yo-yo
48 Motel approver, briefly
50 Estrada of "CHiPs"
51 Hebrew letter before resh
52 Proof finale
53 Minuscule
54 "The Island of the Day Before" author
55 To date
56 Tampa Bay player, for short

by Trip Payne

ACROSS

1 Title car in a 1964 song
4 Month after marzo, in Mexico
9 Indian prince
14 Urban music
15 Tired
16 Uneven, as the border of a leaf
17 Oscar director for "Gentleman's Agreement"
19 ___ Moore stew
20 N.Y. neighbor
21 Oscar actress for "The Accidental Tourist"
23 Dramatist Eugene
25 Taboo
26 Oscar actress for "Shampoo"
30 Doctrine: Suffix
33 Easy golf putt
36 In ___ land (spacy)
37 Make eyes at
38 Pleasingly mirthful
39 Rocker Brian
40 ___ water (facing trouble)
41 In unison, musically
42 Johann Sebastian ___
43 Stop holding
44 ___ de mer
45 Oscar actor for "Forrest Gump"
47 Bank job?
49 Shoot-'em-ups
53 Oscar actor for "The Color of Money"
58 Region
59 Beckon to enter
60 Oscar actor for "Harry and Tonto"
62 Depart
63 Fiend
64 "___ Got Sixpence"
65 Concentrated beam
66 Plant disease
67 Always, to a poet

DOWN

1 Artist El ___
2 Eagle's claw
3 Think out loud
4 Parrot's cry
5 Snoopy, for one
6 Bring down the house
7 Hymn "Dies ___"
8 City northeast of Boston
9 Measles symptom
10 Suffix with sect
11 Oscar actor for "Coming Home"
12 Italian wine center
13 Cries of surprise
18 Dye ingredient
22 "___ Karenina"
24 Pre-Easter season
27 Flash of light
28 Cowhand's home
29 Hilo hello
31 Work long and hard
32 "Take ___ your leader"
33 Monorail unit
34 Verdi opera
35 Oscar actor for "Watch on the Rhine"
37 Poor movie rating
40 Actress Chase
42 Snack for a dog
45 Leather worker
46 Sarge, for one
48 Martini garnish
50 "Sesame Street" regular
51 Christopher of "Superman"
52 Pop singer Leo
53 Cast a ___ over
54 On the briny
55 Walk in the surf
56 60's TV horse
57 "Look ___!"
61 Literary olio

by Thomas W. Schier

140

ACROSS

1 It's hailed by city dwellers
5 "The final frontier"
10 Philosopher David
14 Plow pullers
15 Director Welles
16 Ukraine's Sea of ___
17 One socially challenged
18 Scottish estate owner
19 "Oh, my!"
20 Bad news
23 Philosopher John
24 It comes from the heart
28 Tampa neighbor, informally
31 Maladroit
33 "Common Sense" pamphleteer
34 Equestrian's handful
36 Smidgen
37 Lots of activity
41 Baseball stat
42 Like Superman's vision
43 Less tanned
44 Kickoff response
47 TV journalist Poussaint et al.
48 Highway curves
49 Window cover
51 Like some chicken
57 Talk
60 Alternatives to suspenders
61 Keen
62 One for the road
63 $100 bill
64 Reply to the Little Red Hen
65 "That was a close one!"
66 Planted
67 Word with high or hole

DOWN

1 Chinese society
2 Skater's move
3 Dry: Prefix
4 Slothful
5 Comfort giver
6 Short-sheeting a bed, e.g.
7 Stage remark
8 Part of a parachute
9 Prefix with morph
10 Upper part of a barn
11 Terrorist's weapon
12 Swab
13 "The Three Faces of ___"
21 "Psycho" setting
22 Sturdy furniture material
25 Tot's noisemaker
26 Rose's home, in song
27 Common vipers
28 Globe
29 Ford model
30 Galileo's kinsmen
31 Amos's partner
32 Part of "www"
34 Luke preceder
35 Santa ___, Calif.
38 First-rate: Abbr.
39 Flip over
40 Shoal
45 Confer (upon)
46 Volcano detritus
47 Got the suds out
49 "Look out ___!"
50 Starbucks serving
52 Kindergarten instruction
53 Gambling game
54 The Bard's river
55 Toy with a tail
56 Singer Brickell
57 Beret
58 "Come again?"
59 Noshed

by Brendan Emmett Quigley

ACROSS

1 Bar fare
6 "Merry old" king of rhyme
10 Drivel
13 Shiraz native
14 Moundsman Hershiser
15 Make a pitch
16 Trattoria staple
17 Noodges
18 Atahualpa was one
19 When an actress can see forever?
22 "Gunsmoke" appeared on it
25 Original sinner
26 Kickoff aid
27 Suffix with labyrinth
28 Black-and-white snack
30 Golden Fleece craft
32 Horse opera
34 Jamboree locale
36 Hwy.
37 Obese author's admission?
42 E.R. devices
43 More exquisite
44 Lawn game
47 Terrarium plant
48 China setting
49 A "Road" destination
50 Columbus initials
52 Candle count
54 Strive
55 Masochistic trumpeter's prediction?
59 Fine-edged
60 Peek-___
61 Disconcerted
65 Messes up
66 Oversupply
67 Hopping mad
68 Compass pt.
69 Antitoxins
70 Himalayan kingdom

DOWN

1 Sample, as wine
2 Coach Parseghian
3 Vegas opening
4 Opposed
5 "Cheers" character
6 Orchestral offering
7 Spoken
8 Smoothly, to Solti
9 Old comic actress ___ Janis
10 Learned one
11 Secret
12 Cast member
15 Get a move on
20 Profits
21 Go back into business
22 Caesar's sidekick
23 Source of fiber
24 Highway hauler
29 Kind of nerve
31 Crystal-lined rock
33 Dog from Japan
35 Delivery person?
36 Emotional pang
38 Circus Hall of Fame site
39 Main point
40 One who succeeds
41 Busboy's pickup
44 Part of a road test
45 Edmonton icemen
46 Stick together
47 Gridiron mishap
51 Bucks
53 Puckish
56 Election winners
57 Part of B.Y.O.B.
58 Make out
62 Skip, as commercials
63 Hellenic vowel
64 Singer Shannon

by Richard Silvestri

142

ACROSS
1 Employee's reward
6 Person from Muscat
11 Civil War alliance: Abbr.
14 ___-garde
15 Repairman
16 Cause friction
17 Nervousness
19 Slippery fish
20 Lover of Sir Lancelot
21 Dawn goddess
22 Take it easy
23 Chooses
25 Computer-telephone link
27 Some New Year's resolutions
29 Gallows loops
32 Muppeteer Henson
35 Former pro footballer, briefly
37 Like mountains in winter
38 Very dry
40 Batman's sidekick
42 Yemeni port
43 Hotel employee
45 Words mouthed at a TV camera
47 "We ___ Not Alone" (1939 film)
48 Short sock
50 "Frasier" character
52 Red wine
54 Outline
58 Part of Q.E.D.
60 Prof's deg.
62 Jelly used for fuel
63 Coffee maker
64 Numbskulls
66 Ripen
67 Out-of-date
68 Stan's partner, for short
69 Actress Susan
70 Place for grandma's trunk
71 Yorkshire city

DOWN
1 "___ in Toyland"
2 Small egg
3 Birth-related
4 Loose, as shoelaces
5 Sign painter's aid
6 Not at work
7 Miss's equivalent, in a saying
8 Adage
9 Actor Liam
10 April check payee: Abbr.
11 Certain soft drink
12 Mideast canal
13 Skillful
18 Open up a rip again
22 Hotelier Helmsley
24 ___ Brewery Co., of Detroit
26 Opposite of no-nos
28 Polio vaccine developer
30 Pitcher
31 Auld lang ___
32 Jakarta's island
33 Ayatollah's land
34 Small allowance for a schoolchild
36 Copycat
39 Took out
41 Like a win-win situation
44 "Nightline" host Koppel
46 Cough drop ingredient
49 Formal headgear
51 "The Spectator" essayist
53 Treasure container
55 Papal vestment
56 Ruined
57 What everything's coming up, in song
58 College area
59 Encourage
61 Lucy's husband
64 Bean counter, for short
65 Dry, as wine

by Janet R. Bender

143

ACROSS

1 Start to form, as a storm
5 "___-Dick"
9 Christie's Miss Marple
13 Exude
14 Village Voice award
15 Miser Marner
16 Where this answer goes
19 Singing syllable
20 Mysterious loch
21 Utah mountains
22 Villa d'___
23 Up to the task
24 Goodyear fleet
27 Train storage area
31 W.W. II hero Murphy
32 Seas, to Cousteau
33 Go a-courtin'
34 What this answer does
38 Suffix with ranch
39 ". . . unto us ___ is given"
40 Contemptible one
41 Narrow-necked bottle
44 Cried like a baby
45 Word with slicker or hall
46 Guns, as an engine
47 "Lucky" dice rolls
50 ___ over (carry through)
51 Point of decline
54 What this answer seems to have
57 Book with legends
58 The triple in a triple play
59 Author Bagnold
60 Exude
61 Phoenix neighbor
62 Thanksgiving dishes

DOWN

1 Ring engagement
2 First sound in an M-G-M film
3 Poet Pound
4 Little piggy's cry
5 Some MoMA paintings
6 More than plump
7 Strained pea catchers
8 Biblical affirmative
9 Small bus
10 Heaps
11 Cape Canaveral org.
12 Gentlemen: Abbr.
15 Expertise
17 Without obligation
18 Picasso-Braque movement
22 Bahrain bigwig
23 Hammerin' Hank
24 Bundled, as straw
25 Riches
26 Manner of speaking
27 Scouting mission
28 Horrendous
29 Stir from slumber
30 Parceled (out)
32 Like fine netting
35 Chinese philosopher
36 Football team quorum
37 Starts a crop
42 Polar feature
43 Pixie and Dixie's nemesis, in the cartoons
44 Mythological woman with unruly hair
46 Laughfests
47 Mineral springs
48 Suffix with cigar
49 Reprehensible
50 Veracious
51 Sicilian peak
52 Cup lip
53 Political campaigns
55 Mr. Turkey
56 Susan of "Looker"

by Patrick Jordan

144

ACROSS
1 Abnormal vesicle
5 Longtime Boston Symphony conductor
10 D.E.A. officer
14 Miles per hour, e.g.
15 Suburban San Francisco county
16 Like an octopus's defense
17 Inter ___
18 Parenthetical comment
19 Saintly
20 The Flintstones' favorite track star?
23 "___ pray"
24 NASA launch concern
28 Carl Reiner's "Where's ___?"
32 Daunt
33 Drink from a dish
36 The Flintstones' favorite dancer?
39 Greek concert sites
41 Steal away
42 Cattle encourager
43 The Flintstones' favorite Congressman?
46 Calendar spans: Abbr.
47 Drain
48 Popular Deco lithographs
50 Covets
53 Organize, as an exhibit
57 The Flintstones' favorite baker?
61 Skater Starbuck
64 Bunk
65 Word in many Gardner titles
66 "The Art of Love" poet
67 Fish
68 "¿Cómo ___ usted?"
69 Pebbles, e.g., on "The Flintstones"
70 Actress Patricia et al.
71 Day of ___

DOWN
1 Swimming stroke
2 Bulldog
3 Circus prop
4 Join forces (with)
5 Bradley or Sharif
6 Pitts of "Life With Father"
7 Droughtlike
8 Golf ___
9 Give extreme unction to, old-style
10 Brandy, perhaps
11 Year in Spain
12 "Citizen Kane" studio
13 Dancer Charisse
21 Beginning
22 History
25 Dangerous, colloquially
26 Trial's partner
27 Oboes, e.g.
29 Quarry
30 Ill-gotten gains
31 Put on a pedestal
33 Like oak leaves
34 "There Is Nothin' Like ___"
35 Police blotter types
37 Be on ___ with (equal)
38 Posted
40 Immunity unit
44 Australia's largest lake
45 ___ Sabe
49 Football
51 Wharton's "___ Frome"
52 Best Director of 1986 and 1989
54 Imperial decree
55 Settles in
56 Doctor
58 Hatha-___
59 Word with T or dry
60 Whiskies
61 Psalms preceder
62 Fertility clinic needs
63 Foresail

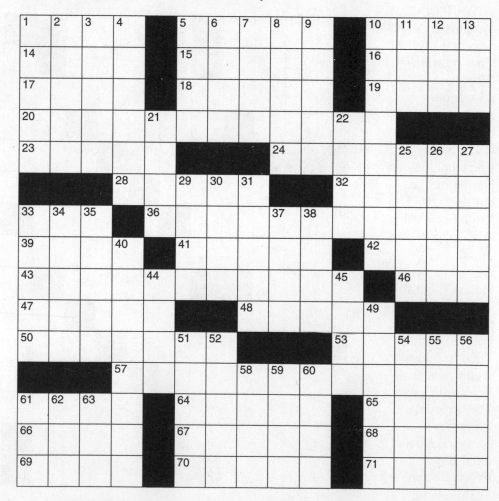

by Mark Elliot Skolsky

145

ACROSS

1 Hairdo
5 Inquired
10 Surrender
14 Stratagem
15 "Mars Attacks!" genre
16 They can take a yoke
17 Cake finisher
18 Guardian of Crete, in classical myth
19 Actor Arnaz
20 Agatha Christie title
23 "All ___ day's work"
24 Legal thing
25 Keats's work on melancholy
28 Biased
32 Grp. that oversees I.C.B.M.'s
35 Ironworker's workplace
37 Decree
38 Kent's state
39 Investigative tool
42 "EZ Streets" actor Ken
43 Mars: Prefix
44 Playful aquatic animal
45 Old TV comedian Louis
46 Hi-fis
48 Aegean, e.g.
49 Worker with a stethoscope
50 Ex-G.I.
52 Dismiss lightly
61 Work over Time
62 Profit
63 687 days on Mars
64 Bridge site
65 Jeune ___ (girl, in France)
66 Word repeated in "It's ___! All ___!"
67 Russian autocrat
68 Skedaddles
69 Word ending a threat

DOWN

1 Lit ___ (college course, informally)
2 "That hurts!"
3 Words of enlightenment
4 Physicist Enrico
5 Stellar
6 Old wound mark
7 Drug shipment, maybe
8 ___ effort
9 Separate
10 Musical finales
11 Prez
12 Where a student sits
13 Geraint's lady
21 Miniature map
22 Scarlet
25 Go ___ a tangent
26 Frilly place mat
27 Bert's "Sesame Street" buddy
29 Ere
30 Gunpowder ingredient
31 California-Nevada resort lake
32 Some immunizations
33 Evangelist McPherson
34 Army attack helicopter
36 Powell or Westmoreland, e.g.: Abbr.
38 Halloween mo.
40 Grain byproduct
41 Units of medicine
46 Drunkard
47 Seeds-to-be
49 Restrain through intimidation
51 Mint family member
52 Lady's escort
53 Altar vows
54 MasterCard alternative
55 Wicked
56 Cotton quantity
57 Make angry
58 Trompe l'___
59 Pre-air conditioning coolers
60 Gratis

by Teresa M. Hackett

ACROSS

1 Singer-actress Lane
5 "___ Mia" (1965 hit)
9 Choreographer Agnes de ___
14 Watery
15 Stratford-Avon link
16 Firefighter Red
17 TV/film actor Jack
19 Comparatively modern
20 Scott's "___ Roy"
21 Got a move on
22 Honeybunch
23 Humdingers
25 Octave followers, in sonnets
28 It's hoisted in a pub
29 T'ai ___ ch'uan
30 Phillips University site
31 Writer Jack
34 Form 1040 completer
35 Scourge
38 Idolize
39 Escritoire
40 "Boola Boola" singer
41 Pugilist Jack
43 Savoir-faire
45 Skater Midori
46 Superaggressive one
50 Barrow residents
52 Licked boots?
54 Grasslands
55 Crash diet
56 Absorbed, as an expense
57 AOL memos
59 Movie actor Jack
61 Haggard
62 "Garfield" dog
63 Grid coach ___ Alonzo Stagg
64 Loquacious, in slang
65 Kind of blocker
66 Sit in the sun

DOWN

1 Oscar and Obie
2 Wisconsin college
3 Psycho talk?
4 Manage to get, with "out"
5 Doll
6 Church recesses
7 Crucifix
8 Gloucester's cape
9 They're combed on a farm
10 Imagine
11 Lyricist Jack
12 "The check is in the mail," maybe
13 Blow it
18 Kind of wine
22 Clears for takeoff?
24 Word of Valleyspeak
25 High-pitched
26 Much of a waiter's income
27 Mount Rushmore's site: Abbr.
29 Former New York governor
32 Transmits
33 "Golden Boy" dramatist
35 ___ noire
36 Griever's exclamation
37 Golfer Jack
39 Twosome
42 Sister of Calliope
44 Some commercial promotions
47 Poisonous atmosphere
48 Caused to go
49 Danish city
51 Like beer
52 Unspoken
53 Actor Milo
55 Bona ___
57 "Rotten" missile
58 Ewe's sound
59 San Francisco's ___ Hill
60 Part of a science class

by Fred Piscop

ACROSS

1 Cheek
5 Runs in neutral
10 Latitude
14 Woody's son
15 State capital or its river
16 Artist Magritte
17 Ham operator's dog?
19 Prefix with hedron
20 Napkin's place
21 Buffalo hunter
22 Feast of Lots honoree
24 Dam
25 Showing a fancy for
26 Cooked cereal
29 Kind of roll
33 Think a thought
34 Reading, for a famous example
35 Mishmash
36 Called the butler
37 Not set
38 Large green moth
39 Work units
40 They're kept under lids at night
41 ___ the hills
42 Drop in
44 Least laugh-out-loud, as humor
45 Parroted
46 Can't stand
47 Two-dimensional
50 Future jr.
51 Leg. title
54 Kharagpur queen
55 Hairdresser's dog?
58 30's migrant
59 Flip chart site
60 Woolen caps
61 Farmer's locale?
62 Metric unit
63 Boxer's stat

DOWN

1 Satirist Mort
2 Gazetteer info
3 Big shot in ice hockey
4 Lay turf
5 Locale of the Cantabrian Mountains
6 Mother hen, e.g.
7 Low-cal
8 Lubbock-to-Fort Worth dir.
9 In a calm manner
10 Diplomat's dog?
11 Poland's Walesa
12 Kitty feed
13 Junior, e.g.
18 Scape
23 Peter and Paul: Abbr.
24 Pilot's dog?
25 Best Actor of 1990
26 Shouts on the links
27 Disjointedly
28 Spoken-word #1 hit of 1964
29 One administering corporal punishment
30 Shake off
31 Hirschfeld hidings
32 Brown
34 Reinforced with a rope
37 Exhibits dyslexia
41 Lawn products brand
43 W.W.II agcy.
44 Parti-colored
46 Noted marine watercolorist
47 Egg on
48 Cottage site
49 Indigo dye
50 Enclosure with a MS.
51 Neighbor of Minn.
52 Pollster Roper
53 Hero of 60's TV and 80's film
56 Toque, for one
57 Six-time home run champ

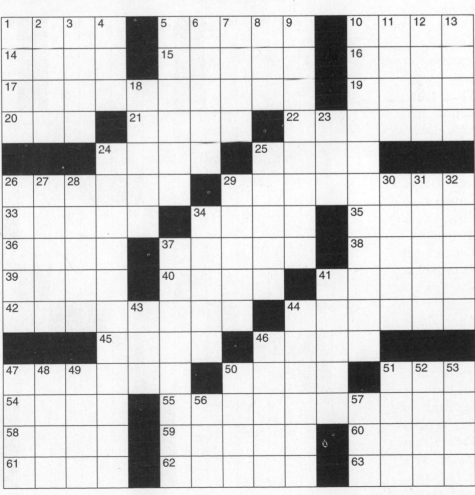

by Norman S. Wizer

ACROSS

1 Enter
5 Throaty utterance
9 Up, as the ante
14 Ancient alphabetic character
15 Singer Guthrie
16 Get straight A's, e.g.
17 Lot of land
18 "Greetings ___ . . ." (postcard opening)
19 Opinions
20 Lose some weight
23 Looks perfect on
24 Not pos.
25 Flier Earhart
29 Part of T.G.I.F.
30 Place to crash
33 Recluse
34 60's hairdo
36 ___ fide
37 Criticize formally
40 God of war
41 Where the Mets meet
42 Pulitzer winner Pyle
43 Actor Beatty
44 Señor Guevara
45 Certain marbles
46 "We ___ the Champions" (Queen tune)
47 He loved Lucy
49 Nears, as a target
56 Hardly the brainy type
57 "Othello" villain
58 Golfer's cry
59 The Little Mermaid
60 Quite a rarity
61 Writer Lebowitz
62 Raison ___
63 Marquis de ___
64 Jodie Foster's alma mater

DOWN

1 Pâté de foie ___
2 "That hurt!"
3 Concerning
4 Exigency
5 Basket material
6 Stop, in France
7 Puts on the brakes
8 Splendor
9 Variety shows
10 Getting rid of
11 Decorated, as a cake
12 Uses needle and thread
13 Overhead trains, for short
21 Blazing
22 "___ of Old Smoky"
25 Nebbishy comic Sherman
26 Sculptor Henry
27 Signed off
28 Diamond, of gangsterdom
29 "___ la Douce"
30 Gist
31 Vanity Fair photographer Leibovitz
32 Palm tree fruits
34 Word with head or heart
35 Enemy
36 Silent film star Theda
38 Hearth residue
39 On the up and up
44 New Orleans cuisine
45 On dry land
46 Yellowish-brown
47 Rigg or Ross
48 Pushed, with "on"
49 Take on, as an employee
50 Leave out
51 Grande and Bravo
52 Questionable
53 "A Doll's House" heroine
54 Like much testimony
55 Hawaii's state bird
56 Good, in street talk

by Stephanie Spadaccini

ACROSS

1 The beans in refried beans
9 Snail ___ (endangered fish)
15 City south of Tijuana
16 Register
17 Battle site where the Athenians routed the Persians
18 Ford flops
19 Scene of Operation Overlord
21 Old paper currency
24 Gaffer's assistant
29 Friends' pronoun
30 Pound part
33 Druidic worship sites
34 Science shop
35 In ___ (properly placed)
36 When Browning wanted to be in England
37 Montana massacre locale
41 Tired of it all
42 Some nest eggs: Abbr.
43 "Take me as ___"
45 Hill dwellers
46 Michael and Peter
48 Sunday seats
49 Site of many flicks
51 Poet Teasdale et al.
52 1781 surrender site
56 Violinist Menuhin
60 1862 Maryland battle site
64 Obliterates
65 Infant
66 Heat up again
67 Candidate Harold et al.

DOWN

1 Opposite of masc.
2 Genetic inits.
3 Neighbor of Leb.
4 Dream girl in a Foster song
5 Where to put the cherry of a sundae
6 "The Wizard of Oz" actor
7 Brother of Jacob
8 Yemen's capital
9 Role in TV's "Hunter"
10 Capp and Gump
11 B.&O. et al.
12 Boot part
13 Add-on
14 "Treasure Island" monogram
20 Peacock network
21 Letters on a Cardinal's cap
22 Where Attila was defeated, 451
23 Religious experience
25 "___ the mornin'!"
26 Obstacle
27 1945 island dogfight site
28 Couturier initials
30 Heating fuel
31 Southwestern Indian
32 Ancient kingdom on the Nile
35 Criterion: Abbr.
36 Cries of delight
38 Exam
39 Like "to be": Abbr.
40 Heating fuel
41 Flock sound
44 What eds. edit
46 Oriental philosophy
47 Hafez al-Assad's land: Abbr.
48 Juries
50 Actress Winona
51 Kind of cheese
53 Okla. neighbor
54 Carpenter's fastener
55 Other: Sp.
56 "Get ___ Ya-Ya's Out!" (Stones album)
57 Poet's "before"
58 Turn left
59 "Land of the free": Abbr.
61 Knot
62 Raggedy doll
63 Brit. sports cars

by Jonathan Schmalzbach

ACROSS

1 Screamer's necessity
6 Manhandle
9 "Peer Gynt" dramatist
14 "Otello," e.g.
15 ___ mode
16 It makes quite a bang
17 Sound of old floorboards
18 When Guy Fawkes Day is celebrated: Abbr.
19 It may be static
20 Cult Canadian comedy troupe, with "The"
23 Operates
24 Tara family
25 Flood stage
28 ___ Xing (sign)
29 "The Gold Bug" author
30 Need air conditioning
32 60's war capital
34 Boy or girl lead-in
35 Twain travelogue, with "The"
41 Season of peace
42 Move stealthily
43 Provided for, as a widow
47 N.Y.C. clock setting
48 Liq. measures
51 Gives the green light
52 Of service
54 Untouched
55 1934 Lillian Hellman play, with "The"
58 Genius
60 Hood's gun
61 Item on a pole
62 Plane seating choice
63 Charlottesville sch.
64 And ___ grow on
65 Gibson, e.g.

66 Gibson, e.g.
67 Victim of a 1955 coup

DOWN

1 Poky
2 Revolt
3 Had to have
4 Not Astroturf
5 H. H. Munro, pseudonymically
6 Roman temple
7 56-Down salutation
8 Isn't decisive
9 If
10 Unwelcome mail
11 Heel style
12 Sea bird
13 Yule serving

21 Peter of Herman's Hermits
22 Hem's partner
26 Home video format
27 Carpenter's nail
29 Campaign money source
31 Harmless prank
32 Reason for darning
33 "___ De-Lovely"
35 Prefix with Chinese
36 Cranny's partner
37 10:00 program
38 Bony
39 "Homage to Clio." poet
40 Diner sandwich
44 Spoiler

45 Immigrant's study, for short
46 Cotton-pickin'
48 Citer
49 Loyally following
50 Address of St. Patrick's Cathedral?
53 Plucky
54 Drop a dime, so to speak
56 See 7-Down
57 Call it a day
58 Farm call
59 Rock's Ocasek

by Brendan Emmett Quigley

ACROSS

1 Greta who never actually said "I vant to be alone"
6 Howled like a hound
11 This instant
14 Extraterrestrial
15 Popeye's sweetie
16 Gardner of Tinseltown
17 Restaurant gadabout
19 Blend
20 Pesky insects
21 Christians' ___ Creed
23 Surfeit
26 Made fractions
27 Fold, as paper
28 One-dimensional
29 Forebodings
30 Zippy flavors
31 Uneaten morsel
34 Chaney Jr. and Sr.
35 Hats' stats
36 Fencing blade
37 Dehydrated
38 Star-to-be
39 The Washington Nationals, once
40 Held responsible (for)
42 "Accept the situation!"
43 Bing Crosby or Rudy Vallee, e.g.
45 Penny-pinching
46 Coarse-toothed tool
47 Stun gun
48 Egyptian snake
49 Dazzling performer
54 Victory sign
55 Cassettes
56 Speak
57 Be mistaken
58 Bewildered
59 Former Russian sovereigns

DOWN

1 Gangster's gun
2 Chicken ___ king
3 Barbecued treat
4 Antwerp residents
5 Unity
6 Pirates' plunder
7 Zurich's peaks
8 Sharp bark
9 Periods just past sunset
10 Infers
11 Egotistical conversationalist
12 Sheeplike
13 Like shiny floors
18 Despise
22 Spy org.
23 Chide, as a child
24 Knight's protection
25 Adolescent rock fan
26 Mel's on "Alice," for one
28 Lolled
30 Track official
32 Try to stop a squeak again
33 Snappish
35 To an extent
36 Quotes in book reviews
38 Rummy variation
39 Depose gradually and politely
41 ___ Angeles
42 Pugilist's weapon
43 Desire deeply
44 Part of a stairway
45 Term of address in "Roots"
47 Overly precious, to a Briton
50 Photo ___ (pol's news events)
51 Local educ. support group
52 Always, in verse
53 Southern Pacific and others: Abbr.

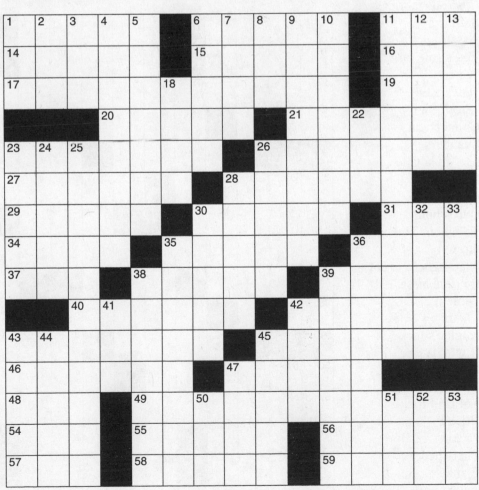

by Patrick Jordan

152

ACROSS

1 Quark's place
5 Some are filled out
10 Org. for 7-Down
14 Command on a submarine
15 Beethoven dedicatee
16 Get ___ the ground floor
17 "Stop" sign
20 Costa del ___
21 Cleanse
22 One of the Brothers Karamazov
23 "Unforgettable" singer
24 Gas or elec., e.g.
25 To pieces
28 Lustrous fabric
30 Sailor
33 Assail
34 Ted's role on "Cheers"
35 "Dies ___"
36 "Stop" sign
40 Connecticut Ivy Leaguers
41 ___ de la Cité
42 Marconi's invention
43 Cub's home
44 To whom Tinker threw
46 Alamogordo event
47 Bouillabaisse, e.g.
48 Table d'___
50 Chairs on poles
53 Angler's luck
54 Guy's date
57 "Stop" sign
60 German article
61 Colorful rock
62 "Pistol Packin' ___"
63 Cherished
64 Wankel engine part
65 Procedure part

DOWN

1 Tacks on
2 Novice: Var.
3 Track shape
4 Kitten's cry
5 Untamed
6 Mount of ___ (site near Jerusalem)
7 Astronaut Sally
8 N.Y.C. sports venue
9 When to sow
10 This meant nothing to Nero
11 Operating without ___ (taking risks)
12 Skyrocket
13 "The King ___"
18 Three sheets to the wind
19 Ugandan dictator
23 Game featuring shooters
24 Where Provo is
25 Invited
26 English dramatist George
27 Supped at home
29 Starwort
30 School division
31 Watering hole
32 Infatuate
35 Furious
37 Exceptional, as a restaurant or hotel
38 Went by plane
39 Gadget for cheese
44 Sicilian volcano
45 Religion of Japan
47 Not a spendthrift
49 Aquatic mammal
50 Scurried
51 Buffalo's lake
52 Actress Merrill
53 Tuckered out
54 Midge
55 Crowning point
56 "Able to ___ tall buildings . . ."
58 Freudian factor
59 Early hrs.

by Gerald R. Ferguson

ACROSS

1 Jim at the bar
5 Long Island town
10 "Want to hear a secret?"
14 It was tender in Turin
15 Actress Gia
16 Bar assoc. member
17 Like a gemologist's drinks?
19 Kisser
20 Migrant's advocate Chavez
21 Sans mixers
22 Latest thing
23 Carafe quantity
25 Fictional hotel hellion
27 First-rate
30 Static ___
31 Film director Wertmuller
32 Adventure hero ___ Williams
35 Grateful?
38 Tailward, on jets
39 Sangria container
41 Gentle handling, initially
42 ___ dicit (legal refusal)
44 Ike's onetime singing partner
45 Luau entertainment
46 Skip over
48 Worker with a scythe
50 "The Song of the Earth" composer
52 Highly hackneyed
54 Baseball's Jesus
55 Actor Guinness
57 Gin flavorers
61 Asset
62 Like a platform diver's drinks?
64 Mislay
65 Fur source
66 Sparkling wine spot
67 Baa-maids?

68 In the poorhouse
69 Two semesters

DOWN

1 Voting group
2 Deutsche article
3 Song and dance, e.g.
4 Gospel's Jackson
5 Mt. Carmel site: Abbr.
6 Treat with tea
7 One who spikes the punch
8 Chase of "Now, Voyager"
9 Drawing that's easy on the eyes
10 Bar regulars, e.g.
11 Like an astronaut's drinks?

12 Deer sirs
13 Melville adventure
18 Lexicographer Partridge
24 TV's Hatcher
26 Detector target
27 Scotch family
28 LP player
29 Like a roofer's drinks?
30 Lawyer Roy
33 Diminutive suffix
34 Sprint rival
36 Word for a madame
37 Lasting impression
39 Barre room bend
40 Bring home
43 Mistreats
45 Vestibule

47 Tap
49 Part of SEATO
50 Fudge flavor
51 Let have
52 Davis of "Now, Voyager"
53 Hurt
56 Miller beer option
58 Seine feeder
59 "¿Cómo ___ usted?"
60 Do a bartending job
63 It may finish second

by Cathy Millhauser

ACROSS

1 Comedian Mort
5 Small dent on a fender
9 Picket line crossers
14 Margarine
15 Cookie with a creme center
16 Diamond weight
17 Vegas card game
19 Dress style
20 Bullfight bull
21 Marx who wrote "Das Kapital"
23 Sault ___ Marie
24 Flue residue
26 Suffix meaning "approximately"
28 Lucille Ball, e.g.
30 Where the Eiffel Tower is
32 Feed bag contents
34 Distinctive doctrines
35 Fast-growing community
37 Housebroken animal
39 Savior
42 Till bill
43 Yearned (for)
46 Weapon in a silo, for short
49 Found's partner
51 Muse of love poetry
52 Organized absenteeism of police officers
54 Turf
56 "The ___ in the Hat" (rhyming Seuss book)
57 Writer Fleming
58 Greek letter
60 Ark builder
62 Greek letter
64 Stew vegetable
68 Build
69 Forearm bone
70 Indonesian island
71 Appears
72 Christmas carol
73 Settled, as on a perch

DOWN

1 Cry loudly
2 Start (and end) of the Three Musketeers' motto
3 London airport
4 Kooky
5 Martial arts schools
6 Rhymester Gershwin
7 Giraffe's prominent feature
8 Racing vehicle
9 Burn with hot water
10 Baseball's Ripken
11 Gets up
12 Small chicken
13 Spirited horses
18 Actress ___ Scott Thomas
22 Set a top in motion again
24 Police radio alert, briefly
25 ___ Paulo, Brazil
27 Inventor Elias
29 ___ and yon (in many places)
31 "Hi, honey!" follower
33 Egyptian symbols of life
36 Verdi opera based on a Shakespeare play
38 Incited
40 Kooky
41 Of the windpipe
44 Greek letter
45 "i" piece
46 Long-billed wading birds
47 Actress Bloom
48 Jumper's cord
50 Exceed in firepower
53 Decrees
55 Basketball's Shaquille
59 Woody Guthrie's son
61 Rhyme scheme for Mr. Eban?
63 1900, on a cornerstone
65 Opposite WSW
66 Rhyming boxing champ
67 Annual basketball event: Abbr.

by Peter Gordon

ACROSS

1 Sluggers' stats
5 Theme of this puzzle
10 Capital of Italia
14 Burn soother
15 Filibuster, in a way
16 Hawaiian music makers
17 Editor's definition of this puzzle's theme
20 Prevent legally
21 Popular beverage brand
22 Shea nine
25 More crafty
26 Allowable
30 Beckon
33 University of Maine site
34 ___-do-well
35 Dickens protagonist
38 Mapmaker's definition of this puzzle's theme
42 Compass heading
43 Pseudonymous short-story writer
44 Backing for an exhibit
45 Peaceful
47 Sentient
48 Insurance giant
51 Negative in Nuremberg
53 Competed in the Hambletonian
56 Ribeye, e.g.
60 Physician's definition of this puzzle's theme
64 Bank claim
65 Battery part
66 Second in command
67 Driver's license prerequisite
68 The ___ Prayer
69 Interested look

DOWN

1 Genre for Notorious B.I.G.
2 Depressed
3 Charged particles
4 Split-off group
5 Stylish auto
6 Man-mouse link
7 Back muscle, familiarly
8 Redding of 60's soul
9 "Open 24 hours" sign, maybe
10 Muss up
11 Animal with zebra-striped legs
12 Actress Oberon
13 Questioner
18 Indian drum
19 Political cartoonist Thomas
23 Kid's make-believe telephone
24 Elude the doorman
26 Canter
27 Ayatollah's land
28 Dunce cap, essentially
29 ___ pinch
31 Where St. Mark's Cathedral is
32 Investment vehicle, for short
35 Famous tower locale
36 Roman road
37 See 49-Down
39 Enzyme suffix
40 Shanty
41 Bird's cry
45 Purpose
46 "Phooey!"
48 Not perfectly upright
49 With 37-Down, famous W.W. II correspondent
50 Big handbags
52 Wight and Man
54 List shortener
55 Singer Martin, to friends
57 Therefore
58 In awe
59 Basketball's Malone
61 Neither's companion
62 Do basic arithmetic
63 Society column word

by Jeff Herrington

156

ACROSS

1 Made fun of
6 Comic Martin
11 Object of invective, often
14 Concert venue
15 Site of Western Michigan University
17 1959 Philip Roth book
19 Part of the Holy Trinity
20 First name on Capitol Hill
21 Cold war side, with "the"
22 Seats with cushions
23 1932 and 1981 "Tarzan" films, e.g.
26 Inevitably
29 Dove rival
30 Coin no longer minted
31 Gen. Powell
32 Charge
35 Hemingway novel of 1929
39 Abbr. for 20-Across, in two ways
40 Watergate co-conspirator
41 Nonsense word repeated in a 1961 hit
42 Chemistry measurements
43 1902 Physics Nobelist Pieter
45 Loudly laments
48 Add color to
49 Seat
50 The "pneumo" in pneumonia
51 Untapped
54 1958 Mario Lanza song
59 Popular motor home
60 Writer Shute
61 Article in France Soir
62 Give
63 Ennoble

DOWN

1 Certain sports cars, informally
2 Suffix with buck
3 Drudge
4 Get rid of
5 Actor Coleman
6 Biases
7 Mediator's skill
8 "Hold On Tight" rock band
9 Kilmer of "The Saint"
10 Aussie bird
11 Language spoken in Tashkent
12 Cursor mover
13 Puts up, as a computer message
16 Home products company
18 Evergreens
22 Jack of 50's–60's TV
23 Come-from-behind attempt
24 Send out
25 Jorge's hand
26 Winglike
27 Never-ending sentence?
28 Scarf
29 Causes of some absences
31 Turns over
32 Gift tag word
33 Austen heroine
34 Cable staple
36 "The Time Machine" race
37 Something left behind
38 Help
42 Cheech of Cheech and Chong
43 Vitamin additive
44 Head of a train
45 More than a scuffle
46 Chill-including
47 Alerts
48 "Presumed Innocent" author
50 Lincoln Log competitor
51 Astronomer's sighting
52 Disney's "___ and the Detectives"
53 Cartoonist Kelly
55 Churchill symbol
56 Surveyor's dir.
57 Pop
58 Latin ruler

by Brendan Emmett Quigley

ACROSS

1 The ex-Mrs. Bono
5 Money owed
9 Pharmacy items
14 Composer Schifrin
15 Anatomical passage
16 Like "The Twilight Zone" episodes
17 Actress Lena
18 This ___ of tears (life)
19 Do watercolors
20 Secondhand store
23 Showed respect for the national anthem
24 Sister of Osiris
25 Mr. O.
28 Cinematographer Nykvist
30 Arthurian sorcerer
32 Harvest goddess
35 Pass, as laws
38 Verdi heroine
39 John Glenn's Mercury spacecraft
43 Type assortment
44 Card catalogue entry after "Author"
45 Before, in verse
46 Overage
49 Boat propellers
51 Loaf with seeds
52 ___ to the throne (prince, e.g.)
55 Laid, as a bathroom floor
58 Member of the police
61 Without ___ in the world
64 Prefix with China
65 Nat King or Natalie
66 ___ says (tots' game)
67 ___-do-well
68 Popular fashion magazine
69 Israeli port
70 Microbe
71 Do one of the three R's

DOWN

1 Drain problem
2 Angels' headgear
3 Ness of "The Untouchables"
4 Musical movements
5 Stockholder's income
6 Catchall abbr.
7 Attorney Melvin
8 Lock of hair
9 Remove from office
10 Harvest
11 Spoon-bender Geller
12 Rummy game
13 Matched items
21 Made on a loom
22 That guy
25 Kicking's partner
26 Contract add-on
27 Nonsensical
29 Political cartoonist Thomas
31 "Norma ___"
32 Bidder's amount
33 Stockholder's vote
34 Subsequently
36 Letter before psi
37 Maverick Yugoslav leader
40 High season, on the Riviera
41 Railroad station area
42 Printing flourish
47 Singer Easton
48 Ocean
50 Deli machine
53 Cake decoration
54 "Walk Away ___" (1966 hit)
56 French school
57 Singer Reese
58 Univ. teacher
59 German border river
60 Marsh stalk
61 Cigarette waste
62 K.G.B.'s cold war foe
63 "___ the only one?"

by Stephanie Spadaccini

158

ACROSS
1 Procter & Gamble bar
6 Native Alaskan
11 Spoil
14 Midwest airport hub
15 Sergeant at TV's Fort Baxter
16 Diamonds
17 Place to place a wallet or handkerchief
19 ___ Na Na
20 Thanksgiving meat request
21 "Entry of Christ into Brussels" painter James
23 Scott Adams's put-upon comics hero
27 Nautical spar
29 Body parts shaped like punching bags
30 W.W. II Philippine battle site
31 Horse in a harness race
32 1924 Ferber novel
33 Little newt
36 It's NNW of Oklahoma City
37 Rounded lumps
38 Nicholas I or II, e.g.
39 Mule of song
40 Nash's two-l beast
41 Hardly elegant
42 Easy two-pointers
44 Concert halls
45 Starts of tourneys
47 Last course
48 Peres's predecessor
49 "___ That a Shame"
50 Eggs
51 "Come on!"
58 ___ canto (singing style)
59 Characteristic
60 Confuse
61 Right-angle joint
62 Steinbeck migrants
63 Dapper

DOWN
1 ___ a plea
2 "Now I see!"
3 Beatnik's exclamation
4 Skill
5 Sweetheart's assent
6 Cancel, as a launch
7 Drub
8 Lodge member
9 Luau instrument
10 Alternative to a purse
11 Err on stage
12 Cause for blessing?
13 Get ready for battle again
18 Average figures
22 Org. for Bulls and Bullets
23 Fools
24 Ex-Mrs. Trump
25 Four-time Emmy-winning comedienne
26 Ran, as colors
27 ___ the Hutt, of "Star Wars"
28 Medical suffix
30 Certain mikes
32 Knee hits
34 Mountebank
35 Lovers' engagement
37 Rather morose
38 Suns
40 Deceiving
41 Nuclear treaty subject
43 "The Greatest"
44 ___ cava (path to the heart)
45 Explore
46 "Bolero" composer
47 They're losing propositions
49 French friend
52 Bother
53 ___ tai (drink)
54 Nutritional abbr.
55 N.Y.C. summer clock setting
56 Model Carol
57 Lock opener

by Brendan Emmett Quigley

ACROSS

1 How the boss wants things done, briefly
5 Ditto
9 Devil dolls, e.g.
14 Kind of chop
15 "Family Ties" kid
16 Dander
17 "Oh, woe!"
18 Chimney covering
19 Nick name?
20 "Don't tell!"
23 "Losing My Religion" rock group
24 Scene of the William Tell legend
25 Norma Webster's middle name
26 Cash substitute
27 Certain corporate career path
33 Beam
34 Carthage founder
35 Julia, on "Seinfeld"
38 "___ Three Lives"
40 Reggae relative
42 Brit. decorations
43 New York county
46 Reaching as far as
49 Easter parade attraction
50 1948 Irene Dunne film
53 Foldaway, e.g.
55 Polit. designation
56 Maiden name preceder
57 ___ Arbor
58 Western mountain range
64 Shade tree
66 Equine shade
67 "Let's Make a Deal" choice
68 "Victory ___" (1954 film)
69 Secular
70 Designer Cassini
71 Forfeits
72 Swirl
73 "And away ___!"

DOWN

1 In ___ (having trouble)
2 George Takei TV/film role
3 Sixth-day creation
4 "Playing" critter
5 Japanese fish dish
6 Facial tissues additive
7 Doorsill cry
8 Obtain by force
9 Poker boo-boo
10 Mouths, anatomically
11 Eastern taxi: Var.
12 Prefix with arthritis
13 SeaWorld attraction
21 Walked (on)
22 Scarce
27 Chamber group, maybe
28 Dutch painter
29 See firsthand
30 Clinic workers, for short
31 Mammy ___
32 Lowlife
36 Linguist Chomsky
37 "¿Cómo ___ usted?"
39 German article
41 Police radio msg.
44 Japanese entertainers
45 Old Dodge
47 Period of a renter's agreement
48 Provo neighbor
51 Channel swimmer Gertrude
52 Grazing area
53 Plot
54 "You're ___ talk!"
59 Way to go
60 Bust, so to speak
61 Handout
62 Film director Nicolas
63 "Cogito ___ sum"
65 Middling mark

by Dean Niles

160

ACROSS

1 Mad dog worry
5 Spy ___ Hari
9 Aware, with "in"
14 Water color
15 Valentine's Day matchmaker
16 Hawaiian veranda
17 "Brilliant idea!"
20 Ice Follies venue
21 Maid's cloth
22 Veteran
26 Pennilessness
30 ___Strait (Russia-Alaska separator)
31 Confront
32 Wide shoe specification
33 Police operation
34 Knob
35 Nos. on a road map
36 Classic Bill Clinton phrase
39 Giant Mel et al.
40 Jazzy Fitzgerald
41 Remove, as a knot
43 Award from the Queen: Abbr.
44 Neighbor of Vietnam
45 Like some kisses and bases
46 Novelist Hesse
48 Sentimentalists, maybe
49 Superlative ending
50 Subject of psychoanalysis
51 1962 Cary Grant/Doris Day movie
59 Actor Bruce of radio's "Sherlock Holmes"
60 Chess finale
61 "God's Little ___"
62 Lachrymose
63 Hardly any
64 Rural carriage

DOWN

1 Sheep's sound
2 Stats for eggheads
3 Egyptian boy king
4 Barber's obstruction
5 Cooking up
6 Change, as a motion
7 Swiped
8 Comic dog's bark
9 Split asunder
10 Jessica of 1976's "King Kong"
11 Prefix with cycle
12 ___ de vie
13 Insult, in slang
18 Pumpkin-colored
19 Food seller
22 Out-of-date: Abbr.
23 Last Beatles album
24 Gadabout
25 Jazzman "Fatha"
26 "The Taming of the Shrew" locale
27 Change names
28 Even smaller
29 "You bet!"
31 April ___ Day
34 Parachute material
35 Babbled
37 Shanty
38 Delay
39 Aah's partner
42 U.S.N. officer
44 Summing-up word
45 Flew alone
47 Olympic race unit
48 Conductor Zubin
50 "Get outta here!"
51 Explosive inits.
52 Hasten
53 ___ Khan
54 Thurman of "Pulp Fiction"
55 Mothers
56 "___ bin ein Berliner"
57 Gun enthusiast's grp.
58 Codebreaker's discovery

by Hugh Davis

ACROSS

1 Farm structure
5 Kon-Tiki wood
10 Boutique
14 Rev. Roberts
15 From the East
16 Windex target
17 Conjointly
19 Killer whale film
20 Till bill
21 Plant part
22 Ham
24 Certain pints
25 Vessel
26 Novelist-screenwriter Eric
29 Person in need of salvation
32 Places to buy cold cuts
33 Dugout
34 Showtime rival
35 Greatly
36 Where Joan of Arc died
37 Wilde's "The Ballad of Reading ___"
38 Catty remark?
39 Vine fruit
40 Snorkeler's sight
41 "O Pioneers!" setting
43 Talkative
44 Joins the team?
45 Stable newborn
46 Insignia
48 Sheryl Crow's "___ Wanna Do"
49 Kind of story
52 Handyman Bob
53 Bobby Vinton hit
56 Word after pig or before horse
57 Burdened
58 Tittle
59 Ribald
60 Works in the cutting room
61 Midterm, e.g.

DOWN

1 Part of London or Manhattan
2 Teheran's land
3 Rural route
4 Like a centenarian
5 Back-and-forth
6 Grate expectations?
7 Actor Neeson
8 ___ Diego
9 "Father Knows Best" family name
10 Lampoons
11 Sidney Sheldon TV series
12 Some time ago
13 Fruit cocktail fruit
18 Tropical getaways
23 Pal, down under
24 Dismounted
25 "We'll go to ___, and eat bologna . . ."
26 Rhett's last words
27 Free-for-all
28 Detailed account
29 Singer Nyro or Branigan
30 German sub
31 Candy on a stick, informally
33 Parts of wine bottles
36 Look like
37 Soccer score
39 Enter a Pillsbury contest
40 Mountain range
42 Hero of early French ballads
43 Punctuation marks
45 Armada
46 Like Satan
47 Bog
48 German auto
49 Gin flavor
50 Scoreboard stat
51 Cop's milieu
54 Youth
55 Bridle part

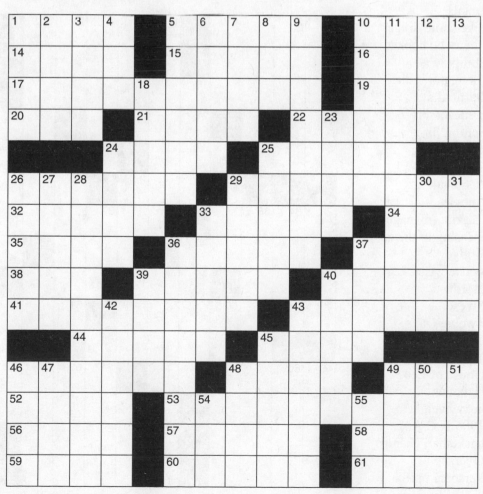

by Gregory E. Paul

162

ACROSS

1 Serve with a summons
5 "Casino" co-star, 1995
10 Castaway's transportation
14 Copper containers
15 Hybrid citrus fruit
16 Perry's creator
17 Egyptian actress?
19 Jar
20 Ar's follower
21 Novelist Jean
22 Come to
24 Last frame, sometimes
26 Chorus syllables
28 Winter resort rentals
30 Like some drugs
33 It may be hooked
36 Philippic
38 Navigator's dir.
39 Garfield's predecessor
41 Setting for a place setting
42 Room to ___
44 "Gotcha!"
45 Guesses
48 ___ out (manages)
49 Pleasing to the ear
51 Bridge
53 Waste gases, e.g.
55 Storm
59 Fivesome
61 Twelve Oaks neighbor
63 Trifle
64 House of Leo?
65 Egyptian heavyweight?
68 1995 N.C.A.A. basketball champs
69 Overact
70 Personal prefix
71 "___ My Girl" (1967 hit)

72 Fabulous
73 Get dewy-eyed

DOWN

1 Hale-Bopp, e.g.
2 People with "O'" names
3 Flirt
4 Paranormal ability
5 Strong praise
6 Where 2-Down live
7 Baby-size
8 Murmur
9 Went all the way, as a smoker
10 Used car deal, e.g.
11 Egyptian second banana?

12 Kind of pipe
13 Ky.-Ala. divider
18 Amount of hair
23 Evanesces
25 Salinger dedicatee
27 Playing marbles
29 "My love is like a red, red rose," e.g.
31 Apropos of
32 Medium grades
33 "Eh?"
34 Island near Kauai
35 Egyptian actor?
37 Commanded
40 Bulgaria's capital
43 Pocket protector items
46 Splash sites
47 Thinner

50 They're cast in a cast of thousands
52 "Immediately!"
54 Sitting place
56 Offhand remark
57 Ancient land on the Aegean
58 Egypt's Temple of ___
59 In addition
60 Individually
62 You have to be upfront about this
66 Big bird
67 Top 10 song, say

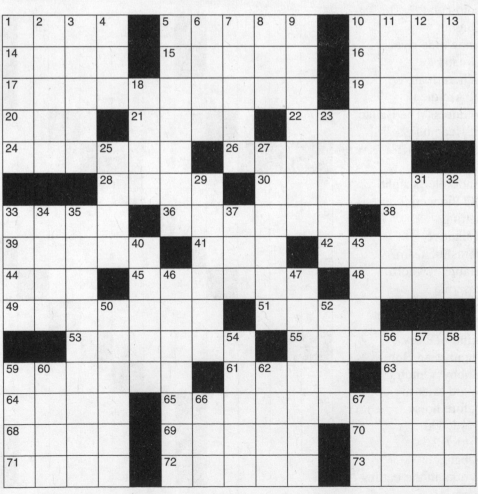

by Norman S. Wizer

ACROSS

1 Meal at boot camp
5 Sell tickets illegally
10 Sam the ___ of 60's pop
14 "Beetle Bailey" dog
15 It's a no-no
16 Car with a meter
17 Lose one's nerve
19 Israeli guns
20 Tennis great Rosewall
21 Bohemian
22 "Gunsmoke" star James
24 Vulgar one
26 Tyke
27 70's–80's Yankee pitching ace
34 Imus's medium
37 Goods
38 "Blue" bird
39 Abba of Israel
40 Opera headliners
41 Stupor
42 ___'easter
43 Sheets, pillowcases, etc.
44 Put on the payroll
45 Old instrument of punishment
48 "Who ___ you?"
49 Sounded, as a bell
53 Prestige
56 Villa d'___
58 Actress Gardner
59 Major league brothers' name
60 Quaint dance
63 "___ the Mood for Love"
64 Actress Samantha
65 Microwave, slangily
66 Grandmother, affectionately
67 Immunizations
68 ___ off (plenty mad)

DOWN

1 Treats cynically
2 Lucy's best friend
3 Children's author R. L. ___
4 League: Abbr.
5 Audiophile's setup
6 Quitter's word
7 "It's ___!" (proud parents' phrase)
8 Singer Rawls
9 Shepherd's pie ingredients
10 Publicity seekers' acts
11 Smog
12 X or Y, on a graph
13 Ole ___
18 Nonmusician's musical instrument
23 Flagmaker Betsy
25 Opposed to, in the backwoods
28 Playground equipment
29 Overhangs
30 Research money
31 Not quite shut
32 Stare, as at a crystal ball
33 Checked out
34 Pull apart
35 "___ Ben Adhem"
36 Jeanne ___ (French saint)
40 Eating alcoves
41 Pickle flavoring
43 Italian money, once
44 Nonsense
46 Hawaiian medicine man
47 Frolicking animals
50 Lash ___ of old westerns
51 Call forth
52 Went out with
53 Old Testament murderer
54 ___ mater
55 Nickel or copper, but not tin
56 Therefore
57 Three-player card game
61 "Yecch!"
62 Blaster's need

by Fred Piscop

164

ACROSS

1 Utters
5 Military plane acronym
10 Desertlike
14 Wyoming neighbor
15 Striped critter
16 Hurting
17 State of financial independence
19 CAT ___
20 Singer Lopez
21 Kett of old comics
22 Little guitars
23 Singer Cara
25 Guard
27 It's a stitch!
29 Mint and sage
32 Stadium sounds
35 Basketball hoop site, often
39 Acorn, in 2020?
40 "Surfin' ___" (Beach Boys hit)
41 Gandhi's title
42 Ryan's "Love Story" co-star
43 Russian space station
44 Puzzle
45 4:1, e.g.
46 Mubarak's predecessor
48 Recipe direction
50 Some Broadway shows
54 Overhead shot
57 Last name in spydom
59 "There ought to be ___!"
61 Suggest itself (to)
63 Thrift shop stipulation
64 "The Birdcage" co-star
66 Possess
67 Whitney Houston's "All the Man That ___"
68 Verve
69 Parrots
70 Chooses actors
71 E-mail command

DOWN

1 Winter bird food
2 Video arcade name
3 Arafat of the P.L.O.
4 Wallflower's characteristic
5 Much-publicized drug
6 Existed
7 Helps in dirty deeds
8 El Greco's birthplace
9 Underworld figure
10 Guarantee
11 Ice cream parlor order
12 "Dies ___"
13 TV rooms
18 ___ qua non
24 1991 Tony winner Daisy
26 "Take ___ Train"
28 When repeated, a fish
30 Like a worn tire
31 T-bar sights
32 Jamaican exports
33 Pacific Rim region
34 Computer part
36 Joplin piece
37 24-hr. conveniences
38 Certain exams, for short
41 Prefix with physical
45 The Scriptures
47 Gets up
49 "___ Fire" (Springsteen hit)
51 Wired, so to speak
52 "The George & ___ Show" (former talk show)
53 Fills up
55 Union rate
56 Chinese province
57 Joker's gibe
58 Rush job notation
60 Stimulate
62 Rip apart
65 Want ___

by Elizabeth C. Gorski

ACROSS
1 Bouquet holder
5 Bouquet makers
10 ___ Offensive
13 Deejay Don
14 Two-time Grand Slam winner
15 Missile housing
16 "Relax!"
19 ___ gratia artis
20 "I have half ___ to . . ."
21 Part of a bouquet
22 The Beatles' last movie
24 Brush, so to speak
25 Baseball's Charlie Hustle
26 Meager
28 Monopoly token
30 Mall component
31 Legal matter
34 "Relax!"
38 Be in hock
39 1977 U.S. Open champ
40 Likable
41 Manipulate
42 Predominant
44 Chiseler
46 James Bond backdrop
49 Not so bold
50 Former Soviet First Lady
52 Guinness specialty
53 "Relax!"
56 Cravings
57 "The Brady Bunch" housekeeper
58 Flying eagle, e.g.
59 Old polit. cause
60 Novelist Dostoyevsky: Var.
61 Trojan ally, in the "Iliad"

DOWN
1 "Myra Breckinridge" author
2 That's a subject for Dean Martin!
3 Summer ailment
4 Therapy fad
5 Like a plum pudding
6 "C'est ___"
7 Kenmore product
8 Crack the books
9 Semicircle
10 Indonesian island
11 Cousin of a gazelle
12 June award
15 Work like a slave
17 Items at a lost-and-found
18 First game
23 With 49-Down, "Say Anything" co-star
24 Cutting remark
26 Lieu
27 True-crime TV series
28 Simpson's criminal-case judge
29 Vulgar
30 Peddle
31 It's found in a runoff
32 And so on
33 1967 Monkees song
35 Zoo section
36 Dr. Atkins's plan
37 Oklahoma town
41 Blubbers
42 Participant at a 90's dance club
43 Jai ___
44 Root on
45 One raising a howl?
46 Pancho's amigo
47 Going stag
48 Signs a lease
49 See 23-Down
50 Preside over
51 Bone-dry
54 Clod
55 Admiral competitor, once

by John D. Leavy

166

ACROSS

1 Prop up
6 Goddess pictured in Egyptian tombs
10 Fraud
14 Old autos
15 Short letter
16 Patriot Nathan
17 Feeling really good
20 Get-out-of-jail money
21 Hors d'oeuvre spread
22 Song for Aida
23 Chomped down
24 "___ cost to you!"
25 Novelist Waugh
27 Batter's goal
29 Frigid
30 "Turandot" slave girl
31 Moon-landing vehicle
32 ___ de Triomphe
33 "I ___ Grow Up" ("Peter Pan" song)
34 Heads of state get-together
38 "It can't be!"
39 Be in session
40 Nothing
41 Peas' holder
42 Pennies: Abbr.
43 Creeks
47 Storm warnings at sea
49 Clinton's #2
50 Wrestler's place
51 Site for a swing
52 Rikki-tikki-___ (Kipling mongoose)
53 Capable of
54 Little that's visible
57 Poker call
58 Mending site
59 Louis XIV, 1643–1715
60 Hawaii's state bird
61 Remove from office
62 Dunne of "I Remember Mama"

DOWN

1 Thick-trunked tropical tree
2 Italian soprano Scotto
3 Clarinetist Shaw and others
4 Refrigerate
5 One of Kreskin's claims
6 Wee one
7 ___ voce (almost in a whisper)
8 Spillane's "___ Jury"
9 Visualize
10 Beach
11 Set of bells
12 Relieving
13 Club ___
18 They expect the best
19 Undulating
24 "Um, excuse me"
25 Like a three-dollar bill
26 Cashew, e.g.
28 "Tickle me" doll
29 Anger
32 Quantity: Abbr.
33 Sly trick
34 Cable channel
35 Support
36 "___ the season . . ."
37 Radial, e.g.
38 Photo ___ (media events)
42 Musical sign
43 Bygone Russian group
44 Electrical unit
45 Female attendant
46 Cheap cigar
48 Sierra ___
49 Scottish Celts
52 10 C-notes
53 Opposite of unter, in German
54 Can's composition
55 Notwithstanding that, briefly
56 Biblical priest

by Eileen Lexau

ACROSS

1 27, to 3
5 Virgule
10 St. Nick accessory
14 The top
15 "Remember the ___!"
16 "Ars Amatoria" poet
17 Surgical site in the Beaver State?
19 Kid's phrase of request
20 Chang's Siamese twin
21 Itch
22 Full moon color
24 Commedia dell'___
25 Rapper who co-starred in "New Jack City"
26 Le Carré character George
29 Methodology
32 Estate papers
33 Gunk
34 Champagne Tony of golf
36 ___ vera
37 Middays
38 Money to tide one over
39 It's west of N.C.
40 Just
41 "What ___ I do?"
42 Nielsen stats
44 Comic Charles Nelson ___
45 Unpleasant task
46 Hospital unit
47 Declarer
50 Swiss river
51 "___ is me!"
54 Glitzy sign
55 Doc from the Old Line State?
58 Cartoonist Al
59 Chorus girls?
60 The first: Abbr.
61 Fashion's Klensch
62 1956 Four Lads hit "___ Much!"
63 It's just for openers

DOWN

1 Supergarb
2 "___ the housetop . . ." (Christmas lyric)
3 Arctic Ocean sighting
4 Phone line abbr.
5 ___-pants (wise guy)
6 Jessica of "Frances"
7 Right-hand person
8 ___-cone
9 Decorated officers
10 Driver's license in the Gem State?
11 Russian "John"
12 Engine knock
13 Actress McClurg
18 Fishing gear
23 ___ room
24 Sound system in the Keystone State?
25 Humor not for dummies
26 Quite a hit
27 Distance runner
28 Actress Massey
29 Chlorinated waters
30 1988 Olympics site
31 Inconsequential
33 Pagoda sounds
35 "Handy" man
37 Rural
41 Goddess of agriculture
43 Suffix with elephant
44 Least cooked
46 "Yippee!"
47 Suffix with utter
48 ___ piccata
49 Kin of "Uh-oh!"
50 Envelope abbr.
51 Alert
52 Leave off
53 Periphery
56 "Strange Magic" rock band
57 1988 Dennis Quaid remake

by Stephanie Spadaccini

168

ACROSS

1 ___ World Service (radio provider)
4 ___ Pet (novelty item)
8 "My Life on Trial" author
13 Mine product
14 Dog : paw :: horse : ___
15 Lacking, with "of"
16 High-risk game
19 Plan
20 "___ to differ"
21 Coral ___
22 Gaze
23 Kind of acid
25 Dumb ___ ox
27 90's House majority leader Dick
31 Hemming and hawing
34 Charles Lamb, to readers
36 Exhibits scorn
37 Rot caused by bark beetles
40 Renaissance type
41 Course
42 ___ Alte (Adenauer)
43 Pulsate
44 Zorro's marks
46 Leg bones
50 Message on a Wonderland cake
54 Pac.'s counterpart
57 Beach, basically
58 Farmer's land
59 Montreal denizens
62 Distance on a radar screen
63 Peter Lorre role Mr. ___
64 Deception
65 Australian export
66 Effect of auto exhaust
67 Actor Mineo

DOWN

1 Tennis's Becker
2 Main thrust
3 Jai alai basket
4 Showy-flowered shrub
5 1956–57 Wimbledon champion Lew
6 Charged particle
7 Pertaining to the second-largest continent
8 Good herder
9 First lady
10 Plenty
11 Miller beer
12 Brainstorm
15 Piece for two
17 Word repeated after "Que"
18 Award bestowed by Queen Eliz.
23 Deep blue
24 Manitoba Indian
26 One of the Waughs
28 "Canterbury Tales" drink
29 Gaelic
30 North Sea feeder
31 Handle text
32 Dr. Westheimer
33 Hollywood Boulevard sight
35 Electric guitar hookup
36 Location
38 Congeal
39 Stupor
45 Hindu garment
47 Scornful cries
48 Co. name ending
49 Monroe's successor
51 Dabbling ducks
52 Craze
53 Collectible Ford
54 Opposite of a buzz cut
55 Pitfall
56 Moon of Jupiter
58 60's–70's Japanese P.M.
60 Zilch
61 Robespierre, e.g.

by Ed Early

169

ACROSS

1 Civil disorder
5 Urban haze
9 Diners
14 Workers' protection org.
15 Variety of fine cotton
16 Hold dear
17 Tizzy
18 The New Yorker cartoonist Peter
19 Chateau-Thierry's river
20 "Petticoat Junction" setting
23 Lyricist Rice
24 Granola grain
25 Copyists
27 Trim, as a tree
32 Arp's art
33 Military address: Abbr.
34 Fishing line
36 The "S" in WASP
39 State north of Ind.
41 Adventures
43 Battle of Normandy objective
44 Big news exclusive
46 Reading lights
48 Ames and Asner
49 Pub orders
51 Practice
53 Edmonton's province
56 Everything
57 Random number generator
58 "Father Knows Best" setting
64 Texas site to remember
66 Have ___ good authority
67 Sewing case
68 Georgia city, home of Mercer University
69 Color of linen
70 Final Four inits.
71 Pronunciation symbol
72 Make-believe
73 Eschew

DOWN

1 ___ ha-Shanah
2 "Money ___ object!"
3 Louisville's river
4 Dragon, perhaps
5 Big Ten team from East Lansing
6 Nuclear missile, briefly
7 Prefix meaning 56-Across
8 London lockups
9 Kodaks, e.g.
10 Nabokov novel
11 "The Phil Silvers Show" setting
12 Sgt. Bilko
13 Looks like
21 Prominent rabbit features
22 Digital readout, for short
26 Mrs. McKinley and others
27 Beavers' constructions
28 Kind of proportions
29 "I Dream of Jeannie" setting
30 Marsh duck
31 "Pomp and Circumstance" composer
35 Shiny fabric
37 Auto pioneer Ransom
38 Victory margin, at times
40 Tunnel
42 Moss for potting plants
45 ___ non grata
47 Prefix with starter
50 Nascar sponsor
52 Little green men
53 Revolutionary leader Samuel
54 Light purple
55 Pisces's follower
59 Scratch it!
60 Nick and ___ Charles
61 Make an aquatint
62 Hilo feast
63 Primatologist Fossey
65 Cut the grass

by Gregory E. Paul

170

ACROSS

1 Support
5 Hindu gentleman
9 Indonesian island
14 Nautical direction
15 Part of the eye
16 Mirror ___
17 Charlemagne's legacy
20 Lepidopterist's equipment
21 Corrida cries
22 Condemned
23 Marking float
24 Tiny memory measures
25 "Nothing ___!"
27 James Buchanan, notably
31 Reign noted for magnificent porcelain
33 Actress Hagen
34 Commentators' page
35 Cricket sides
36 Play start
37 German direction
38 Virginia's nickname
42 Farewells
44 Chips in?
45 Rara ___
46 Semicircles
47 Gene Kelly's activity in the 30-Down
50 Hammett pooch
51 Stage of history
54 Disney realm
57 Draw a bead on
58 Subsequently
59 Venom
60 Cache
61 Stitches
62 Charon's river

DOWN

1 Where to take a Volkswagen for a spin
2 Shampoo ingredient
3 Breton, for one
4 Crucial
5 What John Scopes taught
6 90's House majority leader Dick
7 Partiality
8 Milit. branch
9 Coarse fodder grass
10 Levy
11 Impair
12 Bogeyman
13 Army surgeon Walter
18 Spherical
19 Pronouncement
23 Nickname for the Cowboys' hometown
24 One who sings the part of Boris Godunov
25 Boozehound
26 "And ___ grow on"
27 They were big in the 40's
28 "A Tale of Two Cities" heroine
29 Director Preminger et al.
30 See 47-Across
31 ___ synthesizer
32 Stem joints
36 Termites' kin
38 Render unnecessary
39 Fibbing
40 Forked-tail swallows
41 From early Peru
43 Buxom blonde of 50's TV
46 Crooked
47 B.&O. stops
48 "___ a New High" (1937 Lily Pons song)
49 Verne's captain
50 Lumbago, e.g.
51 Blue-pencil
52 ___-poly
53 Big Board's brother: Abbr.
55 "___ Not Unusual"
56 Literary monogram

by Jonathan Schmalzbach

ACROSS

1 A single time
5 Stephen King's home state
10 Porgy's beloved
14 Gloucester's king
15 Jostle
16 Teatro ___ Scala
17 IRIS
20 Book addendum
21 Striped chalcedony
22 Guest room, frequently
23 Prosciutto
25 IRIS
33 Selfish sort
34 Ring shout
35 Chinese nurse
36 Bridge achievement
37 Snack items
39 In __ (undisturbed)
40 Rival of Rival
41 Darling of the diamond
42 Boobs
43 IRIS
47 Wonder
48 Actor Beatty
49 Play for time
53 Academic term
58 IRIS
61 Shortly
62 Kind of flare or system
63 "___ Named Sue"
64 Well-bred chap
65 Porterhouse kin
66 Kesey and Follett

DOWN

1 One of Chekhov's Three Sisters
2 Tide type
3 Gefilte fish ingredient
4 Mahler's "Das Lied von der ___"
5 Tailor, at times
6 Describing some skiing
7 Old World goat
8 Neither's partner
9 One welcomed to the fold?
10 [Just like that!]
11 Lamb's pen name
12 Blind segment
13 Red-tag event
18 Where Saul consulted a witch
19 Identify
23 Servants
24 "The ___ have it"
25 Arum lily
26 Giraffe's relative
27 Fruit at the bar
28 Bringing off
29 Dated
30 Wrong
31 Hotel charges
32 Consequently
33 Nicholas or Alexander
37 Be exultant
38 Gordie of the N.H.L.
42 European viper
44 Debutante's affair
45 Kind of show or band
46 Shy and modest
49 Small setback
50 Sound quality
51 Bath's county
52 Mardi Gras follower
53 Manche capital
54 Mt. Rushmore's state: Abbr.
55 Start of a Hamlet soliloquy
56 Subj. for an M.B.A.
57 Actor John ___-Davies
59 Suffix with vocal
60 Sorrowful sound

by Nancy S. Ross

172

ACROSS

1 Org. that safeguards pets
5 Prefix with port
9 Liability's opposite
14 Songwriter Gus
15 Plow animals
16 Marvy
17 "Yikes!"
18 Actress Hayworth
19 Mississippi ___
20 Lead singer with Dawn
23 Opposite of 42-Across
24 Alphabet trio
25 Reduced fare
26 ___ la Douce
28 What "hemi-" means
30 Odd
33 Popular record label
36 Cosmetician Elizabeth
37 Treaty
40 Seabees' motto
42 B or better
43 Impassive
45 Horses' home
47 Morning or afternoon travel
49 Vlad the Impaler, e.g.
53 Stallion's mate
54 Water, in Cadiz
56 "Do Ya" rock grp.
57 Kind of testing, in law enforcement
59 Los Angeles suburb
62 Sonata section
64 Mrs. Chaplin
65 Jazz performance
66 Dual conjunction
67 Men's business wear
68 Buster Brown's dog
69 Pirate's prize
70 Nobelist Wiesel
71 TV's "___ Three Lives"

DOWN

1 Artist's rendering
2 Chinese temple
3 Estee Lauder rival
4 Rooney of "60 Minutes"
5 Frightful
6 Banish
7 Free to attack
8 ___ instant (quickly)
9 Neighbor of Spain
10 Go out with
11 60's–70's A's third baseman
12 Ending with Henri
13 Wart-covered creature
21 Stench
22 Morse code click
27 Mrs. Homer Simpson, et al.
29 Bluebeard's last wife
30 Actress Thompson
31 Storm or Tracker, in the auto world
32 Finis
34 Postpaid encl.
35 It's a blast
37 Utilities watchdog grp.
38 From ___ Z
39 "Dirty Dozen" marauder
41 Inflexible
44 Superficial, as a look
46 Emulate Pisa's tower
48 Tetley product
50 Cosmetics applicator
51 Senior years
52 Blew a horn
54 Run ___ of (violate)
55 Bottled spirits
57 Cheerless
58 Banned act
60 Bloodhound's sensor
61 ___ spumante
63 Complete an "i"

by Thomas W. Schier

ACROSS

1 Indian title of respect
6 Love handles, essentially
10 Gad about
14 "Für ___" (Beethoven dedication)
15 Clarence Thomas's garb
16 Second word of many limericks
17 It's not as threatening as it looks
19 Give up
20 Current strength
21 Antiaircraft fire
23 London lavatory
24 "Rocky ___"
25 ___ A Sketch (drawing toy)
26 Old age, in old times
27 Italian cheese
31 ___ Major (southern constellation)
35 Mat victory
36 River of Russia
37 Man ___ (famous race horse)
38 Jive talkin'
40 Running shoe name
41 Marquand's Mr. ___
42 Rotter
43 Does some lawn work
44 Disappear through camouflage
46 Mineral springs
48 Tended to the weeds
49 "High ___" (Anderson play)
50 Photo ___ (camera sessions)
53 Repudiate
56 Horrid
58 It's put off at the bakery
59 Shooter's target
61 Change for a C-note
62 Roof overhang
63 Homes for hatchlings
64 Philosopher
65 Exceeded the limit
66 Gaggle members

DOWN

1 Flower part
2 Bowie's last stand
3 Swimmer in the Congo
4 "Now it's clear!"
5 Additions to an ice cream sundae
6 North Pole-like
7 Theater section
8 Burrows of the theater
9 Chewing out
10 Geologist
11 ___-Day (vitamin brand)
12 Australian hard-rock band
13 Like a milquetoast
18 Party game pin-on
22 New Deal prog.
25 "___ go bragh"
28 Math subject
29 Money brought in
30 Pub quaffs
31 Toothed item
32 Roll call misser
33 Hoops great Archibald
34 Lou Gehrig nickname, with "the"
35 Seat cover
38 Arts' partner
39 Touch down
43 Bringing in
45 ___ Jones
46 Hung around
47 Splendor
50 Corpulent plus
51 Draws, as a line on a graph
52 Good judgment
53 Pencil-and-paper game
54 Brainstorm
55 Carol
56 Garroway of early TV
57 "The African Queen" scriptwriter
60 Drink like Fido

by Fred Piscop

ACROSS

1 They're not to be believed
6 Malice
11 Foot with a claw
14 Good-looker
15 Kind of roll
16 Stat for Yastrzemski
17 "This is ___ two can play!"
18 "Blue Eyes" singer, 1982
20 Deserves
22 Comics cry
23 Balm ingredient
24 "Blue Moon" composer
27 Clinton's attorney general
28 Be a pain
29 Madcap
32 Scarlett's home
35 Biblical gift
39 Leave slack-jawed
40 Story of Jesus
42 Kernel carrier
43 Set down
45 Queens stadium
46 The good guys, in a chase film
47 VCR button
49 Shooter filler
51 "The Blue Knight" author
58 60's TV boy
59 Operated
60 Push beyond limits
62 "Blue Chips" actor
65 Bull: Prefix
66 "Wheel of Fortune" request
67 Shoreline irregularity
68 Encouraged, with "on"
69 Trap, with "in"
70 Oater chasers
71 Scouts' work

DOWN

1 Swindle
2 Even bigger
3 Pong maker
4 Imitation
5 Stew
6 "___ Done Him Wrong" (1933 film)
7 Propelled, as a raft
8 Bury
9 Assumed
10 Directional suffix
11 Manual laborer
12 Hate
13 Pouilly-Fuisse and others
19 Notched
21 Seasonal visitor
25 Bellows
26 Edith Evans, for one
29 Erase, as a PC file
30 Leatherworker's tool
31 King Features competitor
33 Stadium sound
34 Crosswind direction, at sea
36 Classic car
37 Salt-N-Pepa's music
38 Divs. of days
40 Tiniest complaint
41 Gentle ones
44 Alabama native
46 Pluck
48 Prefix with logical
50 Thickly entangled, as hair
51 Old Testament book
52 Imagine
53 Attack dog command
54 Maze parts
55 Pot amounts
56 Meter reader's reading
57 Brought on board
61 Appears to agree
63 Bite
64 Sorbonne summer

by Rich Norris

ACROSS

1 Musicians' copyright grp.
6 King with a golden touch
11 Business fraud monitoring agcy.
14 TV exec Arledge
15 "Be ___ . . ."
16 Spanish gold
17 Grant vs. Bragg, Nov. 1863
19 Tease
20 Sandwich choice
21 Parkers feed it downtown
23 ___-do-well
24 Black Sea port
25 Wakeful watches
28 Bush aide John
30 Neighborhood
31 Idiot
32 Chinese food additive
35 On, as a lamp
36 For fun
38 Place for a hole in a sock
39 Winter clock setting in Vt.
40 Union branch
41 Coal stratum
42 "Old ___" (1957 Disney film)
44 Lines of cliffs
46 Slugged
48 Salon job
49 Perth ___, N.J.
50 Unlike Mr. Spock of "Star Trek"
55 Brock or Costello
56 Rosecrans vs. Bragg, Sept. 1863
58 Continent north of Afr.
59 Eagle's nest
60 Listlessness
61 It follows a dot in many on-line addresses

62 Not our
63 Syria's Hafez al-___

DOWN

1 It may have fallen on a foot
2 Manhattan locale
3 Jacket
4 Cather novel "My ___"
5 Small sea bird
6 Millionaire's home
7 Elvis Presley, in the 50's and 60's
8 "I ___ it!" (cry of success)
9 H.S. math
10 Patrick Ewing specialty

11 Anderson vs. Beauregard, Apr. 1861
12 Attempts
13 Striking snake
18 Good blackjack holdings
22 Poet's dusk
24 ___ about (lawyer's phrase)
25 Caesar's farewell
26 Spring bloom
27 Meade vs. Lee, July 1863
28 Kind of energy or flare
29 ___ Mountains (edge of Asia)
31 Riot queller

33 Ivory, e.g.
34 Onyxes and opals
36 Night prowler
37 Auctioneer's last word
41 Pago Pago residents
43 D.D.E.'s command
44 ___ poor example
45 Sevastopol locale
46 Ancient: Prefix
47 Love affair
48 Fireplace rod
50 Dublin's land
51 1102, in dates
52 Women in habits
53 Tijuana water
54 Deposited
57 Sneaky laugh sound

by Gene Newman

176

ACROSS

1 Bid
6 Mesa dweller
10 Nod off
14 Site of Cnossus
15 Big name in cosmetics
16 German biographer ___ Ludwig
17 "___ looking at you, kid"
18 Lady's man
19 Movers
20 Quirky
21 Impressive achievement
24 Sorbonne, e.g.
26 Tire channel
27 Peer, to his servant
29 Plant with a medicinal root
33 More than peeved
34 Charles's domain
35 Hemispheric assn.
37 Ready to come off the stove
38 Examined, as before a robbery
39 Skip
40 Business mag
41 Lawn
42 "The Taming of the Shrew" setting
43 Spy's byword
45 Police datum
46 Assistance
47 Like toast
48 Final stroke
53 Fate
56 The "A" in A.D.
57 Film ___
58 Pan-fry
60 Harness part
61 Gusto
62 Greek satirist
63 These may be fine
64 On the main
65 Driving hazard

DOWN

1 Cuatro y cuatro
2 N.F.L. receiver Biletnikoff
3 Tropical viper
4 Bastille Day season
5 Give back
6 World Court site, with "The"
7 Finished
8 Thoreau subject
9 Confined, as in wartime
10 Give, as time
11 Gen. Bradley
12 Over-the-counter cold remedy
13 Otherwise
22 Aged
23 Ado
25 ___ d'Azur (French Riviera)
27 Certain skirt
28 Actor Jeremy
29 Long-winded
30 Nouvelle Caledonie and others
31 Pseudonym
32 Julius Caesar's first name
34 W.W. II enlistee
36 Immediately, in the E.R.
38 Sideboard
39 Sculls
41 Part of a crossword
42 Clergymen
44 Poultry offerings
45 Compass tracing
47 Magna ___
48 Dear, as a signorina
49 Unique person
50 Military group
51 "Anything ___" (1934 or 1987 musical)
52 Levitate
54 Siouan tribe
55 Camp shelter
59 Be sick

by Robert Zimmerman

ACROSS

1 Needy
5 Cautious advice
9 Rope fiber
14 Michigan town or its college
15 "___ be in England": Browning
16 Going too far
17 Act of faith
18 Ram
19 Like Dennis the Menace
20 Craze
22 Like some raises
24 Farm distance
25 Pie in the sky
28 Bro, e.g.
29 Not having a surrounding colonnade, in architecture
32 Sixth sense
35 Japanese wraps
38 Sierra ___
39 Guy in the sky
43 City on the Po
44 Function as a medical device
45 6 on the dial
46 Everlasting
48 Diamonds, to a gangster
51 Eye in the sky
57 Go for it
59 "Ben-Hur" garb
60 Bank patron
61 The "her" of "I've Grown Accustomed to Her Face"
63 Bo Derek's first major film
65 Inner tubes, geometrically
66 Musical composition
67 "There oughta be ___!"
68 First name in mystery
69 Shoe material
70 A or O, e.g.
71 Used henna

DOWN

1 Majorcan seaport
2 New York city on the Allegheny
3 Muscat native
4 Canoeist's danger
5 Kind of story
6 Hitting sound
7 Glossy brown fur
8 Some Sunday dinners
9 Foreign film feature
10 Sick
11 Pantry, e.g.
12 Cartoonist Peter
13 "This Gun for Hire" star
21 1996 Olympic torch lighter
23 Rascal
26 Inky
27 "... not always what they ___"
30 Shortly
31 Carson successor
32 Suffix with satin
33 Out of business
34 Swift falcon
36 Ornery farm animal
37 Put ___ good word for
40 Fantastical artist
41 Explain, in a way
42 Successor
47 Flurry
49 "I Love Lucy" appeared on it
50 Overjoyed
52 Premature
53 Abbr. on a CD
54 Banned article of trade
55 Actress Oberon
56 Snooped
57 Ballpoints
58 60's All-Star Felipe
62 From A to ___
64 Wonder

by Stanley B. Whitten

ACROSS

1 Deep sleeps
6 Abbr. before an alias
9 Fragrant oil
14 ___-garde
15 Steal from
16 Push roughly
17 A Roosevelt
18 Afflicted with strabismus
20 Traffic tangle
21 The first "H" of H.H.S.
22 Quilting event
23 Cautious
24 Open a bit
28 Garbage barge
30 Come down
31 Clinton's #2
32 Sigma follower
33 Blue birds
34 Grown-ups
36 Snares
38 Shooting marble
39 Bill settlers
40 Coating metal
41 "Are we there ___?"
42 They're exchanged at weddings
43 Building block company
44 Goofs up
45 Of ships: Abbr.
46 Second-year student, for short
47 Not a beginner
48 Get down from a horse
50 Thesaurus compiler
53 Show with Richie and the Fonz
56 Dancer Astaire
57 Banish
58 Gun grp.
59 Brusque
60 "For ___ sake!"
61 Opposite NNE
62 Industrial city of Germany

DOWN

1 Long-running Broadway show
2 Turkey roaster
3 Paul Reiser/Helen Hunt series
4 President Jackson or Johnson
5 Do, as hair
6 Architectural frames
7 Ones with Seoul custody?
8 "All ___!" (conductor's cry)
9 Helper: Abbr.
10 Where Dutch royals live
11 Plaything
12 "___ Maria"
13 Like Time's border
19 Crafty
25 Pirate flags
26 More pretentious
27 Bowling alley buttons
28 Enter
29 The Great White North
30 Swimmer's regimen
33 Place for pickles
34 ___ time (never)
35 Nov. follower
37 Fasten papers again
38 Visited tourist places
40 Gentle breezes
43 "___ Run" (1976 sci-fi film)
44 Wears away
46 Rock singer Vicious
47 Chatter
49 Caustic solutions
51 Otherwise
52 Adolescent
53 Wise, man
54 Chop
55 Orchestra's location

by Shannon Burns

ACROSS

1 Stage between egg and pupa
6 "Durn it!"
10 Head of hair, slangily
13 "Silas Marner" author
14 Exploiters
16 Eggs
17 Teensy-weensy piece of beef?
19 Seat in St. Paul's
20 ___ Rosa, Calif.
21 1984 World Series champs
23 The sun
26 Johnnie Ray hit of the 50's
27 Biblical king
28 Sleazy
30 Sandlot sport
33 Cottonlike fiber
34 Without
35 Actress ___ Dawn Chong
36 Got 100 on
37 Dot on a monitor
38 Tiny bit
39 ___-de-France
40 Radius, ulna, etc.
41 U.C.L.A. player
42 Big North Carolina industry
44 "Dirty Rotten Scoundrels" actress ___ Headly
45 Kind of bean
46 Old French coin
47 ___ es Salaam
48 Tom Canty, in a Mark Twain book
50 Pedestals, e.g.
52 Mornings, for short
53 What stand-up comics do to keep their material shiny?
58 Soupy Sales missile
59 Long bout
60 Vicinities
61 Catalogue contents

62 Some P.T.A. members
63 Long (for)

DOWN

1 Moon craft, for short
2 Actress MacGraw
3 ___ Tin Tin
4 "Comment allez-___?"
5 Embassy worker
6 Name for a cowpoke
7 Movie pooch
8 Society page word
9 Like a proper rescuee
10 Ride an engine-powered bike?
11 Finished
12 Furry feet
15 Poodle and dirndl, e.g.

18 Professor 'iggins
22 Sailor
23 Sea route
24 Delphic shrine
25 "My gold dress isn't back from the cleaners yet" and others?
27 Sharpens
29 Caesar of "Caesar's Hour"
30 At ___ and sevens
31 Chicana
32 Horseshoes shot
34 Sal of "Giant"
37 Instant picture
38 Anger
40 They're big in gyms
41 Colorful, crested bird
43 Strike lightly

44 "No kidding!"
46 MS. enclosures
48 Madonna's "___ Don't Preach"
49 In the center of
50 Dallas's nickname
51 Achy
54 Meadow
55 Mauna ___
56 It may be pulled in charades
57 ID digits

by Stephanie Spadaccini

180

ACROSS

1 Cockeyed
6 Stirs in ingredients
10 Emily of "Our Town"
14 Trig. function
15 Eye of ___ and toe of frog
16 Oil of ___
17 Gin inventor
19 After-school drink
20 "Cheers" star
21 Fib
23 Cravings
25 "___ giorno!"
26 Bathing facility
29 Spot
31 Flashed one's pearly whites
35 Unagi, at a sushi bar
36 Lymphatic part
38 "Penny Lane," not "Strawberry Fields Forever"
39 Frank Fontaine TV character
43 Thomas Mann's "___ Kröger"
44 Presidential run
45 One below a second lieut.
46 Pursues
48 Government worry
50 Aves.
51 Sir Peter ___, painter of British royalty
53 Kind of toad
55 Leftover
59 Emphatic affirmative
63 Violist's clef
64 "Valley of the Dolls" co-star
66 Sweet dessert
67 "Oh, very funny!"
68 Line of type
69 Blackens
70 Yesteryear
71 Brewer's need

DOWN

1 Like white wine at a restaurant
2 Theme song of Vincent Lopez
3 Alphabet book phrase
4 Info-filled
5 Alpine sounds
6 Member of a colony
7 Fender bender
8 Hardly Mr. Cool
9 Victrola part
10 Not masculine
11 Mideast carrier
12 Neighbor of Java
13 Data unit
18 Diamond segment
22 Arthur Miller character
24 Full-bodied ale
26 Split-off groups
27 Candidate of 1992 and '96
28 George's talk show co-host
30 Put on a border
32 Property securities
33 Order
34 Floor models
37 Once-popular feather source
40 Gobs and gobs
41 On the team?
42 Life, in the early days
47 Like many a winter road
49 Itty-bitty
52 Popular Internet company
54 Compact name
55 Emergency vehicle
56 Miss Cinders of old comics
57 Play the lead
58 1964 Tony winner for "Foxy"
60 "Two Mules for Sister ___"
61 Reply to "Can this be true?"
62 Taken away by force, old-style
65 Caviar

by Elizabeth C. Gorski

ACROSS

1 Throat-clearing sound
5 Fencing weapon
10 Actress Rowlands
14 Exploding star
15 Singer Page
16 Fairy tale's second word
17 St. Paul and Minneapolis
19 Require
20 Comedians Bob and Chris
21 In a wise manner
23 Lawyer's charge
24 "Gee!"
25 Sweatshirt part, perhaps
27 Flush beater
32 Writer Bellow and others
33 Place for a pimento
34 Not the swiftest horse
35 Posterior
36 "Death Be Not Proud" poet
37 Opera star
38 Dog breeder's org.
39 Imply
40 Doled (out)
41 Leaders of hives
43 Like some tea
44 Praise
45 Santa ___, Calif.
46 Refuse to acknowledge responsibility for
49 Post-marathon feeling
54 Quickly, in memos
55 Southern crop, from an economic standpoint
57 Writer Grey
58 Writer Zola
59 Humorist Bombeck
60 Got a good look at

61 Saw socially
62 Profound

DOWN

1 Pot starter
2 Loud laugh
3 More than devilish
4 Part of a car's exhaust system
5 Malice
6 Light bulb unit
7 Elevator inventor
8 Road map abbr.
9 Liquefy
10 Very enthusiastic
11 Fencing weapon
12 Christmas song
13 Raggedy Ann's friend
18 Some college students

22 Tennis great Arthur
24 Quick flashes of light
25 17-syllable poem
26 Precious metal unit of weight
27 Paid, as a bill
28 Arm bones
29 Come together
30 Backed up on disk
31 "Holy cow!"
32 The N.B.A.'s O'Neal, familiarly
36 Exposed as false
37 Poured wine into another container
39 Chew
40 Actor Sal
42 Ran for one's wife?

45 Moved like a shooting star
46 Stun
47 British exclamation
48 Having all one's marbles
49 Tizzy
50 Leer at
51 To be, in Bordeaux
52 Not all
53 Jacket fastener
56 The Monkees' "___ Believer"

by Peter Gordon

182

ACROSS

1. The Hatfields or the McCoys
5. Trip to Mecca
9. Quench
14. Any one of three English rivers
15. "Summertime," e.g., in "Porgy and Bess"
16. Jazzman's cue
17. Woolen wear
20. Bizarre
21. Small ball
22. Makes certain
25. Long, long time
26. Toyota model
28. Govt. agent
32. Fortify, as a town
37. Brit's reply in agreement
38. Spot in a supermarket
41. Cowboys' entertainment
42. Said again
43. Not new
44. Scold
46. Court
47. Riddles
53. Names
58. A lot of Shakespeare's writing
59. Ambassador's stand-in
62. You can dig it
63. Island near Kauai
64. Touches lightly, as with a hanky
65. Soccer shoe
66. Ending with cable or candy
67. Command to Fido

DOWN

1. Drink served with marshmallows
2. Hawaiian feasts
3. Aides-de-camp: Abbr.
4. India's first P.M.
5. "Scots Wha ___" (Burns poem)
6. Sheet music abbr.
7. Goes kaput
8. Quartz variety
9. Oft-televised bishop
10. Polygraph flunker
11. Westernmost Aleutian
12. Canal to the Baltic
13. Raison d'___
18. Debussy's "La ___"
19. Rider's "Stop!"
23. "What's this, Pedro?"
24. "Star Trek" helmsman
27. Kind of lab dish
28. Melt ingredient
29. Catcher's catcher
30. Suit to ___
31. Taped eyeglasses wearer
32. Very light brown
33. Conductance units
34. "Venerable" English writer
35. Passed with flying colors
36. Bout outcome, in brief
37. "___ Sera, Sera"
39. Give up
40. Begin bidding
44. Baskin-Robbins purchase
45. Show off on the slopes
46. Isle of ___
48. Sweet-as-apple-cider girl
49. Diagrams
50. French Revolution figure Jean-Paul
51. Microscopic creature
52. Giving a little lip
53. Electrical letters
54. Former Sen. Gramm of Texas
55. Noggin
56. Killer whale
57. Coal-rich European region
60. Home-financing org.
61. "Fe fi fo ___!"

by Fred Piscop

ACROSS

1 Sports Illustrated's 1974 Sportsman of the Year
4 Steep
9 English poet laureate Nahum ___
13 TV host who does "Headlines"
15 Vietnam's capital
16 Roman Eros
17 Like an inveterate procrastinator
18 Put together
19 Negri of the silent screen
20 Start of a Jonathan Swift quote
23 Col.'s boss
24 Sheriff Taylor's son, in 60's TV
25 Tit for tat?
26 "The Kiss" sculptor
28 Half of CXII
30 ___ Angeles
31 Political losers
32 Select
36 Part 2 of the quote
40 Mother-of-pearl source
41 In a bit
43 Mrs. Nixon
46 J.F.K. regular
47 Played out
48 Lyric poem
50 Largest of seven
53 Bird call
54 End of the quote
58 Surveyor's map
59 Do-___
60 ___-dieu
61 Konrad Adenauer, Der ___
62 Orchestra section
63 Architectural pier
64 "Gentlemen Prefer Blondes" author
65 "Haystacks" painter
66 Word part: Abbr.

DOWN

1 Lively bit of music
2 Omit
3 Plan on it
4 Early rocket traveler
5 Veranda
6 Mindless
7 Drop out, in poker
8 Put away, in a way
9 Tropical animal
10 Without scruples
11 Mid-American Conference team
12 Rubs out
14 Poet's contraction
21 Partner for hither
22 Iodine reaction
27 Mallorca, e.g.
28 Symbol of craziness
29 Hollywood cross street
32 Rock video prizes
33 Hide
34 Arafat's org.
35 Skier's aid
37 "Little Eyolf" playwright
38 Beasts on the royal arms of Scotland
39 Wholeness
42 F.D.R. accomplishment
43 One involved in foreign exchange?
44 Lover of Daphne
45 Campbell's choice
47 Bill
49 Times to remember?
50 "The Age of Anxiety" poet
51 Playground fixture
52 Phrase of explanation
55 Contemptible person
56 Chocolate snack
57 Govt. watchdog group

by Richard Hughes

184

ACROSS
1 "Othello" villain
5 Flat-topped hills
10 Colonel Mustard's game
14 Eschew
15 Some of the Pennsylvania Dutch
16 Feed bag contents
17 Filly's mother
18 "Truly!"
19 Takes advantage of
20 Jalopy
23 Poker starter
24 "Roses ___ red . . ."
25 Like a lot
28 Fawn's mother
31 Necklace units
35 Come about
37 Department of Justice div.
39 Tiny
40 Autumn 1940 aerial war
44 Prior to, poetically
45 Mao ___-tung
46 Tenor Caruso
47 Council of Trent, e.g.
50 Flower holder
52 Spud
53 Lawyer's thing
55 Texas Western, today: Abbr.
57 Mule, e.g.
63 Kind of purse
64 Sidestep
65 Norse Zeus
67 Five-time Wimbledon champ, 1976–80
68 Vintner Ernest or Julio
69 Girl-watch or boy-watch
70 ___-Ball (arcade game)
71 Church officer
72 Marsh plant

DOWN
1 Doctrine: Suffix
2 Captain obsessed
3 Maven
4 Like some diamonds, sizewise
5 "Luncheon on the Grass" painter Edouard
6 Chewed the scenery
7 Fodder storage site
8 "___ I cared!"
9 Yemen, once
10 Grand ___ Dam
11 Word before laugh or straw
12 Salt Lake City students
13 Feminine suffix
21 Toll
22 Regalia item
25 French clerics
26 Hon
27 Time after time
29 Bid
30 Retrocede
32 Lie in store for
33 Winter windshield setting
34 Sir, in Seville
36 What may be followed by improved service?
38 Dander
41 Buckeyes' sch.
42 The "I" in ICBM
43 Cause of an unexpected fall
48 Jellybean flavor
49 ___ Plaines, Ill.
51 Marriageable
54 Old Wells Fargo transport
56 Elizabeth I was the last one
57 Library unit
58 Dublin's land
59 Elliptical
60 Quit, in poker
61 Winning margin
62 Longest river in the world
63 "60 Minutes" network
66 TV's "___ and Stacey"

by Gregory E. Paul

ACROSS

1 "Woe is me!"
5 A wanted man, maybe
9 Miss in the comics
14 ___ Le Pew
15 Oldsmobile, e.g.
16 Sound during hay fever season
17 47-stringed instrument
18 Flair
19 "Jurassic Park" sound
20 Parental advice, part 1
23 ___ Moines
24 "O Sole ___"
25 Antislavery leader Turner
26 Call to Bo-peep
27 Once more, country-style
29 Name
32 See-through wrap
35 Scandinavian capital
36 "The Official Preppy Handbook" author Birnbach
37 Advice, part 2
40 ___ Major
41 Economist Smith
42 Listens to
43 "See ya!"
44 Utopia
45 Served with a meal
46 Choice of sizes: Abbr.
47 Not their
48 Twaddle
51 End of the advice
57 "Silas Marner" author
58 Derby distance, maybe
59 Small field
60 Training group
61 "Zip-___-Doo-Dah"
62 Wedding wear
63 Injured sneakily
64 Back talk
65 Mesozoic and others

DOWN

1 Garden pest
2 What all partygoers eventually take
3 After, in Avignon
4 Fall mo.
5 Flier Earhart
6 "Where's ___?"
7 "Sure, why not?"
8 Letterman rival
9 Hit game of 1980
10 Showy display
11 Call to a mate
12 Search, as a beach
13 Long (for)
21 Mideasterner
22 Merger
26 Where Bear Bryant coached, informally
27 Oriental
28 Grab (onto)
29 ___-a-minute (call rate)
30 Previously owned
31 Chorale part
32 The short end
33 Wrong
34 Floral gift
35 Ye ___ Tea Shoppe
36 Told a whopper
38 Soup scoop
39 "Ta-da!"
44 Hammed it up
45 90's group with the hit "Killing Me Softly," with "the"
46 Boutique
47 Looks at boldly
48 Track car
49 Open-air rooms
50 Skins
51 Isthmus
52 Pearl Buck heroine
53 Coastal flooding factor
54 Holiday season, for short
55 Verdi heroine
56 90's party

by Stephanie Spadaccini

186

ACROSS

1 Monarch until 1979
5 Market amount
9 Texas A & M student
14 Attraction
15 "Button it!"
16 Hush money
17 Omnia vincit ___
18 1992 Edward James Olmos film
20 Travelers' needs
22 Not like a milquetoast
23 #1 hit for Helen Reddy
26 Actor Holbrook and others
30 Red-helmeted rock group
31 Precisely
33 Spheroid
36 Residents of Castel Gandolfo
39 Accommodate
40 Namibia, formerly
43 Paris plaza
44 Does go with them
45 Hipster
46 Making inquiries
48 Tony-winning actress Beryl
50 Parts of itineraries: Abbr.
51 Popular charity
56 Precept
58 ___ spout (water runoff site)
60 Quadrennial athletic event
65 Brooklet
66 Stradivari's teacher
67 Hardly racy
68 White House Scottie
69 Whence the Brahmaputra flows
70 Overpromotion
71 All-too-frequent Buffalo forecast

DOWN

1 Bulgar, e.g.
2 Like greenhouse air
3 Cropped up
4 Miami daily
5 1860's initials
6 Its symbol is an omega
7 Queen's land, once
8 Quarter's worth at a carnival, maybe
9 Fundamentals
10 Grecian Formula target
11 Mixologist's staple
12 PC maker
13 Specification at Thom McAn
19 George Harrison's "___ It a Pity"
21 "Portrait of the Artist" youth
24 Acknowledge
25 Numbskulls
27 Creepy household area
28 Nikon rival
29 French legislature
32 Ref's call
33 Grouchy Muppet
34 Hearty meal
35 Cleveland's ___ Lakefront Airport
37 Pa. hours
38 Sudden fright
41 Around a geographical meeting point
42 "Let Us Now Praise Famous Men" writer
47 Ho lead-in
49 Towers over
52 Below, in poesy
53 "Be that as ___ . . ."
54 Birdy
55 Mello ___ (Coca-Cola brand)
57 Discharge
59 It usually comes on the side
60 To the point
61 "___ Blue?"
62 Pick up
63 Nero, e.g.: Abbr.
64 "Didn't I tell you?"

by Chuck Deodene

ACROSS

1 Tarzan's love
5 Bungle
10 Tickled
14 Johnny Cash's "___ Named Sue"
15 Before the due date
16 Singer McEntire
17 Formative Picasso phase
19 Terrible czar
20 It picks up readings
21 Hustler's tool, maybe
23 Religious council
25 Actor Davis
26 Assail
30 Football Hall-of-Famer Merlin
32 Newspaper publisher Adolph
33 Year, south of the border
34 Wouldn't proceed
39 Center of a 1994 chase
42 Apollo 13 commander
43 Holds
44 Tennis champ Björn
45 Cleaner/disinfectant brand
47 Connection
48 Octagon or oval
52 One of "The Honeymooners"
54 "Carnival of Venice" violinist
56 Tough
61 Jai ___
62 Sophie Tucker was the "last"
64 Opposite of ja
65 Writer Asimov
66 General's command
67 "Auld Lang ___"
68 Tailor
69 Bean counters, for short

DOWN

1 Quick punches
2 Up to the task
3 Verb preceder
4 Potato parts
5 Drunken
6 Paddle
7 July 14, in France
8 Sun blockers
9 F.D.R.'s ___ Park
10 Southern breakfast dish
11 Popular pants since 1850
12 Old-style calculators
13 "Thanks, Gerhard"
18 Hitching ___
22 Sub's "ears"
24 Taboo
26 New Year's Day game
27 22-Down reply
28 Hood's knife
29 Villa d'___
31 Trails off
33 Be ___ in the ointment
35 Earring locale
36 Fort ___ (gold depository site)
37 Stocking shade
38 Labradors and Yorkshires
40 Comedienne DeGeneres
41 Flamboyant Surrealist
46 Most mentally sound
47 Not masc. or fem.
48 Crosses over
49 Alex who wrote "Roots"
50 One more time
51 "Common Sense" pamphleteer
53 "Time in a Bottle" singer Jim
55 Pupil locale
57 Detroit financing co.
58 "The World According to ___"
59 Austen heroine
60 From nine to five, in the classifieds
63 Kubrick's "2001" mainframe

by Mark Elliot Skolsky

188

ACROSS
1 Top piece of a two-piece
4 Italian seaport
11 Timber wood
14 "Alley ___"
15 Zoom-in shot
16 Chinese principle
17 Sex determinant
19 ___ rampage
20 Ready to go
21 Taste test label
23 200 milligrams, to a jeweler
25 Funnyman Philips
28 Not have ___ in the world
29 Spinks defeater, 1978
30 Parallel bar exercises
32 Not nude
33 Complicated situations
37 Debussy contemporary
39 Treasure hunter's declaration
43 Pen
44 Parti-colored
46 Quite the expert
49 Having conflicting allegiances
51 ___ du Diable
52 Kind of fool
54 Wood splitter
55 Quite the expert
57 For adults only
59 Tickle one's fancy
61 Play (with)
62 Twenty-somethings
67 Jargon suffix
68 Earth, wind or fire
69 Squid secretion
70 Texas-Oklahoma boundary river
71 Tennis volleys
72 Gypsy Rose ___

DOWN
1 Word with band or sand
2 Dutton's sitcom role
3 "Art is long, life is short," e.g.
4 Astronaut Carpenter
5 Soprano Gluck
6 Blotto
7 Suffix with lion
8 Rock's ___ Speedwagon
9 Feeling the effects of Novocaine
10 "Don Giovanni," for one
11 Like Schoenberg's music
12 Bullock of "Speed"
13 Took in, in a way
18 Genetic stuff
22 Say "yes" to
23 Auto shaft, slangily
24 "Family Ties" boy
26 Anonymous man
27 Moonfish
31 Fruit/tree connector
34 Deemed appropriate
35 Miscalculate
36 "In Living Color" segment
38 Prefix with propyl
40 Greek portico
41 Salad dressing ingredient
42 Boob tube, in Britain: Var.
45 Hankering
46 Bandleader Les
47 Revolted
48 Not neat at the ends
50 More imminent
53 Pioneer in Cubism
55 Fido and friends
56 "___ recall . . ."
58 Take out
60 "Buddenbrooks" novelist Thomas
63 Surfing site
64 Big bird
65 Opposite SSW
66 Classic Jaguar

by Frank Longo

ACROSS

1 Solipsist's preoccupation
5 Harsh Athenian lawgiver
10 Employ a Singer
13 Anjou, e.g.
14 Casaba, e.g.
15 ___-Ball (arcade game)
16 Heroine of Tennessee Williams's "Summer and Smoke"
17 "___ Help Myself" (Four Tops hit)
18 Phoenician port
19 "Shut up!"
22 ___ broche (cooked on a spit)
24 Coach Parseghian
25 Iranian money
26 Lullaby start
31 Bandleader Shaw
32 They're in galley banks
33 Sow
34 "Flow gently, sweet ___": Burns
36 Yemen's capital
40 Game plan
41 Fancy watch
42 "Pipe down, Pierre!"
47 Hurler Reynolds of the 40's–50's Yankees
48 Go (for)
49 Assist
50 Director's directive
55 Amenhotep IV's god
56 Words repeated at the start of the "Sailor's Song"
57 Like ___ in a trap
60 Bookie's bookings
61 ___ around (near)
62 Rani's attire
63 Come-ons
64 Mystery writer Paretsky and others
65 Book after II Chronicles

DOWN

1 Health center
2 Electric ___
3 Berate
4 German wife
5 Composer Shostakovich
6 Supply with more varnish
7 Astronaut Shepard
8 Rabbit
9 Aware of
10 First U.S. space station
11 In a spooky way
12 Boohoos
15 Narrow furrow
20 Myth
21 City areas, informally
22 Triumphant cries
23 Tackle box item
27 Secreted
28 Smash to smithereens
29 Indochinese language
30 Directional suffix
34 Summer refresher
35 Shriner hat
36 Not worth a ___
37 Much-filmed prison
38 Radar's favorite drink on "M*A*S*H"
39 Fired
40 "___ a man . . ."
41 Popular fast-food chain, informally
42 Crimped, as a piecrust
43 T. S. and George
44 Trifles: Fr.
45 Goddess of wisdom
46 Covers with crumbs
47 Mideast's Gulf of ___
51 Revolutionary orator James
52 Soul singer Hendryx
53 Pre-Soviet royalty
54 Let up
58 Timetable abbr.
59 Aunt, in Madrid

by Jonathan Schmalzbach

190

ACROSS

1 "Quite contrary" nursery rhyme girl
5 Sudden outpouring
10 June 6, 1944
14 Pinza of "South Pacific"
15 "Here ___ trouble!"
16 Straight line
17 Chest organ
18 Make amends (for)
19 Goat's-milk cheese
20 60's TV medical drama
22 Detective Lord ___ Wimsey
23 Guinness suffix
24 Shooting stars
26 World Wildlife Fund's symbol
30 "The Hairy Ape" playwright
32 Gets educated
34 Finale
35 Deep cut
39 Saharan
40 Writer Bret
42 Butter alternative
43 ___ contendere (court plea)
44 Kind of "vu" in a classified
45 Colossus of ___
47 Hardy's partner
50 Get used (to)
51 Medicine injector
54 Neighbor of Syr.
56 Enough to sink one's teeth into
57 Pasternak hero
63 "___ just me or . . . ?"
64 Indian corn
65 Not theirs
66 Rat (on)
67 TV's "Kate & ___"
68 Romance lang.
69 In ___ (actually)
70 She had "the face that launched a thousand ships"
71 Fuddy-duddy

DOWN

1 Blend
2 Côte d'___
3 N.H.L. venue
4 Cartoon bear
5 Oodles
6 Latke ingredient
7 Cupid
8 Rent-controlled building, maybe
9 WNW's opposite
10 British rock group since the mid-70's
11 Because of
12 Take up, as a hem
13 Sophomore and junior, e.g.
21 Low-fat
22 ___ Club (onetime TV group)
25 Downy duck
26 Scheme
27 Prefix with dynamic
28 It gets hit on the head
29 1967 Rex Harrison film role
31 Moxie
33 Shoulder motion
36 Actor Alan
37 Trickle
38 Party thrower
41 Wiry dog
46 Spy Mata ___
48 Unspecified one
49 Tin ___
51 Wallop
52 O.K.'s
53 Train tracks
55 Luster
58 Streamlet
59 Empty
60 Garage occupant
61 Alum
62 Sonja Henie's birthplace
64 ___-jongg

by Gregory E. Paul

ACROSS

1 N.B.A.'s O'Neal, familiarly
5 Nicklaus's org.
8 Orbital point
13 Cape Canaveral grp.
14 E.T. vehicles
15 The Beatles' "You Won't ___"
16 Santa checks it twice
17 Popular adhesive
19 Facility
21 Egg ___ yung
22 And others: Abbr.
23 Canasta relative
26 Cash register key
28 ___ trick (three goals)
29 It kept a princess up
30 Dallas player, for short
31 Small island
32 "Oh, ___ kind of guy . . ."
34 Score in horseshoes
37 New Orleans hot spot
41 Edits
42 Overindulgent parent, e.g.
44 "Meet the Press" network
47 Actress Sue ___ Langdon
48 Feather source
50 ___-Magnon
51 Conditioning, as leather
53 Ham holder
55 Golfer's pocketful
56 Cool ___ cucumber
58 Future atty.'s exam
59 1777 battle site
62 Worst possible score
65 Role player
66 Athlete with a statue in Richmond, Va.
67 Hydrox rival
68 Villa ___ (Italian site)
69 Hair goo
70 Highway entrance

DOWN

1 Variety show since 1975, briefly
2 "Bali ___"
3 O.K.
4 Persian Gulf nation
5 Army rank E-3
6 Disney star
7 Regarding
8 Campfire remnant
9 "For ___ sake!"
10 Washington State airport
11 Relative of a gazelle
12 Old vaudeville actress Blossom
14 1972 Bill Withers hit
18 Longtime Harvard president James Bryant ___
20 Second-biggest movie hit of 1978
23 Touch-tone 4
24 Poetic foot
25 "Cheers" bar owner Sam
27 Recording studio add-ins
30 Raymond of "East of Eden"
33 Shade
35 Tackle's neighbor
36 Custom Royale of old autodom
38 Popular pain relief cream
39 And so on
40 Trillion: Prefix
43 Engine part
44 So-so
45 Writer Ambrose
46 Footballer's footwear
49 Free-for-all
52 "Once ___ Enough"
53 Pay boost
54 Shadow eliminator?
57 Booty
60 Rap's Dr. ___
61 Devils' org.
63 Dream period, for short
64 Alley ___

by Fred Piscop

ACROSS
1 "Battling Bella"
6 Booth in the theater
11 Part of what a biathlete does
14 "Crazy" singer Patsy
15 At any rate
17 1927 Virginia Woolf novel
19 Chem. or biol.
20 Where the wild things are
21 Baltic Sea feeder
22 Relish
23 Fall flat
26 "Java" man
29 Things to strive for
30 Very bright, as colors
31 Bouquet
32 Corp. money man or woman
35 Overly intelligent
39 Baseball's Fernandez
40 Kind of daisy
41 Patron saint of Norway
42 Truckers, perhaps
43 Trounces
45 Tell tale activity
48 Eccentric
49 1970 Kinks hit
50 Wrapped (up)
51 '45 battle site, for short
54 1962 Mitchum/MacLaine film
59 Kind of clause
60 Vampire hunter's weapon
61 Catcher locale?
62 Team for which Gretzky left the Oilers
63 Spoken for

DOWN
1 Groups on the program
2 Coalition
3 Penne alternative
4 Durham sch.
5 Coot
6 "Middlemarch" author
7 What grads earn: Abbr.
8 Crying sound
9 Partisan suffix
10 Utmost
11 Fahd or Faisal
12 Bandleader Kay
13 Rhone tributary
16 Marmaduke's comments
18 Confused
22 Element #30
23 One of the Bonds
24 Prosodic foot
25 Do in
26 Carpenters, e.g.
27 Pope who persuaded Attila not to attack Rome
28 Where the boyz are
29 Lady Jane and Zane
31 Cartoonist Tex
32 Storm preceder
33 Envelope part
34 Switch settings
36 Ear part
37 Phys. activity
38 Catchy part of a song
42 Rub the wrong way?
43 Really impresses
44 "I swear!"
45 Raised platform
46 Obstreperous
47 Part of a bulb
48 Ships' spines
50 Long nap?
51 Dinesen who wrote "Out of Africa"
52 Ship's trail
53 John Irving's "A Prayer for ___ Meany"
55 Fictional planet
56 Slugger's stat
57 Solder material
58 J.F.K. listing

by Brendan Emmett Quigley

193

ACROSS

1 "If I ___ the World" (pop hit)
6 Boutique
10 Kind of carpet
14 Glue
15 Carbonated canful
16 Scarlett's plantation
17 Run to the altar
18 Brother of Cain
19 N.M. neighbor
20 Accounting principle, for short
21 Comic strip witch
23 ___ Steamer (early auto)
25 Land west of Britain
26 Brain wave reading: Abbr.
27 Track records?
29 Sine ___ non
32 Journalist Alexander
35 Isn't on the street?
36 Phoenix fivesome
37 Defeat decisively
40 "Ball!" callers
41 Scolds ceaselessly
42 Birchbark boat
43 Toothpaste type
44 Days of long ago
45 Inclined (to)
46 Feldman role in "Young Frankenstein"
48 Mill in 1848 news
52 Seal tightly, as a coffee can
56 Cleveland's lake
57 Memorable periods
58 Tiny bit
59 Area of corporate investment, briefly
60 1996 Broadway hit
61 Walked (on)
62 Popular watch brand
63 Plumb loco
64 Slangy assents
65 German industrial city

DOWN

1 Movie units
2 Illuminated from below
3 Bath sponge: Var.
4 Square numbers?
5 Hair coloring
6 Hair-raising
7 Traveling tramp
8 Bogus butter
9 Tree with fan-shaped leaves
10 Flight of steps
11 Clown
12 Dry, as a desert
13 Disputed Mideast strip
21 Entreat
22 Towel inscription
24 One of Jacob's wives
27 Unwelcome water on a ship
28 Seth's son
30 Next-to-last word of the golden rule
31 Tennis's Arthur
32 Self-satisfied
33 "Fourth base"
34 Résumé submitter
35 From a distance
36 Specialized police units
38 Outrageousness
39 Sales slip: Abbr.
44 Last word of the golden rule
45 Northern diving bird
47 Bursts of wind
48 Gazillions
49 Sea eagles
50 Chain of hills
51 Alternative to a convertible
52 Sink or swim, e.g.
53 Vicinity
54 Skin opening
55 On the peak of
59 ___ v. Wade (landmark decision)

by Patrick Jordan

194

ACROSS

1 Free ticket
5 Watercress unit
10 Throw off
14 Neighborhood
15 Fraternity ___
16 Fast feline
17 Cheery tune
18 Bewildered
19 Kind of rain
20 1980 Neil Diamond hit
23 Yalie
24 Barker and Kettle, e.g.
25 "Siddhartha" author
27 ___-car
29 Injure
32 Nickname
33 Creature caught only by a virgin maiden
36 Prefix with gramme
37 Secret competitor
40 Beam
41 Liqueur flavoring
42 Kind of stock: Abbr.
43 Sunrise direction, in Sonora
44 Pre-Revolution leaders
48 Solo in Berlioz's "Harold in Italy"
50 Clinton or Kerry: Abbr.
52 Formerly
53 1978 Oscar-winning prison documentary
58 Pessimist's comments
59 Monastery figure
60 Rendezvous
61 Change for a ten
62 Argentine dance
63 Wings
64 About
65 Product of Bethlehem
66 Basketball's Archibald

DOWN

1 Telemarketer
2 Baltimore bird
3 Litigator Belli
4 Toast toping
5 Alexander, formerly of "60 Minutes"
6 "Designing Women" co-star
7 Hurry
8 Words of understanding
9 Trucker's choice
10 Part of NASA
11 Snake oil salesman
12 Go-between
13 June honoree
21 Saudi neighbor
22 Physicist Georg
26 Bruised item
28 Not go straight
29 Guts
30 Lincoln Center subject
31 Memo starter
34 Lupino and others
35 Copper
36 Tacks on
37 Masons, coopers and the like
38 Glance
39 Big insurance carrier
40 N.J.'s Corzine e.g.
43 Pitcher part
45 Bassett of "Waiting of Exhale"
46 Warm up, as leftovers
47 Living room piece
49 Rancher's rope
50 Put on
51 Flynn of film
54 Newts
55 "Phooey!"
56 Kind of curve, in math
57 "___ old cowhand . . ."
58 Constrictor

by Elizabeth C. Gorski

ACROSS

1 You'd better believe it!
5 TV's Hawkeye
9 Bossy
12 "Dies ___"
13 Bloomsbury group writer
15 Showed up
16 Religious leader born in Wadowice, Poland
18 Stone with color flashes
19 Roadhouse
20 Formerly
21 Don sackcloth
23 Method
24 Nota ___
25 Sundae toppers
28 "Annie" showstopper
32 Controversial orchard spray
33 "King David" star, 1985
34 1922 Vincent Lopez hit
35 Actress Singer
36 Silo contents
37 Footnote abbr.
38 Fencer's weapon
39 Radiation units
40 Inlet
41 Minutemen's foe
43 Justice who replaced Brennan
45 Arm part
46 Bamboozles
47 Warehoused
50 Playwright Bogosian
51 Kind of chamber
54 New Zealander
55 Pianist born in Kurilovka, Poland
58 It popped into Descartes's head
59 Pool owner's headache
60 Novelist Paton
61 Cartridge holder
62 Young 'un
63 Motown's Marvin

DOWN

1 Big coconut exporter
2 The King's middle name
3 "Call Me Irresponsible" lyricist
4 Large shoe size
5 Plaques, maybe
6 No-goodnik
7 Nincompoop
8 Foreman's superior
9 Supergarb
10 Arab League member
11 Whipping memento
14 Relief pitchers, so to speak
15 Astronomer born in Torun, Poland
17 Working stiff
22 Roxy Music co-founder
23 Chemist born in Warsaw, Poland
24 Pushkin hero
25 Not so ruddy
26 Run to Reno?
27 Gave a fig
28 The yoke's on them
29 Kind of bomb
30 Ocher-green
31 Heron or egret
33 She vanted to be alone
36 White-bearded geezer, stereotypically
42 Grand ___ Opry
43 Formal bash
44 Exceptional occasion
46 Haunted house noise
47 Pass over
48 Beach sweeper
49 Novelist Wister
50 On pins and needles
51 Any of the Galápagos
52 "Why not?"
53 Common opening time
56 Supermodel Carol
57 Jokester

by John D. Leavy

ACROSS

1 Recipe amts.
5 Send by United Parcel
9 Carried on, as war
14 Big pile
15 Worth a D
16 Irregularly notched, as a leaf
17 NBC's "My name is ___"
18 Mysterious character
19 Singer Furtado
20 Season's greetings from Little Bo Peep?
23 Cut on a slant
24 At ___ rate
25 Take the wrong way?
28 "The Faerie Queene" character
29 Where Lewis and Clark started their expedition
31 Throw a party for
34 Like yard sale items
35 Season's greetings from the Jolly Green Giant?
38 Berth place
40 Request for a hug
41 Flashlight brand
43 Queen Amidala's home planet
48 Swindle
49 Actor with a mohawk
50 Looking like
52 Season's greetings from the cast of "Hair"?
55 Kiwi's language
57 Breakfast, lunch or dinner
58 Not made up
59 Material for some balloons
60 HOMES part
61 "Hamlet" quintet

62 Reagan's attorney general
63 Convinced
64 Modernists

DOWN

1 Clarice Starling's org.
2 Paint basecoat
3 Okay to eat on Passover
4 Bad humor
5 Buyer's bender
6 Pester persistently
7 Scottish isle
8 Was victorious
9 Frosty maker
10 Neck of the woods
11 Event of '49

12 Night school subj.
13 Susan of "LA Law"
21 Nurse Barton
22 Clothing line
26 You can dig it
27 Monetary offer
29 Macho
30 Passé
32 It sounds like an F
33 Pleasant memories
35 Opening in many a door
36 Slip
37 Ask for more Time
38 Outfield throw
39 The holly and the ___
42 Word on a New York license plate

44 "The Kitchen God's Wife" author
45 Author Ambrose of "The Devil's Dictionary"
46 Running unattended
47 Mrs. Shrek, e.g.
50 Exemplar of slowness
51 Caught congers
53 Cousins of 401(k)s
54 Gateway Arch architect Saarinen
55 "Tasty"
56 Congressional approval

by Randy Ross

ACROSS

1 Quick raids
7 Brass component
11 ___ Kosh B'Gosh
14 Getting nowhere fast
15 "On the Waterfront" director Kazan
16 Corp. or Sgt.
17 Kid's carol
19 Rubber ducky's "pond"
20 Addams Family cousin
21 Autumn apple
22 "The Sopranos" network
23 Coal holders
25 Ostrich look-alikes
27 Triumphant carol
32 2001 British Open champion David ___
33 "Telephone Line" band
34 Potting need
36 Black and tan ingredient
37 End of a flight
41 Lab eggs
42 Feeder visitor
44 Slinger's weapon
45 Desert stops
47 Crèche carol
51 Doofus
52 Former Time film critic James
53 Mandy's "Evita" role
54 Heaven on earth
58 Dream Team team
61 Salad topper
62 Lullaby carol
65 Einstein's birthplace
66 Garden of delight
67 Tiny village
68 Hwy. turnoffs
69 Mind readers?: Abbr.
70 ___ Way (ancient Roman road)

DOWN

1 South Pacific island nation
2 "Don't count ___!"
3 Deliver a diatribe
4 Braz. neighbor
5 Brynner of "The King and I"
6 Canned heat brand
7 Jazz duo?
8 Trials and tribulations
9 Cairo's river
10 Havana honcho
11 At large
12 Underwater sightseer
13 Kings of the road
18 Flopola
23 Win ___ landslide
24 "___ cost you!"
26 Visiting times: Abbr.
27 Celebrated TV chef
28 Floods, in a way
29 Gossipy Hopper
30 Connecticut collegian
31 Took the prize
32 Apply lightly
35 "Viva ___ Vegas!"
38 Bordeaux buddy
39 "Sister Act" extra
40 Outta here
43 Water gate
46 It's measured in candles
48 "It's like this . . ."
49 Water conduit
50 Mystery writer Christie
51 Scrub strenuously
55 Ocean motion
56 Designer Cassini
57 Pigs' digs
58 Aptly named tangelo
59 Where to meet the Mets
60 Ltr. routing aid
63 Forty winks
64 Mischievous kid

by Nancy Salomon

ACROSS

1 Wall recess
6 Honolulan's "hi"
11 Asian sash
14 Time with a single chime
15 Starts to take over, as another's territory
17 Sleigh's covering
19 Hip they're not
20 Launch sequence phrase
21 North Pole's covering
27 Klutz
28 "Honest" prez
29 Tax ID
30 Bride's new title
34 They fill tanker trucks and truckers' tanks
36 Reindeer team's covering
41 Prefix with centric
42 Protect, in a box
43 Self-examining question
46 Early 20th-cen. conflict
47 LBJ's successor
48 Elf's covering
55 Mars: Prefix
56 Trims, as a budget
57 Santa's Christmas Eve covering
64 Used a car emergency kit device
65 Staked structures
66 WSW's opposite
67 Mints with Retsyn
68 Milk and a cookie, e.g.

DOWN

1 Eggy quaff
2 Diminutive suffix
3 Animation unit
4 "___ a clue" (was oblivious)
5 Dais introducer
6 Brazilian novelist Jorge
7 Bunches of, in a word

8 Start that means "egg"
9 Bunny's boss, for short
10 Egyptian wriggler
11 Vegetables good for frying or crying
12 Knee-held percussion instrument
13 Visiting the local area
16 Author Fleming and others
18 Pursuer of Bilbo
21 Newborn's last address
22 60's musical
23 "Should that be the case . . ."
24 Not slack
25 Very overweight
26 No petty criminal
31 Ger. neighbor

32 Split evenly
33 Neutral vowel
34 ___ Schwarz
35 Noncom three ranks above cpl.
37 Taking care of the situation
38 Cabbie's charge
39 "Semper Fideles" org.
40 Artist Magritte
43 Fit for growing crops
44 Arthurian magician
45 Conceive
49 ___ Cola
50 Mod painting style
51 Destinies
52 To's partner
53 Turns made on a Nascar oval

54 Ruhr Valley city
58 The Colonel's restaurant
59 Indians, on a scoreboard
60 Canoe conveyer
61 "I'm ___ diet" (common post-Christmas statement)
62 Like Nasdaq trades
63 Bad reaction?

by Patrick Merrell

ACROSS

1 Felix Salten's beloved creation
6 Command at sea
11 Robt. Mueller's org.
14 Jennifer Garner series
15 Beethoven's Choral symphony
16 Row
17 . . . PLEASE DON'T BRING ME A ___
19 "So that's it!"
20 Doled
21 "The Joy Luck Club" author
23 Fortune's partner
26 Bribable
28 Farmer Hoggett's wife, in "Babe"
29 Black Sea port
31 Brian of rock
32 On ___ (equal)
33 . . . OR A ___
35 Gross
36 Real ending
37 "¿Que es ___?"
39 Requirements, briefly
43 . . . OR ___
49 Walt Kelly's cartoon critter
50 Big ___
51 Improve
52 Gymnast Korbut
53 Playing marble
55 Together, musically speaking
56 Hopkins's Oscar-winning role
58 Chicago team
60 Aussie bird
61 . . . OR A ___. THANKS!
66 Bill addition
67 Sarcasms
68 It's black and white all over
69 Place for U.S.A. career men
70 Carmaker Soichiro ___
71 Mrs. Archie Bunker

DOWN

1 Catch
2 Menu words
3 Russian space station
4 ". . . Leroy Brown, the ___ man . . ."
5 Words of understanding
6 Slant
7 Napa Valley figure
8 "Wheel of Fortune" request
9 Brittany tourist destination
10 Joyce Carol Oates novel
11 . . . OR A ___
12 Independent country since 1973
13 Some laundry workers
18 Southwest Indians
22 Word with lunar or solar
23 Daze
24 Nicole in "Cold Mountain"
25 One of the "Little Women"
27 ___ up (paid)
30 Former flyers: Abbr.
34 Kind of vb.
35 Invent
38 Cold and hard
39 Charleston's ___ Festival
40 Attack on another's opinion
41 . . . OR ___
42 Chesterfield, e.g.
44 Permitted
45 Understood
46 Covered up
47 Ft. Worth inst.
48 Lennon/McCartney's "___ Loves You"
50 Hispanic neighborhood
54 Oklahoma's second city
57 D-I connection
59 Lounge
62 Son of, in Arabic names
63 Sports page stat
64 Scrap for Fido
65 Nope

by Nancy Nicholson Joline

ACROSS

1 Design of on-line magazine, e.g.: Abbr.
4 Madrid museum
9 Make sense
14 Woolly female
15 Bridge move
16 Mike ___, the plumber on "Desperate Housewives"
17 Topic for collective bargaining
19 Made something at home, say
20 Times up
21 Wine bottle sound
23 Pen without ink
24 TV sitcom that featured Carlton the Doorman
25 Unaccompanied
27 Concerning
29 Even chances
32 Tricky baseball bouce
36 Nifty
37 Playboy nickname
38 Early auto pioneer
42 Baton Rouge sch.
43 Broadcast letters
45 Doesn't decide right away
47 Room service fate, categorically
51 Movie lioness
52 Like most runway models
54 Word with run or attorney
58 See 61-Across
60 Perimeter
61 With 58-Across, singer with the hit "Rockin' Around the Christmas Tree"
62 1950s middleweight champ "Bobo" ___
64 Insurgents
66 ". . . woman who lived in ___"
67 Georgia university
68 Galoot
69 Have pity toward
70 Awards first given out in 1993
71 Regular: Abbr.

DOWN

1 Scot who invented the vacuum flask
2 Small fraction
3 Music's Bryson
4 Anticipation
5 Ring leaders?
6 ___ Dhabi
7 Drab
8 Uncommon amount
9 Sayings
10 Netherlands city known for its pottery
11 Deliveries to truck stops
12 Army group
13 Yankee Doodle's transport
18 Speeder's concern?
22 Spanish cardinal?
25 Catcalls
26 Nine-digit I.D.
28 Divinity deg.
30 Part of U.T.E.P.
31 Knock for a loop
32 Exiled monarch
33 Blood: Prefix
34 Readily available at stores
35 Monies dishonestly acquired
39 Shouts of encouragement
40 28-Down's field: Abbr.
41 Wipes out
44 Tony Soprano's psychiatrist
46 Kitchen gizmo
48 Letter ___
49 Passé
50 It may be honorary
53 Appears
55 Quechua speakers
56 Proficient
57 Gave off light, in a way
58 Take it easy
59 "So what ___ is new?"
61 Place for bats?
63 Winning tic-tac-toe line
65 Conk

by David J. Kahn

The New York Times

Crossword Puzzle Collections

THE BOOKS THAT ARE ON EVERYBODY'S WISH LIST!

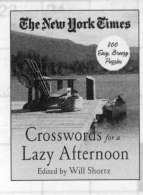

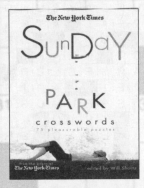

Available at your local bookstore or online at www.nytimes.com/nytstore

 St. Martin's Griffin

1

2

3

4

5

6

7

```
CHIC ■ PAVER ■ PAAR
OATH ■ ALIVE ■ IDLE
RITA ■ GODEL ■ VOID
KRYPTONISOTOPE
■ LODE ■ ATTN
FARINA ■ MARLA
ALENE ■ DICKCLARK
LEI ■ MUNRO ■ RAE
KENTSTATE ■ JERRY
ROADS ■ RINSES
SPED ■ DEBT
MANANDSUPERMAN
JOLT ■ EXCEL ■ ELLA
OLEO ■ RIATA ■ ELIS
ETON ■ DITSY ■ SETH
```

8

```
TYRO ■ BEAM ■ TUBAS
ROAR ■ UCLA ■ USURP
IDLE ■ GRID ■ ROMEO
BELLYBUTTON ■ BAT
ELYSEE ■ VITAL
EGADS ■ LOVEIN
JEB ■ GRITTY ■ EBAY
AMASS ■ SIR ■ FRETS
DILL ■ SCRIBE ■ EEE
ELLIOT ■ SOILS
OPRAH ■ GLEAMS
AGT ■ BREADBASKET
RABBI ■ ELLA ■ TIDE
ABOUT ■ DOIN ■ ERIN
TEXTS ■ SWIG ■ TACO
```

9

```
CANCAN ■ TUTTUT
EPAULET ■ SANREMO
COMRADE ■ WISEMAN
IRES ■ STELES
LTD ■ OUTWAIT ■ BBB
OSBORN ■ BORO
NOS ■ MEAT ■ GOOGOO
ESTOP ■ NIM ■ UNION
CHICHI ■ MESS ■ EKE
KENT ■ REEDIT
SAG ■ MIDRIBS ■ ZOE
MEDUSA ■ POUR
ASIATIC ■ TORONTO
PASSOUT ■ ELOPERS
TOMTOM ■ DEEDEE
```

10

```
EDITS ■ SIGH ■ SLAP
PATIO ■ ACRE ■ HALL
INEED ■ FEAR ■ ESPY
COMPAREDNOTES
■ ISIT ■ DEEP
ASSN ■ PYM ■ STIGMA
TAW ■ ZONED ■ OSLER
BLEWONESOWNHORN
ALEAD ■ TATES ■ ARI
TETRIS ■ SSA ■ STYE
RAMA ■ TRIO
FACEDTHEMUSIC
MEAN ■ LIRE ■ AROMA
OMIT ■ LEOI ■ GELID
BURY ■ SUDS ■ EDENS
```

11

```
NARC ■ FLATS ■ MESA
OLIO ■ ROGUE ■ EMIR
BLOC ■ ACURA ■ TUNE
OUTOFTHEBLUE
DREAR ■ OUTRAGE
YER ■ ORES ■ PAMPAS
STORES ■ AINT
WITHNOWARNING
RATA ■ SEGUED
INBRED ■ ROTH ■ EAT
BEEGEES ■ RANGE
ALLOFASUDDEN
WHIZ ■ EDICT ■ DENS
HATE ■ TARRY ■ LADE
ODOR ■ ESSEX ■ ERAS
```

12

```
JAB ■ IMLATE ■ WINE
AER ■ SUISSE ■ ALEX
NIA ■ AUTHORMILNE
DOWD ■ MAYS ■ OKIES
JUNEAU ■ BRIC
BLUESMANKING
SEPTA ■ PHIL ■ ITER
OUR ■ RESEALS ■ LIE
URIS ■ DORM ■ SLYLY
POETCUMMINGS
DARC ■ ETALII
WHOME ■ USFL ■ TENK
RAPPERCOOLJ ■ ANN
ALEE ■ ELIXIR ■ RIO
POND ■ MARXES ■ NEW
```

13

```
A F T ■ N A T O ■ ■ B A L S A
P R O ■ A I N T ■ G L U E O N
H O W D I D T H E O A K A S K
I D E A L S ■ E P I C ■ D O H
D O L T ■ ■ P R A N K S ■ ■
■ ■ A J A R ■ ■ S H A M U
C D S ■ O B O E ■ P H O B O S
O U T T H E M A P L E T R E E
B E Y O N D ■ T R U E ■ A S S
B L E N D ■ ■ E S P N ■ ■
■ ■ E R S A T Z ■ ■ A G E D
P E R ■ Y A L E ■ E M I L I O
I W O O D P I N E F I R Y E W
C O A X E S ■ A R T S ■ P I N
A K R O N ■ ■ M A S S ■ H O Y
```

14

```
A M O R ■ A V I D ■ E J E C T
R O L E ■ D I N O ■ V A L O R
I T S D E J A V U ■ E Z I N E
A T E S T ■ L O B E ■ Z A N Y
S O N T A G ■ L L A M A ■ ■
■ ■ A L L O V E R A G A I N
T S A R ■ ■ A W E ■ T S E T S E
E L I ■ D S L ■ S H H ■ O A T
R A D I U S ■ ■ E T D ■ I N N S
I T S D E J A V U A L L ■
■ ■ C L A R O ■ Y A L I E S
M E G A ■ W I L D ■ V E R V E
E X E R T ■ O V E R A G A I N
S P A D E ■ ■ S E E D ■ A T A D
H O R S E ■ O D D S ■ L E N S
```

15

```
B A S E D ■ E G A D ■ P A R S
I R E N E ■ R I D E ■ T R O T
G E E N A D A V I S ■ A C M E
■ S M I L E ■ E D I T ■ E E R
■ S U S A N S A R A N D O N
O U T S I D E ■ S E R A ■
A P O ■ N O R D ■ T Y P E A
R O B S ■ N O E A R ■ S H A G
S N E A K ■ ■ B R E T ■ O R E
■ L A S S ■ O P E N E N D
J A C K N I C H O L S O N ■
E M U ■ E C H O ■ A T T I C
T U R K ■ K E V I N B A C O N
E S S O ■ O M E N ■ A T I L T
R E E D ■ F E R N ■ N E A T H
```

16

```
P A L L ■ T A R A ■ R A B I N
L E O I ■ U S E D ■ E L U D E
A R A M ■ R E Q D ■ N O D O Z
T I M B U K T U T U T U ■
E E Y O R E ■ I O T A ■ O C T
■ ■ L Y M E ■ A C T F O R
H A T H ■ O M A H A H A H A
I N S I G H T ■ E N R A G E D
T O K Y O Y O Y O ■ N E N E
I D E A L S ■ E N D S ■ ■
T E D ■ G O A L ■ E M A J O R
■ H O N O L U L U L U L U
S H O U T ■ R O N A ■ A R I L
E A R T H ■ T W I N ■ M O V E
X H O S A ■ A S T O ■ O R E S
```

17

```
S C H E M E ■ T O D O ■ I M P
O L I V E R ■ A M I D ■ T A O
M A K E S A S C E N E ■ L I P
E D E N S ■ H O N G ■ A L D A
■ T U T U ■ B I T T E R
A M C ■ P U L L S A S T U N T
H E A R S T ■ E S T H E R ■
A L L A ■ A N T ■ S N I T
■ C I C A D A ■ A T T U N E
C A U S E S A S T I R ■ P T A
A S L E E P ■ O L A F ■
C H A D ■ I N O N ■ M O R S E
K I T ■ D R A W S A C R O W D
L E O ■ N I T E ■ R A G T A G
E R R ■ A N O N ■ C R E E P Y
```

18

```
A L A R ■ H E E D ■ S M E A R
S A D E ■ A R C O ■ W R E N S
S N O W ■ T O R N ■ A F L A T
H A R R Y H O U D I N I ■
E I E I O ■ ■ I N E X A C T
■ ■ T U T S I ■ G E I G E R
H E L E N H U N T ■ T O D O
E C O ■ G E C K O E S ■ N E V
W O M B ■ H E N R Y H Y D E
E L A I N E ■ D I A N E ■
R I N G E R S ■ ■ C R A P S
■ H E R M A N N H E S S E
J I H A D ■ E Q U I ■ I T A L
A V A I L ■ L U M P ■ A R T E
G E N R E ■ L A B S ■ M O S S
```

19

```
DWEEB  DRAB  EFFS
EAGLE  EARL  SILO
ECOLE  ANTI  PEAL
ROSEGARDENS   SKI
   NELLY  DUSTED
ASS  ELY  LEMMA
CHUMS    AIRPOWER
TOGA  BOWLS  KAVA
SEASCAPE   PEREZ
  RAILS  WAR  ENE
REDIAL  SAVOR
EVA  ORANGEJUICE
BEDS  OLEO  EBBED
UNDO  OMEN  CLING
STYX  MARS  TESTY
```

20

```
AVER  WORST  EDGE
WARE  ANITA  MOLT
ALUM  REFIT  SUET
CUPOFCOFFEE   GNU
SETTER  FRESH
   EDITS  SLINGS
REFS  MOOT  EXULT
EAR  TEACHER  TOA
PRIMO  DIAL  ESPY
SNEAKS  ODETS
  DRYER  MATMAN
APE  ORANGEJUICE
HUGS  ACORN  ANTE
ERGO  PETIT  REED
MESS  EDENS  YODA
```

21

```
OCCAM  JOSH  MARG
SHAME  AXLE  CBER
HAPPY  BEES  SABU
ARISES  NEST  LOM
PAT  RID  PEASOUP
EDAM  GRAY  CANNY
DELI  NET  WINED
  SNOWWHITE
 ABHOR  AOL  SWIT
STAIR  SROS  TITO
EASTMAN  DOC  REL
NTH  SUEY  NOTERS
TUFT  DEAL  NOTAT
TRUE  EZRA  ERATO
OKLA  NYNY  DOPEY
```

22

```
ATEST  SOHO  DCON
CENTS  ELAN  EIRE
SAVEAFTERREBATE
  AROO  TERR
SLAM  RFK  DEIMOS
TIMEOFFER  SEINE
AMERCE  EOE  FLEX
MIR  TIEPINS  EFT
ITIS  TBS  CURARE
NEGEV  BUYONEGET
ADONIS  PAD  CEES
  EVEN  WEAR
NOTSOLDINSTORES
ASEC  EAVE  NOONE
YULE  SKED  OMEGA
```

23

```
AWARDS  COMP  CCS
POTION  OBOE  ARE
ROADWARRIOR  MEN
 ENTER  TENETS
USSR  CDIV  ERIE
MAL  RHODEISLAND
PRIMA  ATOMS
SIDECAR  SNOOKER
 RENEW  KNAVE
ROWEDASHORE  TEN
ORAL  TINA  CENT
TANYAS  TESLA
TNT  RODESHOTGUN
EGO  CYAN  ESTATE
DEN  HAMS  STYLED
```

24

```
VICES  CASAS  BAT
ECLAT  HIPPO  EPA
TEETOTALLER  DAB
 RIPER  ARTDECO
LOIN  EGOS  ECHO
ARC  ONEWHOTAKES
SCARF  LEARN
SALUTED  STANDBY
 BESOS  CAIRO
INVENTORYAT  SAY
NEIN  RIEL  OCTO
TWOSTEP  NERVE
ATL  AGOLFCOURSE
COE  PASEO  ULNAR
TNT  ENTER  TESLA
```

25

```
H B O . G A L A S . R E S I N
A R C . A B O R C . A R I S E
W I T . B O B B Y K N I G H T
S L A L O M . . T O U C H .
E L V I N B I S H O P . T O E
R O E G . . S T E . S G T S
. . . H A S T E . S W E A T S
. . S T E P H E N K I N G .
C H E E S Y . P O I N T .
B O A R . . P L O . O R C A
S E T . E L L E R Y Q U E E N
. . B O G I E . A U T U M N
I R E N E C A S T L E . S E A
M U L E S . S P A T S . E N L
P E T I T . E F L A T . D T S
```

26

```
B E B O P . G A R B O . B L T
I R A N I . I D E A L . R U R
B E D A N D B O A R D . A C E
. . H U E S . . T A C K Y
B A B O O N S . S M I L E Y S
O T O O L E . R H U M B A .
A T O N E . L E A S E . N A T
R A M A . V O I D S . E D N A
S R A . F O G G Y . U N B O X
. N O R T O N . I N C I S E
C A D D I E S . P S A L T E R
R U B E S . A L I I . .
E D U . B O R N A N D B R E D
S I S . E J E C T . E M O T E
T E T . E S T E E . D W E E B
```

27

```
P A S A . G E R A L D . C H E
A L O T . O U N C E S . L E X
B I L L Y G R A H A M . O R A
L O V E M E . S E R . I C B M
O N E A C T S . S N A C K .
. . S A T I E . S L E W E D
T A C T . E L M O . A S I D E
H E R . C R A C K E R . S I N
A R O L L . S E R A . G E T S
N O S O A P . E A S E L .
. . S O D O I . S T R A S S E
R A F T . L C D . S A S H A Y
A L I . P L A Y S I T S A F E
C A R . R E R E A D . E W E R
E S E . O N E D G E . S L R S
```

28

```
N O V . B I O T A . S O A P Y
E R A . I D I O M . T O M E I
Z E N . B A L L O O N P A R K
. . D C L . S E E N . D D E
O N E H I T . B U L B O U S
W A L L O O N P A P E R .
S T L O . D E I . V I S A
. C A R T O O N W R I G H T
H S I A . T O A . I A T E
. D R A G O O N S T R I P
S W E E P E R . D E T E C T
O H M . R U S H . N E W .
L A M P O O N P O S T . I Q S
O M A H A . G A M E R . T O N
N O S I R . E N E M Y . H M O
```

29

```
C P A S . R I S K S . O S H A
D E F T . O S H E A . L U I S
R A R A . L E O N I . A R E S
O N E L I F E T O L I V E .
M U S E D . . B O N . F I B
. T H R E E B L I N D M I C E
. . A M M O . O A R E D
S O D S . S W O R E . T E S S
O D I U M . . P A L S .
F I V E E A S Y P I E C E S
A N I . R N A . A L L O R
. S E V E N Y E A R I T C H
S H I V . M E A T S . P O K Y
P A V E . I S L E S . O R E M
A M E N . A T E S T . N O T E
```

30

```
F I L E . M O L E . G A M U T
A R I D . S P A M . A B A S E
C O N G O G A M E . R A N U P
E N T E R . L A R V A . G A I
. . S A S S . A G E O L D
R E T I N A . C A M E T O .
S L A N G Y . A M P . A F R O
V I N . E G O M A I L . G A P
P E G S . R Y E . R E M O T E
. O N C A L L . E V A D E D
B E L L O C . . I S A K .
A R I . L E A R N . N E R T S
C I N C O . G O B E T W E E N
O C E A N . A M E N . A B R A
N A S T Y . R E D S . R A M P
```

31

```
YEWS ■ CLAW ■ REGAL
ACHE ■ OATH ■ ALINE
WHATISHOO ■ MCRAE
NOT ■ MITZI ■ JILTS
■ ■ IRANI ■ SLED ■ ■
ALSACE ■ CHAT ■ WAS
PAWNS ■ WOODS ■ HOT
HIED ■ SHOWS ■ CARE
INN ■ AWAKE ■ GOTTA
DEN ■ LATE ■ SAMIAM
■ ■ ZITI ■ MAZES ■
PIZZA ■ SCALE ■ WEE
ABUTS ■ WHOISWATT
CANOE ■ YARN ■ ARON
TRIPS ■ ERIE ■ XENA
```

32

```
EDNA ■ BAAS ■ SMELL
GRIT ■ UCLA ■ TALIA
GALE ■ GRAM ■ ALLEY
■ WEATHERBUREAU
■ ■ MAO ■ AMT ■
LIU ■ RUTH ■ PRAISE
ERSE ■ SEER ■ EIDER
HEATHERLOCKLEAR
ANITA ■ MESH ■ SATE
RERUNS ■ NEAR ■ LSD
■ DCC ■ REA ■
■ LEATHERJACKET
SAYSO ■ LAUD ■ IRAQ
ONETO ■ LINE ■ TILE
PEDAL ■ ODES ■ ACED
```

33

```
RABAT ■ GOSH ■ TBSP
IMACS ■ ENTO ■ RATA
BANTU ■ NEAR ■ ORES
■ INDIANAJONES
ATH ■ AYE ■ TUPELO
TRAUMA ■ LAID ■ YEN
VIRGINIAWOOLF ■
SOUL ■ MPH ■ IRIS
■ MINNESOTAFATS
IRS ■ IATE ■ ARENOT
NICELY ■ CRT ■ KOS
STATESPEOPLE ■
AURA ■ ALER ■ ERUPT
NAUT ■ YELP ■ SINAI
ELMS ■ SASS ■ SKILL
```

34

```
SWAN ■ EBAY ■ GETUP
WADE ■ IRMA ■ OPART
ALDA ■ FAIR ■ DOLLS
PETRIFIEDROCK ■
■ SOBBED ■ ETHICS
■ EEL ■ WAH ■ SNIT
SORER ■ MYNAS ■ GTO
CLARIFIEDBUTTER
ALI ■ AUNTY ■ BRODY
MISS ■ NTH ■ STA ■
PEEPED ■ DELPHI
■ CLASSIFIEDADS
CRAIG ■ OWLS ■ OREO
ONICE ■ SIAM ■ OPAL
SANER ■ ANTS ■ ROLE
```

35

```
EMMA ■ ROTOR ■ PAL
LOINS ■ EVADE ■ ELI
CUTTHECARDS ■ ROE
INTERVAL ■ EASED
DDS ■ OIL ■ SPACE ■
■ PULLTHELEVER
SCALD ■ HERS ■ EMU
EASY ■ CARAT ■ ARID
AMS ■ SOLE ■ PIETY
SPINTHEWHEEL ■
■ SEINE ■ UTE ■ NAT
LITER ■ INCREASE
ADA ■ ROLLTHEDICE
MEN ■ ERASE ■ DEVON
BAT ■ DEBAR ■ NETS
```

36

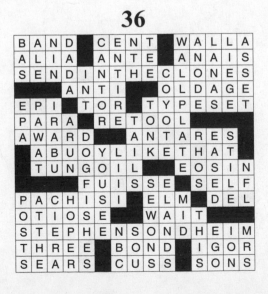

```
BAND ■ CENT ■ WALLA
ALIA ■ ANTE ■ ANAIS
SENDINTHECLONES
■ ANTI ■ OLDAGE
EPI ■ TOR ■ TYPESET
PARA ■ RETOOL ■
AWARD ■ ANTARES
■ ABUOYLIKETHAT
TUNGOIL ■ EOSIN
■ FUISSE ■ SELF
PACHISI ■ ELM ■ DEL
OTIOSE ■ WAIT ■
STEPHENSONDHEIM
THREE ■ BOND ■ IGOR
SEARS ■ CUSS ■ SONS
```

37

```
S A D A . A N I L . L O W L Y
T R I S . Z E N O . E L I T E
I A N S . T O N Y A W A R D S .
G R E A S E . . O V I N E . .
M A R I A C A L L A S . H A L
A T O L L . M I A . . R A R E
. . . U P O N . E S K I M O
. W E S T S I D E S T O R Y .
B A S K E T . S R T A . . . .
E L O I . S A G . L E R O I
G E T . N E W Y O R K J E T S
. E M O T E . . U S E N E T
C A R D S H A R K S . C O L L
A R I S E . T I E S . T I L E
D I C E D . Y O Y O . S R O S
```

38

```
F E T E . A F A R . D A C H A
A C R E . N A S A . E T H A N
T H E G O O D S H E P H E R D
S O X . D I E T . Q U O T E S
. . . V E N D . C U T S . .
P A L E S T . G R A Y . C H E
A C E R S . U R A L . W H O A
T H E B A D N E W S B E A R S
T E C S . R I A L . L E O N E
I S H . M I T T . L A P S E D
. . . P A V E . H A Z Y . .
O C T A N E . J U T E . I C K
T H E U G L Y A M E R I C A N
T E R S E . A V O N . D O M O
O W N E R . M A R T . A N E W
```

39

```
C A S H . S A T I N Y . T E A
O B O E . A T O N C E . A R T
D E M I . L O O K A L I K E S
. . B R E A M . A P I E C E
F I R . S M I T E . I O T A
I D E N T I C A L T W I N S .
T E R I . . N I N A . . . .
. D O P P E L G A N G E R S .
. . I D E E . . V E T S
. S P I T T I N G I M A G E S
S P U D . S T O R E . U T E
A R M O R S . V I T A L .
D U P L I C A T E S . S A T E
A C E . G A L O R E . I R A S
T E D . S T E R N S . A S P S
```

40

```
P S I . A C I D . T H E L M A
O W N . L A Z E . H A V E A T
R E D . S L O B . U N E A S E
T R E E O F D I A M O N D S .
E V E R . . R B I . P E A
R E P A S T . S R S . M I N I
. . . P E A L E . C A P E R
. N O T A T R U S T R E E T
N I K O N . M E T O O . . .
O N L Y . G A S . T W I L L S
D E A . S I N . . N O O N
. T H E T R I L L I S G O N E
M E O W E D . E A S T . P G A
R E M O V E . N I L E . E E K
S N A K E D . D R E W . D R Y
```

41

```
A B B E . Z E A L . . A J A R
T R A X . A D L A I . D E C O
W A S H I N G T O N . A F R O
A V I A R I E S . K N I F E D
R E S U M E S . A W I R E .
. . S A S . P R E V . R E Q
B E R T . E A G L E . S T U
L O O . L I N C O L N . O R E
U N O . A T T E N . O N E S
E S S . U S E S . Y M A
. E R R O R . B E A R C A T
V I V I A N . B O A T S H O W
A P E D . M T R U S H M O R E
I S L E . E V E N T . A R T E
L O T S . A D D S . N E A T
```

42

```
H A V E N S . S E C . S K I D
I D I D I T . T R Y . K E N O
M A R T H A D A N D R I D G E
O N T . R U R . A P S E S
M O U N T V E R N O N . . .
. I R E . O M I C R O N
A M I G O . L O R N . R I P E
V I R G I N I A M I L I T I A
E L A L . A B R A . E S T E R
R O S E L L E . M A T
. V A L L E Y F O R G E
A L I B I . I A N . A O L
C O N T I N E N T A L A R M Y
E R L E . B A T . H A B E A S
D E A N . C R Y . S T E R N E
```

43

```
M E D A L . U S E R . P O C O
A D O R E . R A V E . O V A L
C U P I D C A K E S . S E N D
A C E . O O N A . . D E N S E
W E S . F L U I D S E A S O N
. H A F T S . E E L S . . . .
O N E S . . A M A H . P I A .
F R E U D I A N S L I P I N S
F A T . O R G Y . . . I N C H
. A R O O . A P S E S . . . .
S L I D I N G S H O T . T V A
T U N I C . A C N E . R E L .
E G A D . H I G H D I V I D E
N A N A . E R G O . N I P A T
O R E S . M A Y O . S E E Y A
```

44

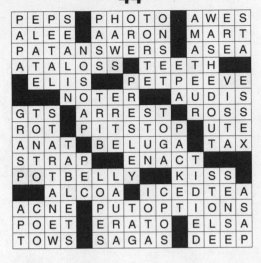

```
P E P S . P H O T O . A W E S
A L E E . A A R O N . M A R T
P A T A N S W E R S . A S E A
A T A L O S S . T E E T H . .
. E L I S . . P E T P E E V E
. . N O T E R . . A U D I S .
G T S . A R R E S T . R O S S
R O T . P I T S T O P . U T E
A N A T . B E L U G A . T A X
S T R A P . E N A C T . . . .
P O T B E L L Y . K I S S . .
. A L C O A . I C E D T E A .
A C N E . P U T O P T I O N S
P O E T . E R A T O . E L S A
T O W S . S A G A S . D E E P
```

45

```
M A Y E R . H A H A . C A L M
I R E N E . A B E T . O L I O
S C A R E D Y C A T . A S E A
S H R O V E . S T A R T O U T
. . L E C H . S C O T . . . .
L E O . S L O P . K O A L A S
A T M . A R E A . M I A T A .
T H E C O W A R D L Y L I O N
T E N O R . S O L E . N N E .
E R S A T Z . N A S H . E E R
. S H I P . I T I S . . . . .
I S O T O P E S . E N C O D E
B A L I . P A P E R T I G E R
E V E N . E C C E . A F L E A
G E O G . R E A L . T I E R S
```

46

```
M A L L . B L E S T . O N K P
O V A L . A O L E R . N A L A
C O M B . H O K E Y P O K E Y
S W E E T . M E N S A . E I N
. . . A A A . . T R U D G E .
C L I N K G L A S S E S . . .
A I T . E I E I O . E S M E .
P E R S O N A L I Z E D P E N
N U Y S . R E L O G . A R G .
. . G R A N D S L A M M E R .
B U S T U P . A D O . . . . .
I B M . S L E E T . S N A P E
J O I N T O W N E R . I R O N
O L L A . M E T R O . C A R Y
U T E P . B R O N C . A T T A
```

47

```
G A Z E . S C A P E . S L O W
I G E T . H A B I T . P A S O
B R I C . A M A N A . O C H O
B A T H S H E B A . K N E E L
. . . A S T . F L A G D A Y .
P A T T Y . O T O O L E . . .
A U G U S T . A R R . C E N T
C R I B . O C H E R . A M A H
T A F T . R O O . E S K I M O
. . H A M L E T . H E L E N .
R E F U G E E . E S O . . . .
A R O M A . S O A P O P E R A
G A R P . U L T R A . A T A D
E T T E . S A T E D . G A Z A
D O E R . S W O R E . E L E M
```

48

```
M A T T . S T E A L . S A I L
A R I A . T E S L A . E T T U
D E E R . I N T E L . N E A L
. . S T I L L E R A N D A L L
S L O . N E B . L O A M Y . .
M I N C E S . S W A N K . . .
A T E U P . D E A N . . G A S
S H O R T E R A N D S W E E T
H E N . G I L D . P A T S Y .
. . L O O P Y . P I S T O N .
. G I A N T . E O N . O P E .
H U N T E R A N D P E C K . .
A I D E . I M A G E . U N I T
U S E S . P E T E Y . T O R O
T E X T . S N O R E . S W A P
```

49

```
A S A I R   A C L U   T W A S
G U I D O   R A I N   E A T A
F I R E S I G N T H E A T R E
A T F   S K U A   E A S E I N
    O K I E S   C A M E R A S
F A R I N A   D O T E L L
L A C T I   C A R E S   O W L
A R E S   O A R E D   S O I E
P E R   A P S I S   B O S S A
    E R R A T A   D U S T E R
A S S A I L S   S A M O A
T H E N C E   N E R D   T S U
E A R T H S H A T T E R I N G
I D V E   C O P T   A B O I L
N E E R   E S S O   L I N T Y
```

50

```
A L E C   A C T U P   A D A M
T E R I   M O U S E   V I B E
N O T T O B E B E L I E V E D
O V E R R I D E   L A R V A E
    I C E   D E M   Y M A
H O W C A N T H A T B E
A P E   S C R A P   S T E A K
L E S S   E A R P S   C A T O
O N T A P   D E L T A   S R O
    G I V E M E A B R E A K
S T A   Q E D   R N A
A R M O U R   S E L E C T E E
Y O U R E N O T S E R I O U S
S O S A   A V A S T   N O R A
O P E L   L A G O S   E N O S
```

51

```
P A T S   M E C C A   S H U E
A C R E   A T A R I   K A R L
S H E R Y L C R O W   E R I E
T E A P O T   N A M E T A G
A D D E D   U N E   I T C H Y
    N A C H O S   S E R
P O E T   L O O   S T R A F E
R I D   J O H N J A Y   N O R
O L D H A T   D U N   S E E R
    Y O N   B A N G L E
C A R T E   E Y E   E A S Y A
I N A S T I R   F A M O U S
G I V E   P E T E R F I N C H
A S E A   S T A L E   L A C E
R E N T   O S S I E   E R A S
```

52

```
T E A C U P   E T D   E R R S
E R R O L L   S E E   N E E T
S I R I C A   A S S   A F A R
    A R E Y O U S I N C E R E
L A Y   R A T   A T R E E
E Y E C A T C H I N G   E N T
E N D A T   O O O   M E D S
    S E A C R U I S E
D U K E   J O N   U R G E D
R N A   K A Y E B A L L A R D
O S T E O   E L L   S A S
W H Y N O T T H E B E S T
N A D A   R I A   E N U R E S
E D I T   A N T   R E F I L L
D E D E   M T S   T R I C K Y
```

53

```
S E P I A   S H O D   M A I L
A G E N T   H O U R   A C N E
T O R S O   A P S E   G A T E
    O N E H I T W O N D E R
P R O F E S S   Z A I R E
R E P A S T   M A N O   A N D
Y E A R   P A C I N O
    F L A S H I N T H E P A N
    S H A P E S   E R A T
T A U   I M E T   F I N A L S
A S T O R   L A S T L A P
S H O O T I N G S T A R
S O P H   T A R A   B A R R E
E R I E   E M I T   E D U C E
L E A D   M E N S   L E G A L
```

54

```
A S H   E D G E D   B E I N G
B O O   L O R R E   A M T O O
S N L   S W E E N E Y T O D D
C O M P A N Y   I R E
A M E R   I M A R O U N D
M A S O N J A R   A L O E
    T O N K A S   T E T E
S T E P H E N S O N D H E I M
H O A R   S O O N E R
I T S O   M E E T W I T H
N O T W H I L E   A C R O
    E L I   F O L L I E S
I M S T I L L H E R E   N A T
R E C O N   T I T A N   G T E
A L I V E   S M E L T   S Y D
```

55

```
CACTI  MANDM  GAP
UBOAT  ALONE  EMU
BEETSAMPRAS  NET
   SOLES   SPENT
BOO PAT MAKESDO
ANKLES  ZENITH
SIREN  MOTET  AMA
ICAN  SINEW  SLAB
LEW  HATER  JULIA
   IMAGES  CANONS
FUNNIES  MAY  TEE
INFOR   FAILS
FIR  PAULINEKALE
ETE  IRKED  NIGEL
REY  NEEDS  ONEAL
```

56

```
ACTS  STRATA  SAW
COAT  PEALED  URI
HOPEDIAMOND  PIN
ELEVEN  USURPED
   ELATED  CHESS
ADD  PLOY  SEER
QUASH  PESO  SCAB
UNVEILS  INDULGE
AKIN  OYEZ  USUAL
   DART  WEAL  BRA
CASTE  FESSUP
APPEASE  STINGS
IRA  PURPLEHEART
RID  ERASES  CIAO
OLE  RELIES  ELBA
```

57

```
GAPED  WATTS  HON
ABACI  IDAHO  APE
SELLSOLDIER  VEX
   ANDES  DECENT
RELIED  BASEHIT
HAIRY  BRA  PLATO
ERGS  FOOTHOLD
ASH  POTSHOT  DNA
   TOUGHIES  COUP
SPLAT  END  GECKO
TRISTAR  BONKED
RETTON  AGENT
OFT  SITSATURDAY
DEE  EMITS  TAUPE
ERR  AESOP  SLOTS
```

58

```
MACAW  SKIM  SASS
OMANI  TILE  TRIP
DORAG  UNIT  EERO
   WEDGEEARNER
TARTAR   FEAST
ALARMED  OHIO
SORE  REFER  APE
THEEDGEOFREASON
EAR  INANE  LIST
   LAUD  DECODER
APIAN   SHEEDY
SEDGEADVICE
TALE  JOIN  WATER
ICER  AROD  EXILE
REDS  RELY  DENIM
```

59

```
CHIEF  COLA  CASH
RODEO  ALAR  LIPO
ALLEN  REST  OSLO
BYE  DEPOSITSLIP
   SURE   SHEETS
TEETERTOTTER
YIKES  FORE  NAB
PREP  DITTY  AONE
OED  RIDE  UNITE
   BUSINESSTRIP
PEORIA   NOES
URBANSPRAWL  REF
TOOK  TEAM  EVITA
IDEE  ETTE  SAGAL
NESS  REEL  STALL
```

60

```
FROG  BLOB  VADIS
LIMO  ROMA  IWONT
ACNE  OBIT  NEWER
THISINSTANT  NRA
   ANC  AAA  STY
THATGOODNIGHT
REL  ESAI  LEHRER
IRES  STA  HEDY
BOXCAR  CLIO  ANA
   THEOTHERWOMAN
PAR  ROO  OED
ODE  ODDSANDENDS
BABES  AHSO  SEEM
ONENO  TUTU  SAFE
YOKEL  ETAT  ARTE
```

61

J	I	M	S	■	Y	A	K	S	■	S	C	A	N	T
I	D	E	A	■	O	R	E	O	■	H	A	T	E	R
B	O	D	Y	G	U	A	R	D	■	E	S	S	A	Y
E	L	S	I	E	■	L	A	D	E	■	H	E	R	S
■	■	■	N	R	A	■	T	E	L	E	C	A	S	T
B	I	N	G	E	D	R	I	N	K	E	R	■	■	■
O	L	E	■	■	Z	E	N	■	■	L	O	F	T	S
M	I	S	D	E	E	D	■	R	E	S	P	I	R	E
B	A	S	I	C	■	■	T	I	C	■	S	U	E	■
■	■	P	H	O	T	O	G	R	A	P	H	E	R	■
B	O	W	L	O	V	E	R	■	U	S	A	■	■	■
O	L	E	O	■	A	N	N	A	■	I	R	O	N	S
A	D	A	M	S	■	T	A	K	E	A	S	H	O	T
S	I	N	A	I	■	E	D	I	E	■	E	I	R	E
T	E	S	T	S	■	D	O	N	E	■	C	O	A	T

62

B	A	A	L	■	R	A	S	H	■	F	L	O	E	S
E	D	G	Y	■	A	D	A	M	■	L	A	U	R	A
A	M	I	N	■	B	O	L	O	■	A	S	T	R	O
M	I	L	D	A	B	R	A	S	I	V	E	■	■	■
S	T	E	A	D	I	E	S	■	N	O	R	M	A	N
■	■	■	I	T	S	■	H	E	R	■	A	L	E	■
A	B	B	I	E	■	■	G	A	P	■	A	V	O	W
G	R	A	D	U	A	T	E	S	T	U	D	E	N	T
L	I	L	O	■	M	U	M	■	■	P	A	N	G	S
O	D	S	■	D	O	G	■	C	O	S	■	■	■	■
W	E	A	P	O	N	■	C	A	R	E	S	S	E	S
■	■	A	N	G	R	Y	P	A	T	I	E	N	T	■
S	P	A	R	K	■	U	N	I	T	■	M	E	T	E
A	L	I	K	E	■	T	I	T	O	■	O	M	E	N
T	O	D	A	Y	■	S	C	A	R	■	N	E	R	O

63

F	R	O	T	H	■	E	D	N	A	■	A	S	T	O
R	O	D	E	O	■	V	E	A	L	■	S	T	I	R
I	M	E	A	N	■	E	E	R	O	■	P	A	N	T
■	P	A	R	D	O	N	M	Y	F	R	E	N	C	H
■	■	■	D	A	H	L	■	■	T	E	N	D	T	O
A	M	O	R	■	D	Y	E	D	■	N	S	A	■	■
R	E	P	O	S	E	■	R	O	U	E	■	S	A	P
U	S	E	P	L	A	I	N	E	N	G	L	I	S	H
T	A	N	■	U	R	L	S	■	H	E	E	D	E	D
■	■	S	A	M	■	O	T	T	O	■	T	E	A	S
S	T	E	P	P	E	■	■	W	O	O	L	■	■	■
T	H	A	T	S	G	R	E	E	K	T	O	M	E	■
E	A	S	E	■	B	A	R	R	■	T	O	U	R	S
E	N	O	S	■	D	R	I	P	■	E	S	S	A	Y
R	E	N	T	■	F	E	E	S	■	R	E	S	T	S

64

L	E	A	P	S	■	J	I	M	I	■	K	A	R	T
A	S	C	A	P	■	I	D	E	S	■	I	G	O	R
B	A	R	R	I	E	H	E	R	O	■	T	R	A	Y
S	U	E	■	G	R	A	M	■	P	A	C	E	R	S
■	■	L	O	A	D	■	P	O	S	H	E	S	T	■
S	A	B	O	T	S	■	S	A	D	I	E	■	■	■
O	M	O	O	■	E	S	P	Y	■	G	N	O	M	E
B	A	C	K	S	■	P	A	N	■	N	I	V	E	N
S	H	A	F	T	■	R	Y	E	S	■	T	A	U	T
■	■	O	O	Z	E	S	■	P	H	E	L	P	S	■
C	H	A	R	L	I	E	■	S	E	A	M	■	■	■
L	A	R	G	E	R	■	S	E	A	R	■	T	I	S
I	N	T	O	■	C	A	M	E	R	A	S	H	O	T
F	O	I	L	■	O	V	U	M	■	S	E	R	T	A
T	I	E	D	■	N	A	T	E	■	S	Q	U	A	B

65

A	G	N	E	W	■	A	F	A	R	■	T	E	S	T
C	R	I	E	R	■	D	I	R	E	■	A	T	M	O
T	A	K	E	I	T	O	N	T	H	E	C	H	I	N
S	S	E	■	T	O	B	E	■	E	S	T	A	T	E
■	■	S	E	R	E	■	P	A	T	■	N	E	D	■
L	I	S	T	O	N	■	B	A	R	E	S	■	■	■
A	G	E	O	F	■	W	E	T	S	■	T	H	I	S
D	O	W	N	F	O	R	T	H	E	C	O	U	N	T
E	R	N	E	■	V	E	T	O	■	A	R	E	N	A
■	■	S	C	E	N	E	■	D	R	E	S	S	Y	■
O	N	E	■	H	R	S	■	M	A	P	S	■	■	■
T	E	N	D	E	R	■	E	A	V	E	■	S	T	E
T	H	R	O	W	I	N	T	H	E	T	O	W	E	L
E	R	O	S	■	D	O	T	E	■	E	V	A	N	S
R	U	N	E	■	E	V	E	R	■	D	A	N	T	E

66

C	A	B	L	E	■	B	A	B	A	R	■	B	R	A
A	L	I	E	N	■	S	I	E	V	E	■	R	A	H
R	E	D	S	Q	U	I	R	R	E	L	■	O	J	O
O	R	O	T	U	N	D	■	T	R	A	M	W	A	Y
M	T	N	■	I	T	E	M	■	S	P	I	N	■	■
■	■	F	R	O	■	A	M	I	■	A	B	E	T	■
A	M	B	L	E	■	C	I	A	O	■	S	E	R	E
C	O	L	O	R	F	U	L	A	N	I	M	A	L	S
C	P	U	S	■	R	E	B	S	■	M	I	R	E	S
T	E	E	S	■	E	R	A	■	A	M	C	■	■	■
■	■	W	I	R	E	■	G	O	G	O	■	R	D	A
R	E	H	E	E	L	S	■	D	I	D	G	O	O	D
I	R	A	■	G	O	L	D	E	N	E	A	G	L	E
T	I	L	■	A	V	A	I	L	■	S	T	E	E	L
Z	E	E	■	L	E	V	E	L	■	T	E	R	S	E

67

```
V I A L S   ■   S H U N   ■   I M P S
I D I O T   ■   A E R O   ■   D U E T
M O R T O N S A L T   ■   O T T O
■   ■   T O A S T   ■   F I L T E R
H A H   ■   D R Y   ■   P U B   ■   O R E
A R A B I C   ■   B E N I G N   ■
R E R A N   ■   B O O N D O C K S
E S P N   ■   C A N N Y   ■   W H O M
M O O N W A L K S   ■   S N O R E
■   O S I R I S   ■   D I S P E L
N O N   ■   L E N   ■   B O G   ■   S A L
E N G U L F   ■   G O I N G   ■
P I U S   ■   R A Y O N F I B E R
A C N E   ■   E L M S   ■   O L I V E
L E S S   ■   E A S T   ■   R A Z E D
```

68

```
G A R P   ■   M E L B A   ■   E A R L
I C E R   ■   I D E A S   ■   A R I A
R U N E   ■   M E D I C   ■   R A M P
D R E S S I N G R O O M   ■
S A W T O   ■   E N T R A N C E
■   O A F S   ■   B R A Y S
A C T   ■   P O O D L E S K I R T
P R E P   ■   A F O O T   ■   S L U E
T O A S T M A S T E R   ■   S S E
T O K Y O   ■   I S O F   ■
O N S C R E E N   ■   I R E S T
■   H O R N O F P L E N T Y
G O B I   ■   R U L E R   ■   N O O K
E X E C   ■   E R A S E   ■   C L U E
E Y E S   ■   D E N T S   ■   H A T S
```

69

```
H E E L   ■   I B E A M   ■   A T M S
E S A I   ■   L Y N D E   ■   P E E P
S Q U A R E R O O T   ■   O R N O
■   ■   R O T O   ■   A F L C I O
E A R L Y   ■   T A B L E L E A F
E R E I   ■   H E I R   ■   D O L L S
N O B A K E   ■   R E N O   ■
■   W A R D R O B E T R U N K
■   L O C A   ■   W A N I N G
T A N Y A   ■   A S S T   ■   D A I S
B R A I N S T E M   ■   M E S T A
O R T E G A   ■   O M A R   ■
N A T L   ■   B A N K B R A N C H
D Y E D   ■   E N N E A   ■   G O R E
S S R S   ■   R E E D S   ■   E R T E
```

70

```
A S P I C   ■   O M E N   ■   S A C K
P E A C H   ■   L O L A   ■   O G R E
R A T I O   ■   D A I S   ■   S L A Y
■   T H E R E S N O S N O O Z E
■   R U D E   ■   T A O   ■   W E D
E R A   ■   S W A B   ■   U R N   ■
B O N E   ■   I D O L   ■   M E A T Y
B U T T O N O N A C A T W H O
S T I N G   ■   G U S H   ■   S E E K
■   A L A   ■   S T E W   ■   D Y E
A T E   ■   E L F   ■   T E A M   ■
W A N T S B R E A K F A S T   ■
A U T O   ■   E A R N   ■   F R U I T
S P E D   ■   D I N G   ■   L I N D A
H E R O   ■   O L E O   ■   E A G E R
```

71

```
I S L E T   ■   T R I A L   ■   F O G
R H I N O   ■   H A N O I   ■   E V A
K I N D O F R I F L E   ■   E A R
E R G   ■   K R O N E   ■   A L L Y
D E O   ■   T A W   ■   R O A R S   ■
■   C O U R T S U M M O N S
B A S H   ■   D U O   ■   R O B R O Y
M E T E S   ■   G N P   ■   K A R E N
O R I E N T   ■   E R S   ■   N Y S E
C O R R O B O R A T E D   ■
■   C U B A N   ■   T A P   ■   B U S
W A R P   ■   L O T T O   ■   O N E
E T A   ■   T R I P L E C R O W N
B I Z   ■   R A N E E   ■   H A Z E D
S T Y   ■   A M E N D   ■   S H E D S
```

72

```
A L O H A   ■   R A C E R   ■   S Y D
W I D O W   ■   E D D I E   ■   H O E
N E E D L E P O I N T   ■   E S S
I N S   ■   S T E P   ■   A P R E S
N O S E   ■   D A T I N G G A M E
G R A S P   ■   L E N O   ■   S T I R
■   P U P   ■   E C O L   ■   O T T
■   T E N N I S   ■   A N Y O N E
S E X   ■   T A C O   ■   E L M   ■
P A P A   ■   N A B S   ■   E I D E R
E R E C T O R S E T   ■   T A X I
C I R C A   ■   C A R T   ■   L A C
I N T   ■   S A F E T Y M A T C H
A T L   ■   K L I N E   ■   E M O T E
L O Y   ■   S I X E D   ■   N I N A S
```

73

```
PAPA . TREE . MAIL
EPICS . ROSY . EINE
THEHOLYSEE . DOSE
TIRELESS . . OILER
YDS . VATICANCITY
. . . BED . . RUE
ACNE . . EHUDBARAK
POPEBENEDICTXVI
BERTLANCE . . ASAP
. . . ORU . MUD
HISHOLINESS . COQ
ONTOP . . ONREPORT
ADAM . JOHNPAULII
RILE . ERIE . SCOOP
DALY . BETA . ERNS
```

74

```
FSTOP . OTTER . SIG
OHARA . CHINO . HOR
POLARICECAP . ONE
SPECTRUM . BIGWIG
. . . LIAR . FLEABAG
LLBEAN . SEESTO .
OIL . LITER . TEARS
ONUS . SONAR . STOW
TEETH . ADLIB . EVA
. BOARDS . FLORET
SNOOZES . ALOU .
PANDAS . EVENTUAL
RMN . ROLLERDERBY
EEE . DREAR . EASEL
EST . STONY . STATE
```

75

```
RIVET . GAGS . SKIP
PRIMO . ULAN . AIME
MARCO . RITA . GNAT
. GETOUTOFDODGE
SHIELD . RUE . EER
HON . EDENS . PURRS
ALII . JAI . STP
HEADFORTHEHILLS
. LIB . TEA . NEAT
ASNER . MYRRH . AKA
GTO . TRY . COPPER
HITTHEHIGHWAY
ANNE . HERA . SUEDE
SKEE . ARID . ALARM
TOWN . BOSS . DARES
```

76

```
MISS . GRAF . LIMO
ACTUP . LULL . ANEW
YOUMACONFUNOFME
ANN . ROVE . OTOES
. ISLE . KATZ .
YOUREAREALBUTTE
AZTEC . STAY . ROM
HAID . OASES . GOTO
ORC . AURA . CRUET
OKAYTROYTOHITME
. ESSO . ABET .
ATIME . STIR . ESE
JUNEAUWHATYADID
ANON . SHIM . LODGE
RANI . HOPI . LYNN
```

77

```
TUBA . PATROL . BOP
ATOP . ERRATA . IDE
LARA . SEASON . GOT
CHECKONCHECKOUT
. HESA . ENTRY
HOMEY . PLATO
ACE . EILEEN . WITS
STANDFORSTANDUP
POLO . FOSSIL . ONE
. THYME . ESSEX
ALAMO . ACCT
TAKEOVERTAKEOFF
BRR . TINIER . WOOL
AGO . ELICIT . EZRA
YEN . REDONE . DEEP
```

78

```
WARD . ADDS . VERGE
AXON . PERT . ODOUL
DISAPPEARINGINK
ESE . LAPTOP . ELSE
. RUR . SPAY . EHS
ABDOMEN . NEEDY
DRIBBLEGLASS
ZASU . HRE . COED
. SQUIRTFLOWER
DATUM . SOARERS
SAP . OISE . RST
APIA . ANDRES . TLC
THEJOKEWASONYOU
UNCAP . AIRE . URGE
PEERS . KNEE . BOOS
```

79

```
S T I L T ▓ T A W S ▓ A T O Z
T O N T O ▓ A T O P ▓ T A L E
E X T R A E X T R A ▓ A X I S
M I R ▓ S L I N K ▓ B R E N T
S C O T T I E ▓ R E M I X ▓ ▓
▓ ▓ R E D D F O X X ▓ E E E
I N J U R E ▓ E O E ▓ C M D R
H E A D S ▓ A D M ▓ T A P I N
O H M Y ▓ I C E ▓ S E N T T O
P I E ▓ P R I X F I X E ▓ ▓
▓ ▓ S T R A D ▓ O N A D A T E
O R F E O ▓ C O R E S ▓ M E R
B E I N ▓ X E R O X T O N E R
I N X S ▓ K L A N ▓ E C O N O
S A X E ▓ E L L E ▓ A T T A R
```

80

```
C I G A R ▓ A L A M O ▓ T R A
E C O L E ▓ B E B O P ▓ W I Z
D O U B L E A G E N T ▓ I C U
E N T A I L S ▓ S K I N N E R
▓ ▓ E L E C ▓ M E E S E
E N D I V E ▓ O B T A I N ▓
S E E M E ▓ S A R A ▓ T G I F
S O U P ▓ F A X E D ▓ H I R E
O N C E ▓ B L E D ▓ P E N A L
▓ E D G I E R ▓ R E R E N T
A T S E A ▓ S E E R ▓ ▓
D O W D I E R ▓ D E F T E S T
A L I ▓ T A B L E F O R T W O
G E L ▓ E V I A N ▓ R E R A N
E T D ▓ R E S T S ▓ M E E T S
```

81

```
D A F T ▓ S H A R K ▓ T K T S
A C R E ▓ N O W A Y ▓ R A R A
W H E N H E L L F R E E Z E S
N Y T I M E S ▓ T A X B A S E
▓ ▓ N O R T H ▓ C L A S S
S I L O S ▓ O S S I E ▓ ▓
P A I N ▓ E S T O P S ▓ W H O
O N C E I N A B L U E M O O N
T S K ▓ G O N E O N ▓ A L O E
▓ ▓ B O W E D ▓ R I F F S
L A P A T ▓ S P A I N ▓ ▓
E M E R I T A ▓ R U M M A G E
T W E N T Y F O U R S E V E N
H A V E ▓ P A N D A ▓ N E R D
E Y E S ▓ E R T E S ▓ U S E S
```

82

```
R E A P ▓ S T I R ▓ C A S E Y
E L M S ▓ P A N E ▓ A L I V E
B E E F P A T T Y ▓ L I N E N
O A R ▓ E R I E ▓ O L G A ▓
U N I T E S ▓ L E M O N T E A
N O N U K E S ▓ V A N ▓ R E P
D R D R E ▓ E D E N ▓ C A K E
▓ ▓ F R I E D R I C E ▓ ▓
D U O S ▓ M Y S T ▓ A R G O T
E A P ▓ S A O ▓ S O M E O N E
F R U I T C U P ▓ R E S E A L
▓ L O I S ▓ H E A T ▓ S T L
A G E N T ▓ H O T C O F F E E
M A N I C ▓ E T A L ▓ R O A R
P I T C H ▓ P O S E ▓ A R R S
```

83

```
A B Y S S ▓ S O D ▓ A L G A
S O O T H E ▓ U N O ▓ V I E D
P I G O U T ▓ D U C K I N T O
S L A P ▓ H I S S ▓ N A D I R
▓ ▓ S P E C ▓ A E R A T E
S Q U I R R E L A W A Y ▓ ▓
P U R G E ▓ R I L E D ▓ Z I G
R A I N ▓ F I E L D ▓ E U R O
Y D S ▓ B I N G E ▓ I G L O O
▓ ▓ M O N K E Y A R O U N D
A S P I R E ▓ E D A M ▓ ▓
T H E S E ▓ W I S E ▓ A G R A
W O L F D O W N ▓ P O N Y U P
A N T I ▓ P I N ▓ T R I P L E
R E S T ▓ T I S ▓ B A S E S
```

84

```
I C B M ▓ T A M E S T ▓ S A O
M O R E ▓ O P E N T O ▓ T A D
P L A Y A D E L R E Y ▓ A L Y
L O V E T O ▓ R A E ▓ B R A S
I N E R T ▓ T O P L A Y E R S
E E L S ▓ L O S T ▓ S A R G E
S L Y ▓ G A L E ▓ K I N S E Y
▓ ▓ W O R D ▓ P L A Y ▓ ▓
M E L I N A ▓ P E E N ▓ R A G
A L O N E ▓ R E N E ▓ C A R L
N E W O R D E R S ▓ P A T I O
A G E S ▓ A S U ▓ A O R T A S
T A R ▓ C R O S S S W O R D S
E N E ▓ P I L E U P ▓ L A N E
E T D ▓ A N D R E S ▓ S P E D
```

85

```
BULBS ■ AMOF ■ ABCS
APOET ■ DIRE ■ TYRA
HINDI ■ ONCE ■ APIA
■ GENTLEASALAMB
CRACKUP ■ ■ VOTES
LUCKOTHEIRISH ■
AIRS ■ ■ STYES ■
NNE ■ INASTEW ■ PLO
■ CROWE ■ ■ AREA
■ WHERESTHEBEEF
ALAIN ■ ■ USURERS
TAKEAMULLIGAN ■
TREF ■ THAI ■ EDITS
HAUL ■ SUMP ■ NENES
ESPY ■ THES ■ EDGER
```

86

```
CAD ■ NICKEL ■ SRTA
UTE ■ EVONNE ■ HERS
BALLRETURN ■ EMIT
ILIAD ■ ROADRACE
CLAW ■ BELLPEPPER
■ FEEL ■ ERA ■
FRAULEINS ■ ASA
BILLOFATTAINDER
IMP ■ SHOWPIECE
■ SOB ■ LOOP ■
BOLLWEEVIL ■ POSH
AXHANDLE ■ LETHE
LEAN ■ BULLDURHAM
MYST ■ UDDERS ■ EVA
YEAS ■ GETSET ■ REN
```

87

```
SPLAT ■ AMFM ■ GELS
GRECO ■ VIDA ■ ORAL
TEDDYBEARS ■ GALA
■ CEO ■ HOOTAT
RAW ■ DOWNPILLOWS
EZIO ■ BOATED ■
MUSHROOMS ■ PUNCH
ARETOO ■ SAHARA
PESOS ■ ENVELOPES
■ CAREER ■ HEAT
BALLOTBOXES ■ SKY
INASEC ■ NEA ■
ZIMA ■ OVEREATERS
ETAT ■ SOLO ■ LOSER
TASS ■ TWIN ■ YMCAS
```

88

```
TSAR ■ SOLD ■ WATCH
RIME ■ CREE ■ ALEUT
OMEN ■ RIAL ■ STABS
WILDGOOSECHASE ■
ELI ■ RUN ■ GAY ■ PRO
LEANON ■ UAL ■ SOON
■ YOGURT ■ SHOOT
SCAVENGERHUNT
STACY ■ RESEAL ■
HULK ■ LES ■ DRAGON
ENO ■ EEL ■ SSE ■ ORE
■ TRIVIALPURSUIT
AMILE ■ TORI ■ PLOT
SEEIN ■ EDIT ■ CELL
INSET ■ DEGS ■ ATEE
```

89

```
CAPS ■ CEDAR ■ BABA
ALOE ■ ORATE ■ EDAM
SPIT ■ WORLDPEACE
HON ■ PEST ■ HANGON
■ TSAR ■ BOT ■ END
SELTZERWATER ■
OREO ■ DAHL ■ NEPAL
LISPS ■ TET ■ STALE
ENSUE ■ IRIS ■ AREA
■ PERFECTPITCH
MIC ■ SHY ■ ABLY
ADAGIO ■ MAYS ■ LAB
SECONDWIND ■ PIPE
TATA ■ EASER ■ ONES
SLIT ■ SHOWY ■ TEXT
```

90

```
DUOS ■ NYSE ■ ALDAS
OTRO ■ AUEL ■ MEETS
LAFF ■ UCLA ■ OATER
THETUSCANSUN ■
SNOWPEA ■ ARENAS
■ AHA ■ URN ■ DIVA
OHARE ■ ANDES ■ CAL
COVEROFDARKNESS
OVI ■ ERTES ■ AORTA
MEOW ■ AAR ■ ATT ■
ERNEST ■ IDEATES
■ THEBOARDWALK
FOAMY ■ AMMO ■ ARIA
ERROL ■ BIBI ■ KOOL
WEEPY ■ ATIT ■ ESTD
```

91

```
J O K E ■ B L A S T ■ S C A R
A S I N ■ A L L A H ■ P O N E
W H E N ■ M O O S E ■ H U G S
S A V E D B Y T H E B E L L ■ I
■ ■ ■ R O D ■ ■ ■ A R D E N
A R R O Y O ■ S L A K E ■ ■
L O A D ■ D I O D E ■ T A M
G I V E S T I T F O R T A T I
A L E ■ A I M A T ■ E X A M
■ ■ R U L E R ■ D E C I D E
S L O A N ■ ■ A I L ■ ■
Y O U C A N C A L L M E A L I
R O T E ■ A O R T A ■ A R E S
U S E R ■ B L E A T ■ R I F E
P E D S ■ S T A R E ■ L A T E
```

92

```
P E S T S ■ S E A R ■ N O V A
R A T O N ■ M L L E ■ A R E S
O R I G I N O F S P E C I E S
■ L O T T O ■ ■ S P H E R E
A C E ■ H T T P ■ H O N E S
H O T E L ■ H A U T E ■ T D S
A R T G U M ■ B R O M O ■ ■
■ R O O T O F A L L E V I L
■ ■ S H O E S ■ D R U M U P
I D S ■ E D I C T ■ A M P L E
S I T A R ■ N O I R ■ E U R
A R O M A S ■ ■ N I C E R ■
B E G I N N I N G O F T I M E
E L I S ■ O B O E ■ O N A I R
L Y E S ■ B M W S ■ S A L T S
```

93

```
S C R A P ■ S H A G ■ L A M B
K O A L A ■ P U R R ■ E W E R
Y O G I S ■ A N T I ■ A F R O
■ ■ ■ S I T T I N G D U C K
I S R A E L ■ E G O ■ L Y E
S T A N D I N G R O O M ■ ■
L O R D ■ E Y E ■ D E N E B
A V E R ■ D U N E D ■ R U L E
M E R E S ■ I I I ■ I D E A
■ ■ W A L K I N G S T I C K
A G E ■ K A I ■ I N S E T S
R U N N I N G M A T E ■ ■
I N T O ■ D A U B ■ A E S O P
E K E S ■ E L S E ■ K R A F T
L Y R E ■ D I E T ■ Y E N T A
```

94

```
S C A T S ■ W O P ■ M E S S
A L C O A ■ N O V A ■ A R N O
G A R Y C O O P E R ■ D I E M
E P E E ■ U G A R T E ■ C A M
■ ■ D O N O T F O R S A K E
L O B ■ N C O ■ E N O L ■ ■
A B E T T E D ■ D E S I G N S
H I G H ■ ■ ■ ■ N O O N
R E S O L V E ■ M I S G A V E
■ ■ T O O N ■ A L K ■ D O E
M E O H M Y D A R L I N ■ ■
A L P ■ B A O B A B ■ I C E D
I D E M ■ G R A C E K E L L Y
Z E R O ■ E S T A ■ I C A M E
E R A S ■ S E E ■ D E M O S
```

95

```
G R I N ■ L A G O ■ F E D E X
R E N O ■ A B U T ■ A D E L E
A S S T ■ S O L E ■ R I L E S
P A P E R O R P L A S T I C ■
E W E ■ A R T ■ L I I ■ ■
■ C R E D I T O R D E B I T
■ S T U ■ A V A ■ S E N A T E
N E I L ■ E K E ■ G R A D
A M O E B A ■ E N D ■ E L L
W I N D O W O R A I S L E ■
■ ■ N O R ■ M A I ■ Y M A
R E G U L A R O R D E C A F
L O P E S ■ T E R I ■ L O N I
A L I N E ■ E P E E ■ B R E R
S E C T S ■ S O D S ■ A N T E
```

96

```
O T B S ■ B E A D ■ A L C O A
N O O N ■ A L L I ■ G I R L S
T W O E G G S O V E R E A S Y
A N E A R ■ ■ T O T E ■ Z E E
P E R K I N S ■ T H E R E N T
■ ■ E L E N A ■ E T E ■ ■
F O U R L E A F C L O V E R S
G U S ■ ■ F O O ■ ■ G U T
S I X F I G U R E I N C O M E
■ ■ U N O ■ E U B I E ■ ■
T O R N A D O ■ R E C R O O M
E L I ■ S O P S ■ H E N N A
E I G H T T R A C K T A P E S
M V I I I ■ A L A I ■ L O G O
S E D E R ■ H E R D ■ S T A N
```

97

T	H	A	W	S		C	A	T		A	S	K	E	D
V	I	N	C	I		A	W	E		A	C	E	L	A
A	S	D	F	G	H	J	K	L		R	O	Y	A	L
		I	N	T	O	W		D	O	U	B	L	E
A	C	H	E		S	L	A	M	I	N	T	O	
C	O	U	L	D		E	R	A	S		S	A	P	S
C	O	N	D	O	R		D	R	A	B		R	A	E
O	P	T	S	O	U	T		T	R	E	A	D	L	E
R	E	A		M	B	A	S		M	A	N	I	A	S
D	R	N	O		E	M	U	S		V	I	S	T	A
		D	R	O	N	E	B	E	E		S	T	E	W
E	X	P	A	T	S		G	R	E	T	E	
L	E	E	C	H		T	O	U	C	H	T	Y	P	E
U	N	C	L	E		H	A	M		U	T	U	R	N
L	A	K	E	R		E	L	S		D	E	M	O	S

98

A	D	A	M	S		S	O	F	A		I	N	G	E
B	A	D	A	T		A	W	E	S		N	E	O	N
A	N	D	C	R	O	W	N	T	H	Y	G	O	O	D
S	I	S		I	L	O		A	T	O	M	
E	S	T		D	E	F	S		R	R	A	T	E	D
	H	O	M	E	O	F	T	H	E	B	R	A	V	E
	A	S	S		R	H	E	A		D	E	B
B	A	A	S		H	A	H		P	A	N	T
A	R	T		O	L	I	N		I	P	O	
L	E	T	F	R	E	E	D	O	M	R	I	N	G	
M	A	N	I	A	C		S	U	M	O		A	A	S
	S	L	A	B		G	I	G		B	T	U
W	I	T	H	B	R	O	T	H	E	R	H	O	O	D
O	D	I	E		R	A	N	T		A	B	B	R	S
W	A	N	D		E	T	T	A		M	O	S	S	Y

99

T	R	E	K	S		T	A	C	K		S	E	C	T
E	A	G	L	E		O	B	O	E		I	N	R	E
A	N	G	E	R		U	L	N	A		X	D	I	N
	S	E	A	N	P	E	N	N	S	P	E	N	S
N	A	H		T	E	R	I		I	M	A	G	E
B	R	E	A	T	H	E		V	I	M		R	E	D
C	E	L	L	O		D	E	N	I	M	
	A	L	A	N	L	A	D	D	S	L	A	D	S
	S	E	E	D	S		A	R	R	A	Y
D	A	D		D	I	M		P	E	R	S	O	N	A
A	E	I	O	U		I	M	A	X		P	E	W
B	R	A	D	P	I	T	T	S	P	I	T	S	
S	A	L	E		B	O	W	S		T	A	H	O	E
A	T	I	T		A	N	T	E		S	T	O	R	M
T	E	N	S		R	E	F	S		Y	A	T	E	S

100

A	B	C	S		D	I	S	C		E	L	E	N	A
M	E	L	T		O	N	E	A		R	O	O	F	S
O	B	E	Y		C	A	P	N	C	R	U	N	C	H
K	O	A	L	A		T	O	A	S	T	
	P	R	E	S	S	G	A	N	G		I	M	P	S
	S	H	O	O		S	E	A	S	A	L	T
A	G	O		C	L	E	O		T	H	R	O	E
L	A	B		A	I	R	L	I	F	T		I	D	A
B	B	G	U	N		E	T	R	E		A	S	K
U	L	Y	S	S	E	S		C	A	M	E	
M	E	N	E		P	U	S	H	U	P	B	R	A
	L	E	E	C	H		T	B	I	R	D
C	H	E	E	S	E	C	U	R	L		I	G	O	R
A	M	A	S	S		O	L	E	O		N	O	S	E
T	O	R	S	O		R	A	P	T		G	R	E	W

101

A	L	P	S		S	P	E	C	K		V	A	S	E
S	E	R	A		W	I	L	L	A		E	L	A	N
H	A	I	L	C	A	E	S	A	R		L	A	I	D
E	S	C	O	R	T		W	E	E	V	I	L	S
S	T	E	N	O		T	W	E	L	V	E	
	C	R	E	E	D		A	T	L	A	S
A	T	M	S		I	R	A		I	N	F	A	N	T
V	E	I	L		T	I	T	A	N		O	N	T	O
E	X	C	U	S	E		H	U	T		G	A	S	P
S	T	A	S	H		M	E	L	O	N	
	H	A	Z	A	R	D		A	F	T	E	R
H	O	F	F	M	A	N		E	T	O	I	L	E
A	C	L	U		P	U	R	P	L	E	R	A	I	N
S	T	A	N		P	A	I	R	S		T	R	O	T
P	O	N	D		A	L	B	E	E		E	A	T	S

102

D	O	C	S		S	T	U	M	P		S	T	A	R
U	R	A	L		R	I	G	O	R		O	H	I	O
F	I	N	E	W	I	T	H	M	E		W	A	R	Y
F	O	N	D	A		M	E	A	N	T	
E	L	O		L	I	P	S	Y	N	C		S	D	I
L	E	T	S	D	O	I	T		S	T	P	A	U	L
	C	O	N	T	A	C		S	E	G	A	L
M	O	O	R		S	H	R	U	B		P	O	L	S
A	S	K	E	W		S	E	R	I	F	S	
T	H	E	W	H	O		A	L	L	R	I	G	H	T
H	A	Y		I	N	S	T	Y	L	E		M	I	A
	D	A	M	U	P		S	K	I	D	S
T	A	O	S		S	U	R	E	W	H	Y	N	O	T
O	N	K	P		E	R	I	C	A		R	O	U	E
E	Y	E	S		S	T	O	O	D		A	R	T	S

103

```
E S S A Y   W H A T   S W A P
N E H R U   I A G O   M A M A
D R O P C O F F E E M A K E R
E V A   A B E T   L U C E N T
D E L E T E   S T O C K
    D A Y S   O O H   A B S
A L I G N   H O P P O C K E T
L O S E   T I R E S   L I R A
P O P S Q U E A K   M A N G Y
S K Y   U R L   A D A M
    K I N D S   Y E S I A M
P O T A T O   C H E W   C O Y
S H O P O F T H E D E S E R T
S I T U   F E M A   S W A T H
T O O T   S L O T   T E X A S
```

104

```
H O G S   I S N T   L A P P S
A L E E   S E A R   A T E U P
G L O W   R E D O   N O R M A
A I R   M A R A T H O N M A N
R E G G A E   S O L E
  Y E L L O W   L I S B O N
A N G L E   M A V E N   O N O
L O I S   V I V I D   W R I T
E R R   G A T E S   C A S T E
C A L M E D   R E C A N T
    O N E A   R E T A R D
W O N D E R W O M A N   L E O
A R I E S   A M E N   A B E L
H E N R I   R E N E   C O V E
L O A N S   E N D S   E Y E S
```

105

```
A M P   D E P P   P A N T Y
R O O K   O W E R   A L O H A
N O W A Y J O S E   G E T U P
O K E Y D O K E Y   E X A M
L I R A S   T O M S   T B S
D E S K   G I A N T   P A S O
    D A N S   F I L L U P
A T F A U L T   R U D O L P H
G O O G O O   B A J A
E B R O   S C I F I   P R O F
D E G   S H A G   F R E R E
  S E R A   N E V E R E V E R
P U T O N   A Y E A Y E S I R
A R I S E   P E N S   N U D E
P E T E R   E D D Y   P A T
```

106

```
A T R I A   C O U P   A R C H
N O O N S   E A S E   C O L O
K N O C K E D F O R A L O O P
A S T A I R E S   R U S S O
    N E D   F A G   T E N
G U L A G   A L L Y
A R A B   S A M U E L   A P E
D I S C O M B O B U L A T E D
S S T   R O B U S T   T O R I
    I G O R   K A P U T
W A S   E S T   I R A
A G A I N   S T A R T R E K
F R U S T R A T E D N O E N D
T E N N   A T O M   A T A C K
S E A T   P E W S   K O R E A
```

107

```
Z I P S   P I L E D   T A M S
O M I T   E N E R O   I L I E
L O T U S E A T E R   C O R E
A N T   E D N A   M A T T E D
  T R E E   I O N A
  N U M B E R C R U N C H E R
P O R E S   H O S E   A L Y
C H A N   A L I N E   N U D E
T O N   E B A N   P E T E S
S W O R D S W A L L O W E R
    E G O S   A U N T
F E E D E R   C O L T   S M U
L A T H   B O O T L I C K E R
A R N O   E R A S E   A Y E S
P S A T   D A T E D   B E T A
```

108

```
S N A G   D E F T   L E M A T
C O V E   E L L A   I R A N I
A M I N   D U E T   L A I N E
R O S E B U D W A S A S L E D
      A C E   I C E
S P A R S E   B I G   S P I C
T A R O S   E A R N   E N O
A P E W O R L D I S E A R T H
R E N   O I L S   A L I E N
T R A P   G A Y   F R I L L S
    L E E   A I L
S H E I S R E A L L Y A M A N
T O N G S   P I L L   R A R E
A L O H A   I D E E   C R E W
T E S T Y   C E N T   H E A T
```

109

```
WANT  OMAHA  TOUT
AREA  ROSAS  WISE
DIAL  PRATT  ELAN
EARLTHEPEARL
   OAS    EVADE
CAVERN  ATHLETES
AVERS  ATEE  TIS
DENNISTHEMENACE
END  ETON  CHIEN
TUESDAYS  GRANDE
SEETO  SOU
   WILTTHESTILT
YOGI  AHOOT  ODOR
APOS  SARAH  ALOE
KEPT  STOLE  DYNE
```

110

```
EWERS  SCRAP  BEG
LAMAR  ELOPE  RNA
EYESOFLAURAMARS
CORP  HERE  NONOS
TUG  BASK  SUBDUE
STEAL  JET  ITS
    HOUSTON  ASE
   DOWNTOEARTH
   SOY  TINYTIM
TEN  FIR  TEMPI
AVENUE  USDA  EER
CEDAR  ESTE  HARI
ONETOUCHOFVENUS
MTA  RATER  ARISE
AOL  SWORE  TREES
```

111

```
CABAL  AROAR  WAG
ABATE  GOOSE  IGO
PARTNERSHIP  TAO
STAINLESS  LUCID
   MOLE  DAPHNE
PATENS  BIONIC
IBIS  CADET  RIG
NAP  BOATERS  ALA
ESP  ARIES  AFAR
   ERRAND  MARTYR
FACIAL  DATA
ALAMB  STARTLING
TIN  BLOODVESSEL
ECO  AIRED  SETAE
SEE  SEEDY  TASTE
```

112

```
CAPE  BOMBE  SPEC
ARLO  ELIOT  LEVI
GOOSEFLESH  ETAT
END  LOINS  SWEDE
   SAGE  IGNORE
MACON  SHERIFF
AVOIDS  ISIT  IER
MILL  PARTS  ONCE
ADD  BALE  TOUCHE
   TOOTERS  ATHOS
   MUSTER  PCTS
PERCH  TAHOE  THO
ILKA  PIGEONTOED
UBER  INERT  ELLA
SAYS  AGREE  ALLY
```

113

```
LECH  STRAD  MAIN
ASHE  COUPE  OSLO
STAY  ABLEBODIED
EER  ALEE  ARE
RELAYED  ACERBIC
   ICER  FULLNAME
SLED  SLIDES  KIN
CIRCA  IFI  EVENT
ALI  UPSETS  IRES
BACKROAD  AIDS
SCHOOLS  JUJITSU
   WRY  PORK  RON
DELTABURKE  MELD
OLEO  URIEL  PETE
CLAW  SUERS  STIR
```

114

```
CAFE  ETHANE  DAB
UNIT  THEBAN  ADA
JAVATHEHUTT  LAS
OPE  AID  IMAMS
   ALCAPPUCCINO
APPLES  ROSEN
LOUTS  OPERATIC
MOLE  EBBED  MISO
APPROVAL  SANER
   EVADE  SCREEN
IMOGENEMOCHA
MANOR  POM  PRO
ART  AULAITOLSEN
GIA  CLIENT  DALY
ESP  TENSES  STYX
```

115

```
CACTI ▪ TRADE ▪ ABS
ALIEN ▪ RULER ▪ TAP
BLOCKBUSTER ▪ OBI
▪ NASH ▪ ADMAN
BABOONS ▪ MATISSE
ADAPTS ▪ SADISM ▪
SECTS ▪ ATTIC ▪ ARC
ELKS ▪ SIREN ▪ ISEE
DAB ▪ MALAY ▪ SCHED
▪ ROONEY ▪ CHEESE
CLEAVED ▪ CHARRED
LEASE ▪ POEM ▪
INK ▪ SAFECRACKER
ONE ▪ UMIAK ▪ NOOSE
SYR ▪ PINKY ▪ SOPPY
```

116

```
GAS ▪ GAPS ▪ ARCADE
ACT ▪ AREA ▪ PAUSES
GREENMEN ▪ OLDHAT
AILED ▪ PEALE ▪ ERE
▪ DACHA ▪ FLIP ▪
▪ INDIGOGIRLS
SLAP ▪ DISH ▪ HOOEY
LONI ▪ ISAAC ▪ UMAS
OCTET ▪ MINE ▪ SEPT
WHITELADIES ▪
▪ AHOY ▪ SPLAT
CAD ▪ EASES ▪ ROBOT
ABOARD ▪ BLUEBOYS
SUNDAE ▪ BIKE ▪ NEA
ATTEND ▪ STES ▪ ERR
```

117

```
SCAB ▪ REBA ▪ FAIRE
ILLE ▪ EDEN ▪ ERROR
LAIT ▪ BIEN ▪ NIKES
VIVELAFRANCE ▪
AMENITY ▪ YESMAN
▪ OLE ▪ FUSS ▪ ADO
ATRIA ▪ PUGS ▪ BRAT
CHERCHEZLAFEMME
TELE ▪ OOZY ▪ OASES
UTA ▪ BONY ▪ GNU ▪
PAYSUP ▪ DIDGOOD
▪ CESTLAGUERRE
SPOON ▪ BOZO ▪ SILL
TABOO ▪ ABEL ▪ TOOL
EMITS ▪ REDO ▪ ENNA
```

118

```
PASTA ▪ RTES ▪ TSAR
ACERB ▪ EIRE ▪ ITTO
SEMIS ▪ SNAILMAIL
TRAVESTY ▪ NIBBLE
▪ PINES ▪ RETESTS
ITHACA ▪ SEDER ▪
ORO ▪ ETHIC ▪ REMET
NERD ▪ SALUT ▪ DORA
SKEIN ▪ TATER ▪ RST
▪ SIDES ▪ NOISES
CHARTED ▪ DOONE ▪
AUBURN ▪ SURFACES
GRAPEVINE ▪ ERODE
ERST ▪ EDIT ▪ RODIN
DYES ▪ ROTO ▪ SWEET
```

119

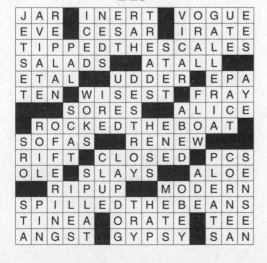

```
JAR ▪ INERT ▪ VOGUE
EVE ▪ CESAR ▪ IRATE
TIPPEDTHESCALES
SALADS ▪ ATALL ▪
ETAL ▪ UDDER ▪ EPA
TEN ▪ WISEST ▪ FRAY
▪ SORES ▪ ALICE
▪ ROCKEDTHEBOAT
SOFAS ▪ RENEW ▪
RIFT ▪ CLOSED ▪ PCS
OLE ▪ SLAYS ▪ ALOE
▪ RIPUP ▪ MODERN
SPILLEDTHEBEANS
TINEA ▪ ORATE ▪ TEE
ANGST ▪ GYPSY ▪ SAN
```

120

```
SLAP ▪ ANJOU ▪ CHAW
PANE ▪ LEARN ▪ RARA
ASTI ▪ BANFF ▪ EVEN
THEGRATEFULDEAD
▪ NANO ▪ REO ▪
RATON ▪ MERE ▪ FOB
APHID ▪ ZERO ▪ ROUE
MERRYWIDOWWALTZ
PROS ▪ AGES ▪ ASIDE
SSW ▪ URSA ▪ STOOL
▪ SRI ▪ HAHA ▪
KILLINGMESOFTLY
ERIE ▪ ENERO ▪ ASIA
MARE ▪ SATON ▪ RANK
PSAT ▪ STANG ▪ IRKS
```

121

```
FACT ▪ PARA ▪ SPARK
ALOE ▪ EVER ▪ HEMAN
IANS ▪ DODO ▪ AZURE
LITTLEWOMEN ▪ ▪ SEE
▪ ▪ RYES ▪ ARGUERS
JAI ▪ STEP ▪ AHS ▪ ▪
ALVA ▪ ALAS ▪ AISLE
WEEWILLIEWINKIE
SEDAN ▪ ARCH ▪ GIRL
▪ ▪ IVE ▪ STOW ▪ NAY
TEXTILE ▪ DEAF ▪ ▪
IMA ▪ TINYBUBBLES
PIXIE ▪ RUIN ▪ BIDE
SLICE ▪ OMNI ▪ INIT
YESES ▪ LAST ▪ ETTA
```

122

```
JAGS ▪ BASIS ▪ CEDE
OGRE ▪ ERICA ▪ AXEL
IRONMAIDEN ▪ SPAM
SEPTET ▪ EDITIONS
TEE ▪ NIA ▪ TANS ▪ ▪
▪ ▪ PUTTERAROUND
ADDIS ▪ TRURO ▪ ROY
LION ▪ DERBY ▪ FETE
PEW ▪ MANOR ▪ ROSES
SUNDAYDRIVER ▪ ▪
▪ GOLD ▪ CIA ▪ ESC
SORCERER ▪ SCAMPI
THAT ▪ ELIJAHWOOD
UNDO ▪ ALONG ▪ ETRE
BOER ▪ METRE ▪ SEER
```

123

```
BASH ▪ PLEB ▪ LAPIN
UPTO ▪ LAIR ▪ ALONE
BRER ▪ ATNO ▪ RILKE
BORNINKENTUCKY ▪
ANN ▪ NNE ▪ CREE ▪ ▪
▪ ITE ▪ OHO ▪ DAM
RAISEDININDIANA
OGDEN ▪ NEA ▪ RODDY
LIVEDINILLINOIS
ONE ▪ TOL ▪ OVA ▪ ▪
▪ DCCV ▪ LGE ▪ PEA
▪ ABRAHAMLINCOLN
SHOOT ▪ TEAC ▪ ANEW
SONIC ▪ ERMA ▪ ETNA
WYETH ▪ SEAL ▪ NEAR
```

124

```
DELI ▪ ELLAS ▪ AFEW
ELON ▪ MEADE ▪ COLA
JACKSONKENTUCKY
ANISETTE ▪ AMIES
▪ ▪ TIE ▪ SAXE ▪ ▪
MADISONILLINOIS
IRONON ▪ DOA ▪ KOA
MORAN ▪ ZIP ▪ APING
ILS ▪ MAO ▪ ASONIA
CLINTONMICHIGAN
▪ OHMY ▪ LEI ▪ ▪
ALONE ▪ NOTEPADS
JEFFERSONOREGON
ANNA ▪ PAGAN ▪ AURA
ROOT ▪ MOOSE ▪ LAMP
```

125

```
SPACE ▪ BACH ▪ EGGO
POPPY ▪ OBOE ▪ GOAD
APPLE ▪ NEVERGOTO
RTE ▪ WASTE ▪ EIDER
TOA ▪ ANA ▪ ROANS
APLASTICSURGEON
▪ OHS ▪ HUTS ▪ ADO
RISK ▪ NAP ▪ STEW
ASH ▪ BEEP ▪ RNA
WHOLOVESTHEWORK
▪ OARED ▪ HEW ▪ NEE
MITZI ▪ ARRAY ▪ ESE
OFPICASSO ▪ OFTEN
ASAN ▪ LAVA ▪ ROWEL
BORG ▪ APPT ▪ KOOKY
```

126

```
WORD ▪ DIMS ▪ SHEBA
IDIO ▪ EPEE ▪ PINED
SANG ▪ AHME ▪ EPODE
PYGMALION ▪ APSES
▪ ALEG ▪ AFRO ▪ ▪
RES ▪ DRED ▪ ASLANT
ARENA ▪ NEED ▪ YEAR
ZOLA ▪ SINUS ▪ TRIO
ODER ▪ MAIM ▪ GAILY
RESCUE ▪ MESO ▪ ESS
▪ ITES ▪ NAGS ▪ ▪
WORST ▪ PHILOMELA
ANISE ▪ LEDA ▪ OMAR
LEMUR ▪ IRED ▪ TINE
TRESS ▪ TOSS ▪ ERAS
```

127

```
F D I C . B A R D S . A S P S
L U N A . U B O A T . N E A L
E R I C . R O U S E . T R I O
D O T H E R I G H T T H I N G
. . . E C O L E . . H E F T S
A L E P H . . W H A M . . .
D A D O O R O N R O N . A L P
A S I T . O N A I R . I D E A
M E T . M O U N T A I N D E W
. . C O T S . . . B A S K S
S L O A N . A S P I C . . .
P O S T A G E D U E S T A M P
O N C E . N A M E R . I C E R
R E A R . A V E R S . V I N E
E R R S . T E N S E . E D D Y
```

128

```
P I E S . T E M P E . C H E R
A N A T . E V E R Y . R A T E
S P R Y . R E N E E . I R A N
T U T . V E N U S D E M I L O
A T H E I S T . . R A E .
. . A N N A . C R O S S S E A
M O N D E . E R U P T . A R C
E G G S . A R I E S . S T A R
A G E . A B I E S . M O U S E
L I L A B N E R . C A R R .
. . C O O . B A N A N A S
M E R C U R Y L Y N X . N R A
O L E O . M A I N E . D I E T
O M A R . A L T E R . A N N O
G O L D . L E E R S . D E A N
```

129

```
B O T H . J I H A D . S K I M
A U R A . A D E L A . A N N O
B R I N G M E A U N I C O R N
A S O N E . A L M A S . C E O
. . A N T . S N E A K .
H I G H E R U P . G E R A R D
I S R . V I S O R . O B O E
T E E N A G E W E R E W O L F
I R A E . S E N O R . U F O
T E T H E R . R E P A R T E E
. . F I X E S . E S E .
U M A . E N L A I . E L A T E
R E L U C T A N T D R A G O N
G A L S . A V O I R . C O R D
E L S A . L E N N Y . E G O S
```

130

```
C A R L . S H O A L . A U N T
A B I E . E A R L E . G N A W
S U G G E S T I V E . O B I E
S T A I R S . O A R S . A V E
. . O N I O N . E A G L E T
. B U N I O N . E D I N A .
D A N . E N E M Y . D U N C E
E S P Y . S W E E T . S C O W
B E R E T . A L L E S . E T E
. . E A R L Y . E L A N D S .
S O P H I A . S T E V E .
A L A . P U P U . F E E L E R
F I R E . D I S C O R D A N T
E V E N . E T H A N . L I T E
R E D D . R H I N O . E N O S
```

131

```
C M O N . E L L A . S A C R E
R O P E . D U E T . A C R E S
A N E W . M A S T . M E A N T
M A D A B O U T Y O U . C E E
. . . R O N . . S T R I K E S
B A C K S T O P . C A N E .
O U R . C O M A S . I N D I A
A R A B . N I N E S . S I B S
R A Z E S . T E P E E . C A P
. . Y A N G . S T A R T E R S
S E Q U I N S . . C I O .
A S U . C U C K O O C L O C K
S T I C K . A L K A . E L L E
H A L L E . M E L S . D E A N
A S T I R . P E A T . O O P S
```

132

```
A S A P . F A D E . A N D G O
D A V E . I L E X . S I R E D
S C A R . L O B E . S T Y N E
. . J A M E S S T E W A R T .
A B D U L . . I R I S E S
G E O R G E C S C O T T . .
A R T Y . S H E A . S A M S
I L E . S I N C E . . H A P
N E R O . L O T S . L A R A
. . F R E D R I C M A R C H
E S S A I S . . A D D O N
S P E N C E R T R A C Y . .
T O R A H . A E O N . B A T S
O S A G E . C A S T . U H O H
P A L E R . K L E E . G A M Y
```

133

```
A L A S _ T R E N T _ D R A B
R O S A _ R U L E R _ A O N E
M A I N _ E N L A I _ N O T E
_ D A D D Y W A R B U C K S _
_ _ W A S A _ E S E _ _ _ _
R E S I N _ Y O M _ E R N I E
E R E C T S _ T A P _ O N S _
F A T H E R C H R I S T M A S
I T T _ O R E _ E T H A N E
T O O T S _ I R S _ A R D E N
_ O P S _ H U G O _ _ _ _
_ P A P A H E M I N G W A Y _
T A M P _ A V A I L _ O N E S
L I M E _ C A R T E _ U T A H
C L O D _ K N E E D _ T I R E
```

134

```
S W A G S _ S C U P _ C R O C
A P L E A _ E R N E _ H E R O
M A L T L I Q U O R _ I T E M
_ U N T R U E _ M E N A G E
D E V O _ M E L T I N G P O T
A R I _ B A L _ O T T _ E N O
G A U Z E _ E M M E T _ _ _
_ M I L T O N B E R L E _
_ P A R E D _ E C L A T
I R E _ T A I _ A D D _ O L E
M O L T E N L A V A _ U N I T
B O U N D S _ B A L I N G
I N D O _ M U L T I G R A I N
B E E T _ I D E A _ O U T R E
E Y R E _ T E R R _ R H E T T
```

135

```
A L A _ S P A S M _ F A S T _
V I N _ T E S L A _ A T E A M
E T A _ O R I O N _ Z O R R O
R E L I V I N G T H E P A S T
_ R Y N E _ R O D _ P U T
M A Z E _ U N M A N _ A H S O
A T E _ O N E A _ O H M _
B I R T H D A Y P R E S E N T
_ H O E _ A K E Y _ P A R
M A R X _ R A N G E _ S I Z E
O R A _ S G T _ P I C A
B A C K T O T H E F U T U R E
I R E N E _ A A R O N _ R E A
L A M E R _ C L I N K _ E T S
_ T E E N _ K E N T S _ S H Y
```

136

```
S A L A D _ B A S K _ N E S T
I M A G E _ A N T I _ O V E R
N A V A L _ A G E S _ M O V E
_ P U L L U P S T A K E S
S E C E D E _ S P E E D E R S
H M O _ E T C _ E R A _
A C N E _ G A S _ C A F F E
H E A D F O R T H E H I L L S
S E N S E _ Y E N _ M O A T
_ T S P _ P I E _ O R E
P R E A C H E D _ A S I D E S
H I T T H E B R I C K S _
O P A L _ I B I S _ I L I A D
T O G A _ K L E E _ M E N S A
O N E S _ S E R E _ O S C A R
```

137

```
C H I C _ M I N U S _ D O T
H A L O _ A T O N E S _ E V E
E L K S _ N E T H E R _ T A X
F E A S T O R F A M I N E
_ E A R _ A M S _ O R A L
G E S T E _ S I P _ T E R R A
R A H S _ M O R E O R L E S S
I T O _ M O M _ R A Y _ N O S
N O W O R N E V E R _ A C N E
D U C T S _ W E D _ P R E S S
S T A T _ S H E _ U A R
_ S O O N E R O R L A T E R
L E I _ R A R I N G _ Y A L E
O W N _ G R E E C E _ E C O N
B E G _ E S S E S _ D O N T
```

138

```
R E C _ S H A W L _ A C E R B
E A R _ T A L I A _ L A T E X
P R E S I D E N T O F I R A Q
O T T E R _ K E A N U
S H A Q _ S K I E R S _ S O O
T A N _ B A R Q S _ S C A M
_ A U D I T _ T A T A R S
_ Q A N D A S E S S I O N S
A T R E S T _ S C A L P
R I O T _ S T A R S _ P C T
C P U _ A T E S T S _ A E R O
_ S E N O R _ Q A T A R
Q W E R T Y K E Y B O A R D S
E E R I E _ I C E U P _ E L O
D E S K S _ N O T C H _ L E S
```

139

```
G T O   A B R I L   R A J A H
R A P   W E A R Y   E R O S E
E L I A K A Z A N   D I N T Y
C O N N   G E E N A D A V I S
O N E I L L     N O N O
    L E E G R A N T   I S M
T A P I N   L A L A   O G L E
R I A N T   E N O   I N H O T
A D U E   B A C H   L E T G O
M A L   T O M H A N K S
    L O A N   O A T E R S
P A U L N E W M A N   A R E A
A S K I N   A R T C A R N E Y
L E A V E   D E M O N   I V E
L A S E R   E D E M A   E E R
```

140

```
T A X I   S P A C E   H U M E
O X E N   O R S O N   A Z O V
N E R D   L A I R D   Y I P E
G L O O M A N D D O O M
    L O C K E   A O R T A
S T P E T E   A W K W A R D
P A I N E   M A N E   T A D
H U S T L E A N D B U S T L E
E R A   X R A Y   P A L E R
R U N B A C K   R E N E E S
E S S E S   B L I N D
    S H A K E A N D B A K E
C H A T   B E L T S   A V I D
A U T O   C N O T E   N O T I
P H E W   S O W E D   K N E E
```

141

```
S A L A D   C O L E   P A P
I R A N I   O R E L   H U R L
P A S T A   N A G S   I N C A
    I N A C L A I R E D A Y
C B S   E V E   T E E   I N E
O R E O   A R G O   O A T E R
C A M P S I T E   T P K
A N I T A L O O S W E I G H T
    I V S   D A I N T I E R
B O C C I   F E R N   A S I A
R I O   O S U   A G E   T R Y
A L H I R T M Y S E L F
K E E N   A B O O   F A Z E D
E R R S   G L U T   I R A T E
S S E   S E R A   N E P A L
```

142

```
B O N U S   O M A N I   C S A
A V A N T   F I X E R   R U B
B U T T E R F L I E S   E E L
E L A I N E   E O S   L A Z E
S E L E C T S   M O D E M
    D I E T S   N O O S E S
J I M   L A R A M   S N O W Y
A R I D   R O B I N   A D E N
V A L E T   H I M O M   A R E
A N K L E T   N I L E S
    M E D O C   C O N T O U R
Q U O D   P H D   S T E R N O
U R N   C H E E S E H E A D S
A G E   P A S S E   O L L I E
D E Y   A T T I C   L E E D S
```

143

```
B R E W   M O B Y   J A N E
O O Z E   O B I E   S I L A S
U A R E O N E(B)A C K T O S Q
T R A   N E S S   U I N T A S
    E S T E   A B L E
B L I M P S   R A I L Y A R D
A U D I E   M E R S   W O O
L C I R C L E(C)O M E S F U L
E R O   A S O N   L O U S E
D E M I J O H N   M E W L E D
    C I T Y   R E V S
S E V E N S   T I D E   E B B
P T I C K E T(R)O U N D T R I
A T L A S   O U T S   E N I D
S E E P   M E S A   Y A M S
```

144

```
C Y S T   O Z A W A   N A R C
R A T E   M A R I N   I N K Y
A L I A   A S I D E   G O O D
W I L M A R U D O L P H
L E T U S     W E A T H E R
    P O P P A   S C A R E
L A P   F R E D A S T A I R E
O D E A   E L O P E   P R O D
B A R N E Y F R A N K   Y R S
E M P T Y   E R T E S
D E S I R E S   M O U N T
    B E T T Y C R O C K E R
J O J O   H O O E Y   C A S E
O V I D   A N G L E   E S T A
B A B Y   N E A L S   R E S T
```

145

```
C O I F ■ A S K E D ■ C E D E
R U S E ■ S C I F I ■ O X E N
I C E R ■ T A L O S ■ D E S I
T H E M I R R O R C R A C K D
■ ■ ■ I N A ■ ■ R E S ■ ■ ■
O D E ■ S L A N T E D ■ S A C
F O R G E ■ F I A T ■ O H I O
F I N E T O O T H E D C O M B
O L I N ■ A R E O ■ O T T E R
N Y E ■ S T E R E O S ■ S E A
■ ■ ■ D O C ■ ■ V E T ■ ■ ■
G I V E T H E B R U S H O F F
E D I T ■ A V A I L ■ Y E A R
N O S E ■ F I L L E ■ M I N E
T S A R ■ F L E E S ■ E L S E
```

146

```
A B B E ■ C A R A ■ M I L L E
W E A K ■ U P O N ■ A D A I R
A L B E R T S O N ■ N E W E R
R O B ■ H I E D ■ D E A R ■
D I L L I E S ■ S E S T E T S
S T E I N ■ C H I ■ E N I D ■
■ K E R O U A C ■ C P A
B A N E ■ A D O R E ■ D E S K
E L I ■ D E M P S E Y ■
T A C T ■ I T O ■ R A M B O
E S K I M O S ■ T O A D I E D
■ L E A S ■ F A S T ■ A T E
E M A I L ■ N I C H O L S O N
G A U N T ■ O D I E ■ A M O S
G A S S Y ■ B E T A ■ B A K E
```

147

```
S A S S ■ I D L E S ■ P L A Y
A R L O ■ B O I S E ■ R E N E
H E A D S E T T E R ■ O C T A
L A P ■ C R E E ■ E S T H E R
■ ■ W E I R ■ I N T O ■ ■
F A R I N A ■ C R E S C E N T
O P I N E ■ G A O L ■ O L I O
R A N G ■ R U N N Y ■ L U N A
E R G S ■ E Y E S ■ O L D A S
S T O P O V E R ■ D R I E S T
■ ■ A P E D ■ H A T E ■ ■
P L A N A R ■ S O P H ■ S E N
R A N I ■ S H A M P O O D L E
O K I E ■ E A S E L ■ T A M S
D E L L ■ S T E R E ■ T K O S
```

148

```
G O I N ■ R A S P ■ R A I S E
R U N E ■ A R L O ■ E X C E L
A C R E ■ F R O M ■ V I E W S
S H E D A F E W P O U N D S ■
■ ■ F I T S ■ N E G ■ ■
A M E L I A ■ I T S ■ P A D
L O N E R ■ A F R O ■ B O N A
L O D G E A C O M P L A I N T
A R E S ■ S H E A ■ E R N I E
N E D ■ C H E ■ A G A T E S
■ ■ A R E ■ D E S I ■ ■
■ H O M E S R I G H T I N O N
B I M B O ■ I A G O ■ F O R E
A R I E L ■ O N E R ■ F R A N
D E T R E ■ S A D E ■ Y A L E
```

149

```
F R I J O L E S ■ D A R T E R
E N S E N A D A ■ E N R O L L
M A R A T H O N ■ E D S E L S
■ ■ N O R M A N D Y ■ ■
S C R I P ■ ■ B E S T B O Y
T H E E ■ O U N C E ■ O A K S
L A B ■ S I T U ■ A P R I L
■ L I T T L E B I G H O R N ■
B O R E D ■ I R A S ■ I A M
A N T S ■ T S A R S ■ P E W S
A S H T R A Y ■ ■ S A R A S
■ ■ Y O R K T O W N ■ ■
Y E H U D I ■ A N T I E T A M
E R A S E S ■ N U R S L I N G
R E W A R M ■ S T A S S E N S
```

150

```
L U N G S ■ P A W ■ I B S E N
O P E R A ■ A L A ■ N I T R O
C R E A K ■ N O V ■ C L I N G
K I D S I N T H E H A L L ■
U S E S ■ O H A R A S ■ E B B
P E D ■ P O E ■ S W E L T E R
■ H A N O I ■ ■ A T T A
I N N O C E N T S A B R O A D
N O E L ■ ■ S K U L K ■
D O W E R E D ■ E D T ■ Q T S
O K S ■ U S A B L E ■ P U R E
■ C H I L D R E N S H O U R
B R A I N ■ G A T ■ T O T E M
A I S L E ■ U V A ■ O N E T O
A C T O R ■ M E L ■ P E R O N
```

151

```
GARBO  BAYED  NOW
ALIEN  OLIVE  AVA
TABLEHOPPER  MIX
  GNATS  NICENE
SATIETY  DIVIDED
CREASE  LINEAR
OMENS  TANGS  ORT
LONS  SIZES  EPEE
DRY  COMER  EXPOS
  BLAMED  FACEIT
CROONER  MISERLY
RIPSAW  TASER
ASP  SHOWSTOPPER
VEE  TAPES  UTTER
ERR  ATSEA  TSARS
```

152

```
ATOM  FORMS  NASA
DIVE  ELISE  INON
DRAWBRIDGEAHEAD
SOL  LAVE  DMITRI
  COLE  UTIL
APART  SATIN  GOB
SETAT  SAM  IRAE
KEEPOFFTHEGRASS
ELIS  ILE  RADIO
DEN  EVERS  ATEST
  STEW  HOTE
SEDANS  BITE  GAL
PRIVATEENTRANCE
EINE  AGATE  MAMA
DEAR  ROTOR  STEP
```

153

```
BEAM  ISLIP  PSST
LIRA  SCALA  ATTY
ONTHEROCKS  TRAP
CESAR  NEAT  RAGE
  LITER  ELOISE
CHOICE  CLING
LINA  REMO  ASHES
AFT  PITCHER  TLC
NIHIL  TINA  HULA
  ELIDE  REAPER
MAHLER  BANAL
ALOU  ALEC  SLOES
PLUS  WITHATWIST
LOSE  OTTER  ASTI
EWES  NEEDY  YEAR
```

154

```
SAHL  DING  SCABS
OLEO  OREO  CARAT
BLACKJACK  ALINE
  TORO  KARL  STE
ASH  ISH  REDHEAD
PARIS  OATS  ISMS
BOOMTOWN  PET
  WHITEKNIGHT
  ONE  HUNGERED
ICBM  LOST  ERATO
BLUEFLU  SOD  CAT
IAN  IOTA  NOAH
SIGMA  GREENBEAN
ERECT  ULNA  BALI
SEEMS  NOEL  ALIT
```

155

```
RBIS  COLON  ROMA
ALOE  ORATE  UKES
PUNCTUATIONMARK
  ESTOP  SNAPPLE
  METS  SLIER
LICIT  INVITE
ORONO  NEER  PIP
PANAMACANALCITY
ENE  SAKI  EASEL
  IRENIC  AWARE
AETNA  NEIN
TROTTED  STEAK
INTESTINALORGAN
LIEN  ANODE  GORE
TEST  LORDS  OGLE
```

156

```
JAPED  STEVE  UMP
ARENA  KALAMAZOO
GOODBYECOLUMBUS
SON  NEWT  WEST
  PEWS  REMAKES
ALWAYS  CAMAY
LIRA  COLIN  FEE
AFAREWELLTOARMS
REP  LIDDY  BOMP
  MOLES  ZEEMAN
BEWAILS  TINT
REAR  LUNG  NEW
ARRIVEDERCIROMA
WINNEBAGO  NEVIL
LES  ENDOW  EXALT
```

157

```
CHER . DEBT . DRUGS
LALO . ITER . EERIE
OLIN . VALE . PAINT
GOODWILLSHOP . . .
. STOOD . ISIS . ARI
. . SVEN . MERLIN .
OPS . ENACT . AIDA .
FRIENDSHIPSEVEN .
FONT . TITLE . ERE .
EXCESS . . OARS . . .
RYE . HEIR . TILED .
. . PEACEOFFICER .
ACARE . INDO . COLE
SIMON . NEER . ELLE
HAIFA . GERM . READ
```

158

```
CAMAY . ALEUT . MAR
OHARE . BILKO . ICE
PANTSPOCKET . SHA
. . DARK . ENSOR
DILBERT . JIBBOOM
UVULAS . BATAAN .
PACER . SOBIG . EFT
ENID . GLOBS . TSAR
SAL . LLAMA . TACKY
. LAYUPS . VENUES
PRELIMS . DESSERT
RABIN . AINT . . .
OVA . GIMMEABREAK
BEL . TRAIT . ADDLE
ELL . OKIES . NATTY
```

159

```
ASAP . SAME . MOJOS
JUDO . ALEX . IRISH
ALAS . SOOT . SANTA
MUMSTHEWORD . REM
. URI . RAE . IOU
THEMOMMYTRACK .
RAY . DIDO . ELAINE
ILED . SKA . DSOS .
OSWEGO . UPTO . HAT
. IREMEMBERMAMA
COT . IND . NEE . .
ANN . SIERRAMADRE
BEECH . ROAN . DOOR
ATSEA . LAIC . OLEG
LOSES . EDDY . WEGO
```

160

```
BITE . MATA . CLUED
AQUA . AMOR . LANAI
ASTROKEOFGENIUS
. RINK . RAG . .
OLDHAND . POVERTY
BERING . FACE . EEE
STING . NODE . RTES
. IFEELYOURPAIN .
OTTS . ELLA . UNTIE
OBE . LAOS . STOLEN
HERMANN . MOONERS
. EST . SELF . .
THATTOUCHOFMINK
NIGEL . MATE . ACRE
TEARY . ATAD . SHAY
```

161

```
SILO . BALSA . SHOP
ORAL . ASIAN . PANE
HANDINHAND . ORCA
ONE . STEM . EMOTER
. ALES . CRAFT . .
AMBLER . LOSTSOUL
DELIS . CANOE . HBO
ALOT . ROUEN . GAOL
MEW . BERRY . CORAL
NEBRASKA . CHATTY
. YOKES . FOAL . .
EMBLEM . ALLI . SOB
VILA . BLUEONBLUE
IRON . LADEN . IOTA
LEWD . EDITS . TEST
```

162

```
CITE . PESCI . RAFT
ORES . LIMON . ERLE
MIAPHARAOH . STUN
ESS . AUEL . AWAKEN
THEEND . LALALA .
. SKIS . GENERIC
WORM . TIRADE . NNE
HAYES . MAT . SPARE
AHA . OPINES . EKES
TUNEFUL . SPAN . .
. OXIDES . ASSAIL
PENTAD . TARA . SOU
LAIR . LEONSPHINX
UCLA . EMOTE . IDIO
SHES . SUPER . TEAR
```

163

```
MESS SCALP SHAM
OTTO TABOO TAXI
CHICKENOUT UZIS
KEN ARTY ARNESS
SLEAZE TOT
GOOSEGOSSAGE
RADIO WARES JAY
EBAN DIVAS DAZE
NOR LINEN HIRED
DUCKINGSTOOL
ARE TOLLED
CACHET ESTE AVA
ALOU TURKEYTROT
IMIN EGGAR NUKE
NANA SHOTS TEED
```

164

```
SAYS AWACS ARID
UTAH ZEBRA SORE
EASYSTREET SCAN
TRINI ETTA UKES
IRENE SENTRY
SEAM HERBS
RAHS GARAGE OAK
USA MAHATMA ALI
MIR ENIGMA ODDS
SADAT STIR
DRAMAS SMASH
HARI ALAW OCCUR
ASIS NATHANLANE
HAVE INEED ELAN
APES CASTS SEND
```

165

```
VASE FLORA TET
IMUS LAVER SILO
DONTHAVEACOWMAN
ARS AMIND PEONY
LETITBE BEARD
ROSE SCANT
IRON STORE RES
TAKEADEEPBREATH
OWE VILAS NICE
WIELD MAIN
CHEAT COLDWAR
SHYER RAISA ALE
KEEPYOURSHIRTON
YENS ALICE CENT
ERA FEDOR ARES
```

166

```
BRACE ISIS SCAM
AEROS NOTE HALE
ONTOPOFTHEWORLD
BAIL PATE ARIA
ATE ATNO EVELYN
BASEHIT ICY LIU
LEM ARC WONT
SUMMITMEETING
OHNO SIT NIL
POD CTS STREAMS
SWELLS GORE MAT
TREE TAVI UPTO
TIPOFTHEICEBERG
IMIN HOLE LEROI
NENE OUST IRENE
```

167

```
CUBE SLASH PIPE
APEX MAINE OVID
PORTLANDOR CANI
ENG URGE ORANGE
ARTE ICET
SMILEY PROCESS
WILLS GOOP LEMA
ALOE NOONS LOAN
TENN ONLY COULD
RATINGS REILLY
ONUS WARD
AVOWER AARE WOE
NEON BETHESDAMD
CAPP ALTOS ORIG
ELSA NONOT ANTE
```

168

```
BBC CHIA BELLI
ORE HOOF DEVOID
RUSSIANROULETTE
INTEND IBEG SEA
STARE ACETIC
ASAN ARMEY
ERS ELIA SNEERS
DUTCHELMDISEASE
ITALIC PATH DER
THROB ZEES
TIBIAE EATME
ATL SAND SPREAD
FRENCHCANADIANS
RADIUS MOTO LIE
OPALS SMOG SAL
```

169

```
RIOT SMOG CAFES
OSHA PIMA ADORE
SNIT ARNO MARNE
HOOTERVILLE TIM
    OAT SCRIBES
DECORATE DADA
APO SNELL SAXON
MICH SAGAS STLO
SCOOP LAMPS EDS
  ALES REHEARSE
ALBERTA ALL
DIE SPRINGFIELD
ALAMO ITON ETUI
MACON ECRU NCAA
SCHWA SHAM SHUN
```

170

```
BACK BABU TIMOR
ALEE IRIS IMAGE
HOLYROMANEMPIRE
NET OLES DOOMED
  BUOY BITS
  DOING BACHELOR
MINGDYNASTY UTA
OPED ONS ACTI
OST OLDDOMINION
GOODBYES ANTES
  AVIS ARCS
SINGIN ASTA ERA
THEMAGICKINGDOM
AIMAT THEN BILE
STORE SEWS STYX
```

171

```
ONCE MAINE BESS
LEAR ELBOW ALLA
GARDENPERENNIAL
APPENDIX AGATE
   DEN HAM
  COLOREDEYEPART
TAKER OLE AMAH
SLAM CHIPS SITU
ALPO RON ASSES
RAINBOWGODDESS
  AWE NED
STALL SEMESTER
NOVELISTMURDOCH
ANON SOLAR ABOY
GENT TBONE KENS
```

172

```
SPCA HELI ASSET
KAHN OXEN NEATO
EGAD RITA DELTA
TONYORLANDO BAD
CDE DIET IRMA
HALFOF STRANGE
  ARISTA ARDEN
PACT CANDO GOOD
STOIC STABLE
COMMUTE DESPOT
  MARE AGUA ELO
DNA SANFERNANDO
RONDO OONA SCAT
ANDOR SUIT TIGE
BOOTY ELIE ILED
```

173

```
SAHIB FLAB ROAM
ELISE ROBE ONCE
PAPERTIGER CEDE
AMPERAGE ACKACK
LOO III ETCH
  ELD RICOTTA
CANIS PIN URAL
OWAR SLANG NIKE
MOTO CAD EDGES
BLENDIN SPA
  HOED TOR OPS
DISOWN DAMNABLE
ODOR CLAYPIGEON
TENS EAVE NESTS
SAGE SPED GEESE
```

174

```
SHAMS SPITE PAW
CUTIE HONOR RBI
AGAME ELTONJOHN
MERITS EEK ALOE
 RICHARDRODGERS
  RENO NAG
ZANY TARA MYRRH
AWE PARABLE EAR
PLACE SHEA COPS
  REC AMMO
JOSEPHWAMBAUGH
OPIE RAN STRAIN
NICKNOLTE TAURO
ANE INLET EGGED
HEM POSSE DEEDS
```

175

```
ASCAP ■ MIDAS ■ FTC
ROONE ■ ADOLL ■ ORO
CHATTANOOGA ■ RIB
HOTORCOLD ■ METER
■ NEER ■ ODESSA ■
VIGILS ■ SUNUNU
AREA ■ MORON ■ MSG
LIT ■ ASALARK ■ TOE
EST ■ LOCAL ■ SEAM
■ YELLER ■ SCARPS
PASTED ■ PERM ■
AMBOY ■ EMOTIONAL
LOU ■ CHICKAMAUGA
EUR ■ AERIE ■ ENNUI
ORG ■ THEIR ■ ASSAD
```

176

```
OFFER ■ HOPI ■ DOZE
CRETE ■ AVON ■ EMIL
HERES ■ GENT ■ VANS
ODD ■ TOURDEFORCE
■ ECOLE ■ RUT ■
MILORD ■ GINSENG
IRATE ■ WALES ■ OAS
DONE ■ CASED ■ OMIT
INC ■ GRASS ■ PADUA
■ SECRECY ■ ARREST
■ AID ■ CRISP ■
COUPDEGRACE ■ LOT
ANNO ■ NOIR ■ SAUTE
REIN ■ ZEST ■ TIMON
ARTS ■ ASEA ■ SLEET
```

177

```
POOR ■ STOP ■ SISAL
ALMA ■ OHTO ■ ULTRA
LEAP ■ BUTT ■ BLOND
MANIA ■ MERIT ■ ROD
ANIDLEPROMISE ■
■ SIB ■ APTERAL
ESP ■ OBIS ■ LEONE
THEMANINTHEMOON
TURIN ■ LASE ■ MNO
ETERNAL ■ ICE ■
■ GOODYEARBLIMP
PAR ■ TOGAS ■ SAVER
ELIZA ■ ORCA ■ TORI
NONET ■ ALAW ■ ERLE
SUEDE ■ TYPE ■ DYED
```

178

```
COMAS ■ AKA ■ ATTAR
AVANT ■ ROB ■ SHOVE
TEDDY ■ CROSSEYED
SNARL ■ HEALTH ■
■ BEE ■ WARY ■ AJAR
SCOW ■ LAND ■ GORE
TAU ■ JAYS ■ ADULTS
ENTRAPS ■ STEELIE
PAYERS ■ ZINC ■ YET
IDOS ■ LEGO ■ ERRS
NAUT ■ SOPH ■ PRO ■
■ ALIGHT ■ ROGET
HAPPYDAYS ■ ADELE
EXILE ■ NRA ■ TERSE
PETES ■ SSW ■ ESSEN
```

179

```
LARVA ■ DANG ■ MOP
ELIOT ■ USERS ■ OVA
MINUTESTEAK ■ PEW
■ SANTA ■ TIGERS
SOL ■ CRY ■ HEROD
TRASHY ■ SOFTBALL
RAMIE ■ MINUS ■ RAE
ACED ■ PIXEL ■ IOTA
ILE ■ BONES ■ BRUIN
TEXTILES ■ GLENNE
■ CACAO ■ SOU ■ DAR
PAUPER ■ BASES ■
AMS ■ POLISHJOKES
PIE ■ SIEGE ■ AREAS
ADS ■ DADS ■ YEARN
```

180

```
INANE ■ ADDS ■ WEBB
COSEC ■ NEWT ■ OLAY
ELIWHITNEY ■ MALT
DANSON ■ TELLALIE
■ YENS ■ BUON ■
SPA ■ SITE ■ SMILED
EEL ■ NODE ■ ASIDE
CRAZYGUGGENHEIM
TONIO ■ TERM ■ NCO
STALKS ■ DEBT ■ STS
■ LELY ■ TREE ■
RESIDUAL ■ YESSIR
ALTO ■ SHARONTATE
FLAN ■ HOHO ■ SERIF
TARS ■ YORE ■ YEAST
```

181

```
AHEM  SWORD  GENA
NOVA  PATTI  UPON
TWINCITIES   NEED
ELLIOTTS   SAGELY
     FEE   GOSH
  HOOD   FULLHOUSE
SAULS  OLIVE  NAG
HIND  DONNE  DIVA
AKC  GETAT  METED
QUEENBEES   ICED
    LAUD   ANA
DISOWN  SORENESS
ASAP  KINGCOTTON
ZANE  EMILE  ERMA
EYED  DATED  DEEP
```

182

```
CLAN  HADJ  SLAKE
OUSE  ARIA  HITIT
CASHMERESWEATER
OUTRE   SPHERULE
ASSURES   EON
    SUPRA  TMAN
EMBATTLE   QUITE
CHECKOUTCOUNTER
RODEO   REPEATED
USED  CHIDE
    WOO  ENIGMAS
APPOINTS   DRAMA
CHARGEDAFFAIRES
DITCH  OAHU  DABS
CLEAT  GRAM  STAY
```

183

```
ALI  CLIFF  TATE
LENO  HANOI  AMOR
LATE  INALL  POLA
EVERYMANDESIRES
GEN  OPIE  TRADE
RODIN  LVI  LOS
OUTS  APPOINT
TOLIVELONGBUT
  ABALONE  ANON
PAT  SST  TRITE
EPODE  ASIA  CAW
NOMANWOULDBEOLD
PLAT  ORDIE  PRIE
ALTE  REEDS  ANTA
LOOS  MONET  SYL
```

184

```
IAGO  MESAS  CLUE
SHUN  AMISH  OATS
MARE  NOLIE  USES
 BUCKETOFBOLTS
   ANTE   ARE
ADORE  DOE  BEADS
BEFALL  FBI  WEE
BATTLEOFBRITAIN
ERE  TSE  ENRICO
SYNOD  URN  TATER
   RES   UTEP
 BEASTOFBURDEN
COIN  AVOID  ODIN
BORG  GALLO  OGLE
SKEE  ELDER  REED
```

185

```
ALAS  AWOL  PEACH
PEPE  MAKE  ACHOO
HARP  ELAN  CLOMP
IVETOLDYOUMAYBE
DES  MIO  NAT
  BAA  AGIN  DUB
SARAN  OSLO  LISA
TWOMILLIONTIMES
URSA  ADAM  HEEDS
BYE  EDEN  FED
   SML  OUR  PAP
NOTTOEXAGGERATE
ELIOT  MILE  ACRE
CADRE  ADEE  VEIL
KNEED  SASS  ERAS
```

186

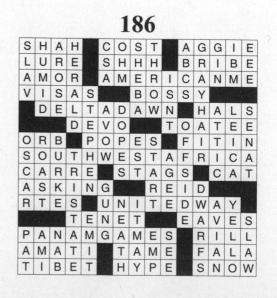

```
SHAH  COST  AGGIE
LURE  SHHH  BRIBE
AMOR  AMERICANME
VISAS  BOSSY
 DELTADAWN  HALS
   DEVO  TOATEE
ORB  POPES  FITIN
SOUTHWESTAFRICA
CARRE  STAGS  CAT
ASKING  REID
RTES  UNITEDWAY
  TENET   EAVES
PANAMGAMES  RILL
AMATI  TAME  FALA
TIBET  HYPE  SNOW
```

187

J	A	N	E	■	B	O	T	C	H	■	G	L	A	D
A	B	O	Y	■	E	A	R	L	Y	■	R	E	B	A
B	L	U	E	P	E	R	I	O	D	■	I	V	A	N
S	E	N	S	O	R	■	C	U	E	S	T	I	C	K
■	■	■	S	Y	N	O	D	■	O	S	S	I	E	■
B	E	S	E	T	■	O	L	S	E	N	■	■	■	■
O	C	H	S	■	A	N	O	■	B	A	L	K	E	D
W	H	I	T	E	F	O	R	D	B	R	O	N	C	O
L	O	V	E	L	L	■	H	A	S	■	B	O	R	G
■	■	L	Y	S	O	L	■	N	E	X	U	S	■	■
S	H	A	P	E	■	A	L	I	C	E	■	■	■	■
P	A	G	A	N	I	N	I	■	R	U	G	G	E	D
A	L	A	I	■	R	E	D	H	O	T	M	A	M	A
N	E	I	N	■	I	S	A	A	C	■	A	R	M	Y
S	Y	N	E	■	S	T	Y	L	E	■	C	P	A	S

188

B	R	A	■	S	A	L	E	R	N	O	■	A	S	H
O	O	P	■	C	L	O	S	E	U	P	■	T	A	O
X	C	H	R	O	M	O	S	O	M	E	■	O	N	A
■	■	O	N	T	A	P	■	■	B	R	A	N	D	X
C	A	R	A	T	■	E	M	O	■	A	C	A	R	E
A	L	I	■	■	D	I	P	S	■	C	L	A	D	■
M	E	S	S	E	S	■	S	A	T	I	E	■	■	■
■	X	M	A	R	K	S	T	H	E	S	P	O	T	■
■	■	W	R	I	T	E	■	M	O	T	L	E	Y	■
B	U	F	F	■	T	O	R	N	■	■	I	L	E	■
A	P	R	I	L	■	A	X	E	■	M	A	V	E	N
X	R	A	T	E	D	■	A	M	U	S	E	■	■	■
T	O	Y	■	G	E	N	E	R	A	T	I	O	N	X
E	S	E	■	E	L	E	M	E	N	T	■	I	N	K
R	E	D	■	R	E	T	U	R	N	S	■	L	E	E

189

S	E	L	F	■	D	R	A	C	O	■	■	S	E	W
P	E	A	R	■	M	E	L	O	N	■	S	K	E	E
A	L	M	A	■	I	C	A	N	T	■	T	Y	R	E
■	■	B	U	T	T	O	N	Y	O	U	R	L	I	P
A	L	A	■	A	R	A	■	■	R	I	A	L	S	■
H	U	S	H	L	I	T	T	L	E	B	A	B	Y	■
A	R	T	I	E	■	■	O	A	R	S	■	■	■	■
S	E	E	D	■	A	F	T	O	N	■	S	A	N	A
■	■	■	I	D	E	A	■	R	O	L	E	X	■	■
■	F	E	R	M	E	Z	L	A	B	O	U	C	H	E
A	L	L	I	E	■	■	T	R	Y	■	A	I	D	■
Q	U	I	E	T	O	N	T	H	E	S	E	T	■	■
A	T	O	N	■	T	O	S	E	A	■	A	R	A	T
B	E	T	S	■	I	N	A	N	D	■	S	A	R	I
A	D	S	■	S	A	R	A	S	■	■	E	Z	R	A

190

M	A	R	Y	■	S	P	A	T	E	■	D	D	A	Y
E	Z	I	O	■	C	O	M	E	S	■	R	U	L	E
L	U	N	G	■	A	T	O	N	E	■	F	E	T	A
D	R	K	I	L	D	A	R	E	■	P	E	T	E	R
■	■	■	E	S	T	■	M	E	T	E	O	R	S	■
P	A	N	D	A	■	O	N	E	I	L	L	■	■	■
L	E	A	R	N	S	■	E	N	D	■	G	A	S	H
A	R	I	D	■	H	A	R	T	E	■	O	L	E	O
N	O	L	O	■	R	I	V	■	R	H	O	D	E	S
■	■	■	L	A	U	R	E	L	■	A	D	A	P	T
S	Y	R	I	N	G	E	■	I	S	R	■	■	■	■
M	E	A	T	Y	■	D	R	Z	H	I	V	A	G	O
I	S	I	T	■	M	A	I	Z	E	■	O	U	R	S
T	E	L	L	■	A	L	L	I	E	■	I	T	A	L
E	S	S	E	■	H	E	L	E	N	■	D	O	D	O

191

S	H	A	Q	■	P	G	A	■	A	P	S	I	S
N	A	S	A	■	U	F	O	S	■	S	E	E	M	E
L	I	S	T	■	S	C	O	T	C	H	T	A	P	E
■	E	A	S	E	■	F	O	O	■	E	T	A	L
G	I	N	R	U	M	M	Y	■	N	O	S	A	L	E
H	A	T	■	P	E	A	■	M	A	V	■	C	A	Y
I	M	T	H	E	■	L	E	A	N	E	R	■	■
■	B	O	U	R	B	O	N	S	T	R	E	E	T
■	E	M	E	N	D	S	■	D	O	T	E	R
N	B	C	■	A	N	E	■	E	M	U	■	C	R	O
O	I	L	I	N	G	■	R	Y	E	B	R	E	A	D
T	E	E	S	■	A	S	A	■	L	S	A	T
B	R	A	N	D	Y	W	I	N	E	■	Z	E	R	O
A	C	T	O	R	■	A	S	H	E	■	O	R	E	O
D	E	S	T	E	■	G	E	L	■	R	A	M	P

192

A	B	Z	U	G	■	E	D	W	I	N	■	S	K	I
C	L	I	N	E	■	L	E	A	S	T	W	A	Y	S
T	O	T	H	E	L	I	G	H	T	H	O	U	S	E
S	C	I	■	Z	O	O	S	■	■	O	D	E	R	■
■	■	Z	E	S	T	■	M	I	S	F	I	R	E	■
A	L	H	I	R	T	■	G	O	A	L	S	■	■	■
N	E	O	N	■	A	R	O	M	A	■	C	F	O	■
T	O	O	C	L	E	V	E	R	B	Y	H	A	L	F
S	I	D	■	O	X	E	Y	E	■	■	O	L	A	F
■	■	■	C	B	E	R	S	■	W	H	O	M	P	S
A	R	C	H	E	R	Y	■	K	O	O	K	■	■	■
L	O	L	A	■	■	S	E	W	N	■	I	W	O	■
T	W	O	F	O	R	T	H	E	S	E	E	S	A	W
A	D	V	E	R	B	I	A	L	■	S	T	A	K	E
R	Y	E	■	K	I	N	G	S	■	T	A	K	E	N

193

R	U	L	E	D	■	S	H	O	P	■	S	H	A	G
E	P	O	X	Y	■	C	O	L	A	■	T	A	R	A
E	L	O	P	E	■	A	B	E	L	■	A	R	I	Z
L	I	F	O	■	B	R	O	O	M	H	I	L	D	A
S	T	A	N	L	E	Y	■	E	I	R	E	■	■	■
■	■	E	E	G	■	B	E	T	S	■	Q	U	A	
S	H	A	N	A	■	A	I	N	T	■	S	U	N	S
M	O	P	T	H	E	F	L	O	O	R	W	I	T	H
U	M	P	S	■	N	A	G	S	■	C	A	N	O	E
G	E	L	■	Y	O	R	E	■	A	P	T	■	■	
■	I	G	O	R	■	■	S	U	T	T	E	R	S	
V	A	C	U	U	M	P	A	C	K	■	E	R	I	E
E	R	A	S	■	I	O	T	A	■	R	A	N	D	D
R	E	N	T	■	T	R	O	D	■	O	M	E	G	A
B	A	T	S	■	Y	E	P	S	■	E	S	S	E	N

194

C	O	M	P	■	S	P	R	I	G	■	S	H	E	D
A	R	E	A	■	H	O	U	S	E	■	P	U	M	A
L	I	L	T	■	A	T	S	E	A	■	A	C	I	D
L	O	V	E	O	N	T	H	E	R	O	C	K	S	
E	L	I	■	M	A	S	■	■	H	E	S	S	E	
R	E	N	T	A	■	M	A	I	M	■	T	A	G	
■	■	U	N	I	C	O	R	N	■	A	E	R	O	
■	A	R	R	I	D	E	X	T	R	A	D	R	Y	
G	R	I	N	■	A	N	I	S	E	E	D	■	■	
O	T	C	■	E	S	T	E	■	T	S	A	R	S	
V	I	O	L	A	■	■	S	E	N	■	N	E	E	
■	S	C	A	R	E	D	S	T	R	A	I	G	H	T
B	A	H	S	■	F	R	I	A	R	■	M	E	E	T
O	N	E	S	■	T	A	N	G	O	■	A	L	A	E
A	S	T	O	■	S	T	E	E	L	■	N	A	T	E

195

F	A	C	T	■	A	L	D	A	■	■	C	O	W	
I	R	A	E	■	W	O	O	L	F	■	C	A	M	E
J	O	H	N	P	A	U	L	I	I	■	O	P	A	L
I	N	N	■	E	R	S	T	■	R	E	P	E	N	T
■	■	M	O	D	E	■	B	E	N	E	■	■	■	
P	E	C	A	N	S	■	T	O	M	O	R	R	O	W
A	L	A	R	■	G	E	R	E	■	N	O	L	A	
L	O	R	I	■	G	R	A	I	N	■	I	B	I	D
E	P	E	E	■	R	E	M	S	■	C	O	V	E	
R	E	D	C	O	A	T	S	■	S	O	U	T	E	R
■	U	L	N	A	■	C	O	N	S	■	■	■		
S	T	O	R	E	D	■	E	R	I	C	■	I	O	N
K	I	W	I	■	P	A	D	E	R	E	W	S	K	I
I	D	E	E	■	A	L	G	A	E	■	A	L	A	N
P	E	N	■	■	T	Y	K	E	■	G	A	Y	E	

196

T	S	P	S	■	S	H	I	P	■	W	A	G	E	D
H	E	A	P	■	P	O	O	R	■	E	R	O	S	E
E	A	R	L	■	R	U	N	E	■	N	E	L	L	Y
F	L	E	E	C	E	N	A	V	I	D	A	D	■	
B	E	V	E	L	E	D	■	A	N	Y	■	R	O	B
I	R	E	N	A	■	M	I	S	S	O	U	R	I	
■	■	R	E	G	A	L	E	■	U	S	E	D		
■	P	E	A	S	O	N	E	A	R	T	H	■		
P	I	E	R	■	H	O	L	D	M	E	■	■		
E	V	E	R	E	A	D	Y	■	N	A	B	O	O	
G	Y	P	■	M	R	T	■	S	E	E	M	I	N	G
■	H	I	P	P	I	E	N	E	W	Y	E	A	R	
M	A	O	R	I	■	M	E	A	L	■	T	R	U	E
M	Y	L	A	R	■	E	R	I	E	■	A	C	T	S
M	E	E	S	E	■	S	O	L	D	■	N	E	O	S

197

F	O	R	A	Y	S	■	Z	I	N	C	■	O	S	H
I	N	A	R	U	T	■	E	L	I	A	■	N	C	O
J	I	N	G	L	E	B	E	L	L	S	■	T	U	B
I	T	T	■	■	R	U	S	S	E	T	■	H	B	O
■	■	B	I	N	S	■	■	R	H	E	A	S		
■	J	O	Y	T	O	T	H	E	W	O	R	L	D	
D	U	V	A	L	■	E	L	O	■	S	O	I	L	
A	L	E	■	L	A	N	D	I	N	G	■	O	V	A
B	I	R	D	■	M	U	D	■	O	A	S	E	S	
■	A	W	A	Y	I	N	A	M	A	N	G	E	R	■
S	C	H	M	O	■	■	A	G	E	E	■	■		
C	H	E	■	U	T	O	P	I	A	■	■	U	S	A
O	I	L	■	S	I	L	E	N	T	N	I	G	H	T
U	L	M	■	E	D	E	N	■	H	A	M	L	E	T
R	D	S	■	E	E	G	S	■	A	P	P	I	A	N

198

N	I	C	H	E	■	A	L	O	H	A	■	O	B	I
O	N	E	A	M	■	M	O	V	E	S	I	N	O	N
G	O	L	D	C	O	A	T	O	F	P	A	I	N	T
■	■	N	E	R	D	S	■	■	N	O	G	O	■	
W	H	I	T	E	C	O	A	T	O	F	S	N	O	W
O	A	F	■	■	■	A	B	E	■	S	S	N	■	
M	I	S	S	I	S	■	F	U	E	L	S	■	■	
B	R	O	W	N	C	O	A	T	S	O	F	F	U	R
■	■	E	T	H	N	O	■	■	E	N	C	A	S	E
A	M	I	■	W	W	I	■	■	■	R	M	N		
R	E	D	C	O	A	T	O	F	F	L	E	E	C	E
A	R	E	O	■	■	P	A	R	E	S	■	■	■	
B	L	A	C	K	C	O	A	T	O	F	S	O	O	T
L	I	T	A	F	L	A	R	E	■	T	E	N	T	S
E	N	E	■	C	E	R	T	S	■	S	N	A	C	K

199

B	A	M	B	I		A	V	A	S	T		F	B	I
A	L	I	A	S		N	I	N	T	H		O	A	R
G	A	R	D	E	N	G	N	O	M	E		O	H	O
		D	E	A	L	T		A	M	Y	T	A	N	
F	A	M	E		V	E	N	A	L		E	S	M	E
O	D	E	S	S	A		E	N	O		A	P	A	R
G	A	G	T	S	H	I	R	T		C	R	A	S	S
		T	O	R		E	S	O						
S	P	E	C	S		R	E	D	T	I	G	H	T	S
P	O	G	O		B	E	N		E	N	R	I	C	H
O	L	G	A		A	G	A	T	E		A	D	U	E
L	E	C	T	E	R		B	U	L	L	S			
E	M	U		F	R	I	L	L	Y	A	P	R	O	N
T	I	P		G	I	B	E	S		Z	E	B	R	A
O	C	S		H	O	N	D	A		E	D	I	T	H

200

D	T	P		P	R	A	D	O		A	D	D	U	P
E	W	E		R	E	B	I	D		D	ELF	I	N	O
W	ELF	A	R	E	F	U	N	D		A	T	E	I	N
A	T	B	A	T	S		G	L	U	G		S	T	Y
R	H	O	D	A		B	Y	O	N	E	S	ELF		
		A	S	T	O		T	O	S	S	U	P	S	
S	H	O	R	T	H	O	P			N	E	A	T	
H	E	F		E	D	S	ELF	O	R	D		L	S	U
A	M	F	M			S	L	E	E	P	S	O	N	
H	O	T	ELF	O	O	D		E	L	S	A			
		H	I	P	L	E	S	S		T	R	I	A	L
L	E	E		E	D	G	E		B	R	E	N	D	A
O	L	S	O	N		R	E	B	ELF	O	R	C	E	S
A	S	H	O	E		E	M	O	R	Y		A	P	E
F	E	ELF	O	R		E	S	P	Y	S		S	T	D